Praise for *The Eye of the Dragonfly*

'Tracey Holmes sits comfortably within the most celebrated and storied history of Australian sporting journalists. To be in the conversation as one of the greats is quite something, in a great sporting nation. It requires a reverence and simultaneous scepticism of sport, a balance only the best can strike. Tracey, in a long career, struck it out of the park.' CRAIG FOSTER

'If I was to describe Tracey in one word it would be "fearless". Unafraid to ruffle feathers, she digs deeper, uncovers the facts and then presents them with confidence and care – a difficult balance to strike. While Tracey may not always be the most popular person in a press room, she is definitely one of the most respected.' CATE CAMPBELL

'By my count, on great sporting issues that you and I have strongly disagreed on, you are leading 5–2 on who's been proven right, even as we head into the top of the ninth innings, with the bases loaded.' PETER FITZSIMONS

The Eye of the Dragonfly

my life seeing the world through sport

Tracey Lee Holmes

SIMON & SCHUSTER

New York · Amsterdam/Antwerp · London · Toronto · Sydney/Melbourne · New Delhi

THE EYE OF THE DRAGONFLY: MY LIFE SEEING THE WORLD THROUGH SPORT
First published in Australia in 2025 by
Simon & Schuster (Australia) Pty Limited
Level 4, 32 York St, Sydney NSW 2000

10 9 8 7 6 5 4 3 2 1

New York Amsterdam/Antwerp London Toronto Sydney/Melbourne New Delhi
Visit our website at www.simonandschuster.com.au

For more than 100 years, Simon & Schuster has championed authors and the stories they create. By respecting the copyright of an author's intellectual property, you enable Simon & Schuster and the author to continue publishing exceptional books for years to come. We thank you for supporting the author's copyright by purchasing an authorised edition of this book.

No amount of this book may be reproduced or stored in any format, nor may it be uploaded to any website, database, language-learning model, or other repository, retrieval, or artificial intelligence system without express permission. All rights reserved. Inquiries may be directed to Simon & Schuster, 1230 Avenue of the Americas, New York, NY 10020 or permissions@simonandschuster.com.

© Tracey Lee Holmes 2025

All rights reserved. No part of this publication may be reproduced, stored in a retrieval system, or transmitted in any form or by any means, electronic, mechanical, photocopying, recording or otherwise, without prior permission of the publisher.

'Beds Are Burning'
Written by Hirst / Moginie / Garrett
© Sprint Music
Licensed by Sony Music Publishing (Australia) Pty Limited

 A catalogue record for this book is available from the National Library of Australia

ISBN: 9781761428685

Cover design: Laura Thomas
Cover images: main photograph, supplied by the author; dragonfly on spine, Shutterstock/Iraida Bearlala; dragonflies on front cover, Shutterstock/AESTRO STUDIO
Typeset by Midland Typesetters, Australia

To Mum and Dad who had me,
To my sister Jodi who laughed with me,
To Stan who loved me,
To Jesse who came to me,
To Dylan, John and Lowanna who accepted me,
To my teachers who taught me,
To my bosses everywhere who fought for me,
To my colleagues around the world who put up with me,
To the many people who have shared their stories with me,
To the women of Afghanistan who inspire me,
To the unsung people whose stories may never be known but whose efforts have supported me,
To the young reporters around the world who agreed to be mentored by me,
To the critics, non-believers, and enemies who challenged me,
To Tonglam who brings clarity to me,
To the one great ocean without borders or judgement that connects every living person to me,
To you all,
Thank you.

Contents

Introduction—Hope: Afghanistan ... 1

Part One—First Stories
Dad ... 25
Mum ... 34
Life Without Borders—Home ... 45
When the World was Black and White—South Africa ... 49
Driving Between Tombstones—Hawaii ... 57

Part Two—Life Stories
The ABC and Me—Women in Sport 1989 to
    FIFA Women's World Cup 2023 ... 67
An Improbable Introduction to F1 ... 80
Grandstand ... 86
Pelé ... 97
Managing the Media—Sydney 2000 ... 103
Living Like Locals—China: Part One ... 121
Another Move, Another World ... 135
Meeting My Monk—China: Part Two ... 143
The Ticket ... 151

Part Three—World Stories

The Olympic Flame—Atlanta 1996	163
Pressure—France 1998	169
The Loneliest Games—Tokyo 2020	172
Welcome to My Country—Qatar 2022	177
Matildas Mania—Australia and New Zealand 2023	193
Olympic Moments	203

Part Four—Developing Stories

The Games of a New Era—Paris 2024: Part One	209
Boxing—Paris: Part Two	221
Sport, a Cold War Propaganda Weapon	229
Captaincy, a Bad Night Out, and the Emperor's New Clothes: Sam Kerr	236
Economies of (Male) Scale	248
Wrestling with Power	261
The Olympics in a Fractured, Political World	269

Part Five—Future Stories

Brisbane 2032	283
The Future is Abbie from *HER WAY*	289
The Future is Technology	297
The Future is Now	311
Circling Back—The Zakia Khudadadi Story	319

Acknowledgements	323
About the Author	326

The distant mountains
Are reflected in the eye
Of the dragonfly

– Kobayashi Issa (1763–1828)

Introduction
Hope: Afghanistan

'I feel so much pain. I feel angry. I feel devastated.'

That's the voice of Khalida Popal, the former captain of Afghanistan's women's football team, who lived under Taliban rule before fleeing and settling in Denmark. She knows the devastation that is now unfolding for the current generation of female Afghan athletes.

It is 16 August 2021. I am in hotel quarantine at the Marriott at Circular Quay in Sydney. I am one of the lucky ones. In Afghanistan, all hell has broken loose.

Four days ago, I flew back into Sydney from the loneliest Games ever, the COVID-delayed Tokyo 2020 Olympics. Throughout, I had been keeping one eye on the Taliban making its way across Afghanistan, reclaiming province after province from the tottering democratic government America and its allies were abandoning. From each territory, hearing the Taliban was coming for them, women athletes would rush to Kabul to hide with relatives. But it was only a matter of time before the long-bearded men in flowing robes would ride into the capital with their weapons and brutal ideology, forever changing Afghans' lives.

Stuck in my hotel, I flick between CNN, BBC and Al Jazeera, and check websites of local news agencies in and around the Middle East, trying to get a complete picture. As soon as CNN confirms the Taliban have reached the capital and overthrown the government, I call Khalida from my makeshift studio in room 1515. She, more than almost anyone, can paint a picture of what is now unfolding in her former homeland.

This is what I do. I am a journalist. When so many run from an emergency in fear, we want to run towards it. We are witnesses to history. We need to document significant moments in as complete a picture as possible. I am not here to swallow the political propaganda from any side but to put my feet in the shoes of those most impacted, to do what I can to share their stories, so that the world can know what is happening.

Khalida responds to my request for a Zoom interview. My TV screen shows allied forces packing planes and exiting quickly. This is a place they have occupied for nearly two decades, and just like that, they are gone. The locals have been left to fend for themselves against the militia born of the Pashtun areas of Pakistan and Afghanistan, who desire to impose the most austere form of Sharia law on all 41 million of the country's inhabitants.

Who will forget the images of Afghan men and boys desperately chasing after a US military plane taxiing down the Kabul runway, some crouching on the wings? The would-be stowaways, clinging on with what little hope they have as the plane lifts skywards, one by one fall to the ground.

The Eye of the Dragonfly

Hope had failed these men of Afghanistan. So too the foreign governments who had sold them a false promise. And the women?

'I see women stuck there. I hear their voices, the shaky voices of women being scared and afraid . . . I feel helpless . . . It's nonstop.' Khalida's voice is trembling. I send her interview to ABC News.

As the Americans, Brits, French and Australians pack up and depart, the sewage-filled moat around Kabul airport gradually thickens with Afghans begging to leave with them.

During moments like these, I do not sleep. I do not want to miss a single detail that may become a significant final piece in the jigsaw of understanding. My focus is intense. Work colleagues have described how I go into a zone that is calm and controlled, where I clearly lay out what everyone must do. My mother sees it differently. She thinks I need to find my panic button and switch it on. It infuriates her that I am not excitable. She thinks I'm mad, unnecessarily covering stories that may carry retribution. Not my husband though. Stan is a journalist too. He knows what drives us. Unlike me, he has been to Afghanistan and covered wars there. He knows the people, knows the landscape, knows the drama of a place that is so beautiful yet continues to be surrounded by mayhem and tragedy.

There is work to do. I send texts to people I know, and Twitter messages to those I don't, lining up interview after interview, in the hope that those who hear them might be able to do something significant to stop the tragedy Khalida describes. There's that word again, *hope*. It is a word I have a love-hate relationship with. Over and over, history shows us it is misplaced. Time and again, we revert to it. Hope is the cornerstone on which civilisations are built. The word itself sounds like a breath, without any physical form – *hope* – and yet it is our constant bedrock.

The former coach of the Afghanistan women's football team, American Kelly Lindsey, is my next call.

'Ask the question of the politicians that make decisions to enter in a country and make these fake promises and then leave it like this: what about the women of Afghanistan? The people of the world need to come together and just get them to safety. It can't be about, "Do you have the right paperwork, do you have the right identity card, do you have a passport?" because I'm going to tell you, so many women in Afghanistan don't have an identity.'

Kelly's words are like a dart hitting a bullseye. How is it that the liberal democratic world can go into a country with a culture so unlike our own to 'save them' with slogans of freedom and equal opportunity, then abandon them at their greatest hour of need?

News travels fast. The sports world is highly connected. My number is shared with those in Afghanistan. This sets off a frenzied week of voice messages pinging through the day and night with people, in desperation and panic, asking for help. Their voices are haunting, most of them women with messages like this:

'Day by day, the situation is getter harder, so I just wanted to check with you if there is any chance that you can help us to evacuate to any country, because we are in a very difficult situation without hope or any assistance.'

And another:

'I think all Afghans are being threatened and sold out. And I don't know who is playing their game. Because we are just ordinary people, just doing our job and getting our salary, and working for our country. Who is behind this? Who? Which country? Who doesn't want us to live a good life? Or to improve our country, to live in a peaceful country?'

The messages keep coming.

In a little over a week, the Paralympics are due to begin. Does Afghanistan have a Paralympic team? Are they still in Afghanistan? Can someone help get them out? I scour Twitter again. I find the Chef de Mission of the Afghanistan team, who is living in London.

Arian Sadiqi's interview is powerful, but he too is devastated, feeling helpless against the force of the Taliban and the retreat of the West.

'I think words can't explain what is actually going through their minds,' Arian tells me.

Even connecting with his team of two athletes is difficult. Intermittent power failures, phone lines cut, the internet going down means communication is sporadic, frequently impossible. There are security risks too. When contact is made, what should be left unsaid? When interviews are broadcast around the world, the Taliban are watching and listening. They come knocking in the night. Family members are taken away, never to be seen again.

Arian forwards me a video message from one of his athletes, the first Afghan woman selected for taekwondo at the Paralympic Games, Zakia Khudadadi. Her history-making achievement is seemingly disappearing in front of her eyes.

'With all the struggles I've been through, I am currently imprisoned inside the house,' she says in a video she hopes to post to social media, which Arian has forwarded to me. 'I cannot even go outside this house with confidence and with security to buy just a few things for myself, to train, to check on how anyone else is. My intention is to participate in the Tokyo Games. Please hold my hand and help me. Please, I urge you all – from the women around the globe, institutions for the protection of women, from all government organisations – to not let the rights of a female citizen of Afghanistan in the Paralympic movement to be taken away so easily.'

Zakia proves to be one of the most resilient people I have ever come across in a lifetime of criss-crossing the globe, meeting people from the backstreets to the halls of power. In the same way that little excites me, there are very few people I hold in awe. Zakia is an exception. She had to leave her parents' home in Herat province weeks earlier, as that was one of the first areas to fall under Taliban rule. She had gone to stay with relatives in Kabul to be closer to the airport when it came time to fly to Tokyo – *if* she could fly to Tokyo. Now the Taliban are in Kabul.

Arian, the Chef de Mission, explains: 'She is with extended relatives, a family of ten who are already struggling to put food on the table given the Taliban situation. She said, "Please advise me what to do." I said, "What can I say? What can I do?" She said, "I am not losing hope yet. I still have hope that somebody out there will help."'

I send his interview to the ABC too, then call him back for an off-the-record chat.

Have you asked the International Paralympic Committee (IPC) what they can do? Yes, Sadiqi says: nothing. That's not good enough, I reply. The president of the IPC, Andrew Parsons, is my next interview. What can you do? Very little, is his response. 'Our influence is limited,' he says. I just don't believe that. What is the International Olympic Committee (IOC) doing? What is the Centre for Sport and Human Rights doing? What is the International Taekwon-Do Federation doing? And World Athletics, the governing body for Arian's other Paralympian, sprinter Hossain Rasouli? Surely, combined, these organisations have all the access and contacts they need to help these athletes in such a time of need.

Governments around the world spend large sums of money hosting major sporting events controlled by organisations such as the IOC and IPC. The presidents of international sports bodies are often photographed with presidents and prime ministers of nations, who in turn enjoy their invitations to private boxes at mega sporting events. But what is the value of the relationship if, when at the time of greatest need, there is either no influence that can be brought to bear or, worse, an unwillingness to even try? At this moment, it appears sports authorities are failing their athletes.

I pass on as many contact names and numbers as I can, encouraging Arian to call them and suggest they face up to their responsibilities. He takes to Facebook to issue a plea for help on behalf of the women of Afghanistan. I edit a one-hour special edition of my podcast, *The Ticket*, to be aired on ABC NewsRadio. It focuses entirely on the women athletes and the lack of response from so many people who were happy to ride on the back of their success, yet so quickly dropped them in the heat of battle.

My friend Nikki Dryden, a human rights lawyer and former Canadian Olympic swimmer, rings me before the podcast has finished airing. She is the embodiment of the Nike sportswear motto 'Just do it.'

'We have to save these women,' she says to me over the phone.

Almost immediately, Nikki teams up with two fellow human rights lawyers to kickstart a rescue mission. Together with Alison Battisson, who established the non-profit Human Rights for All, and Kat Craig, the founder and CEO of Athlead, a not-for-profit consultancy dealing specifically with sport and human rights, Nikki sets up a 24/7 tag-team operation run from their bedrooms-turned-COVID-offices in Sydney and London.

As women in Afghanistan reach out to me, I pass their details on to Nikki. Together, the trio of human rights lawyers coordinate the collection of the Afghan women's details and applications for emergency visas, and devise exit strategies for them. Other sporting alumni become part of the group – former Socceroo captain Craig Foster, Olympic skier and independent member of parliament Zali Steggall, and Paralympic legend Kurt Fearnley. All use whatever influence they can muster. They leave sports governing bodies in their wake.

About 30 hours into this grassroots rescue operation, Nikki phones again, frantic. 'We have no contact inside the airport!' Even with emergency papers, which are starting to come through, the women are being beaten back into the sewage-filled moat around Kabul airport. The last of the military planes are being loaded for their final departure. 'I know who to call. I'll get back to you,' I tell her.

'Neil, it's Tracey. Do you know anybody inside Kabul airport that can help get a couple of athletes out so they can get to the Paralympic Games?'

'Yes, what do you need?'

The Eye of the Dragonfly

Neil Fergus is head of Intelligent Risks, a company that has played a role in protecting athletes, dignitaries and heads of state at almost every Olympic Games in living memory, as well as advising on many Olympic bids and organising committees on security arrangements. Our paths first crossed during the intense security planning around the Sydney 2000 Olympics, when I worked for SOCOG, the organising committee, and he was executive director of security, risk and intelligence for the Olympic and Paralympic Games. Neil has experience working for the Department of Foreign Affairs and Trade, a good knowledge of the Middle East, and vital senior contacts inside the Australian army and the Royal Australian Air Force.

The Paralympic Games opening ceremony in Tokyo will happen on 24 August. As midnight on 22 August ticks over into 23 August, I get a WhatsApp message from Neil. The Paralympians Zakia and Hossain have now been joined by a larger cohort of Afghan athletes the team has managed to locate, including the women's football team. They have been moving from one gate to the next trying to get on a flight to Australia with their emergency-issued visas.

> 12:00 am, NF: I'm waiting on the confirmation – comms have a got a little messy.
>
> 12:00 am, TH: Ok.
>
> 12:06 am, NF: The first info is all should now be through – but as link with ADF Ops Centre I'm waiting for confirmation no-one got separated or left behind.
>
> 12:07 am, TH: I cannot thank you enough. Thank you for everything Neil. I don't know what to say.

12:09 am, NF: Okay – nearly all through and accounted for – unfortunately the 2 Paralympians got separated and haven't been located yet. Need to send some urgent comms . . .

12:12 am, TH: Ok. If their phones aren't dead would the Chef de Mission be of any use trying to locate them since he speaks Farsi?

12:15 am, NF: We've located them. Poor network making comms problematic. I've recommended 1RAF patrol goes and gets them . . . or if they won't then one of our Afghan group needs to volunteer to go and retrieve them . . . standby.

I send a satellite photo of the gate they are standing at, which has been sent to me on a separate WhatsApp group message.

12:16 am, TH: That's where they are, presume you have it.

12:19 am, NF: ADF has it – this is now going high risk. ADF worried why they didn't follow the instructions and stay with the group.

12:19 am, TH: Shit.

12:45 am, NF: They're still outside and too far back from the gate. They have to push on to the gate – it's not safe for ADF to go out and bring them in.

12:47 am, TH: I have told Arian to tell the team to carry Zakia as though she has fainted – anything – to push through to the gate.

The Eye of the Dragonfly

12:50 am, NF: 👍 Then he must stop calling them so the group inside can talk to them.

12:50 am, TH: On it.

12:51 am, TH: He's told them and won't ring them now.

1:09 am, NF: Just waiting for confirmation they are in ✌️✌️✌️

1:09 am, TH: OMG

1:18 am, NF: They're traversing the gate system.

1:18 am, TH: Phew.

1:19 am, NF: Almost there.

1:20 am, TH: Am standing by.

1:24 am, NF: Three layers to get through the perimeter and inside, but they are in it and weren't rejected at the UK outer cordon so I expect ADF should now be moving to facilitate/receive them.

1:24 am, TH: Fan bloody tastic. Does Arian know?

1:26 am, NF: I don't know. However I understand Nikki has been talking with him so he probably does by now.

The mission continues through the early hours of the morning, into the night, and into the following day. More calls are coming every hour from people needing help to leave.

The story emerges that Zakia, the Paralympian, had been close to exhaustion, about to give up. An ITV crew from London had been filming in the moat at the airport and captured video of her wiping tears from her face, weak at the knees. Teammate Hossain looked to be in a daze. Arian Sadiqi's younger brother was there to support them, urging them forward.

Zakia and Hossein didn't make it onto an RAAF plane. For a short time, there was confusion, then we heard they boarded a French plane to Paris before flying on to Tokyo for the Paralympic Games.

In their first interview following their escape, Arian Sadiqi organised for me to speak to Zakia and Hossain from inside the Paralympics athletes' village while he interpreted and filled in the missing pieces.

'I remember messaging the British Paralympic Association,' Arian said. 'I ask them, "Please can you help us? Because our athletes are literally behind the British gate." She forwards the message to the GB Paralympics secretary general. He contacted the British ambassador directly. Suddenly the gates were open, they were in.'

It was the first time I had seen Arian smile since the saga began.

'I feel that goodness and happiness awaits us, the good life,' Zakia said. 'But we'd be much more happy to have our family next to us, because we are here and our hearts are there.'

Both athletes got to make history competing at the Games and have now settled in France. They carried the Afghanistan flag at the Tokyo Paralympic Games closing ceremony. It is another image I will never forget. What they had been through. How their lives had changed so irrevocably. What future now lay ahead?

—

Another group emerged from the Australian sport network – former cricketer and now commentator Mel Jones, cricket administrator Emma Staples, and University of Canberra sports integrity expert Dr Catherine Ordway – and managed to coordinate a months-long evacuation of the Afghanistan women's cricket team. Twenty-two of them now live in Australia. With support from Cricket Australia and the England and Wales Cricket Board, they worked tirelessly to have the International Cricket Council (ICC) recognise them as a team in exile. They continued to train and play, hoping their sporting dreams would one day be realised.

After one too many negative headlines and three years of inaction, the ICC made an out-of-the-blue announcement in April 2025. A task force dedicated to supporting the Afghanistan women's cricket team would be established, with funding to help them secure training facilities, coaches and mentors. It would be a joint effort by the ICC and cricket authorities in India, England and Australia. I couldn't help but wonder how much difference a single question at a recent press conference might have made. In early March, just weeks before the IOC elected Kirsty Coventry as its first female president, I asked her during a 'Meet the Presidential Candidates' conference hosted by the International Sports Press Association (AIPS) whether she would advocate for the Afghanistan women's cricket team given that cricket was making a return to the Olympic Games in Los Angeles in 2028. Coventry said she had a meeting scheduled with the chairman of the ICC, Jay Shah, in the next week and would raise it with him. She contacted me privately afterwards to say it was a 'very insightful' meeting, with a key part of the conversation focused on the Afghan women. I thanked her for following through on her promise but remained sceptical about any real development. Sports governing bodies have a long tradition of meeting often, saying much and doing little, with a few exceptions. Weeks later, the ICC's publicly stated commitment both floored and thrilled me. You can imagine the impact on the players. If only I could have been a fly on the wall in that meeting between Kirsty Coventry and Jay Shah, two of the most powerful people in world sport given the offices they occupy and the influence they have.

The captain of the Afghanistan women's team, Nahida Sapan, told me such a commitment from the powerful and influential ICC would reverberate beyond the team itself.

'This is really big news – not just for me, not just for the Afghan women's cricket team, it's very big and very surprising news for all Afghan women.'

Teammate Firooza Afghan – who once famously put on her joggers and ran from her home into Melbourne's CBD to confront the president of the Afghanistan Cricket Board while he was dining in a restaurant where her sister worked – said she was determined 'not to cry' at the announcement, because this was a day that each and every female Afghan cricketer deserved to celebrate. 'But we couldn't help it,' she said, wiping away her own tears.

The Eye of the Dragonfly

More than 100 Afghan athletes from numerous sports, as well as a few of their family members, now call Australia home. Neil Fergus and his colleagues at Intelligent Risks are still organising papers, sponsorships and evacuations from Afghanistan more than four years after my initial call. He jokes with me often about my initial request to help two Paralympians, which suddenly became a few more athletes, then dozens more, then more than a hundred and still counting.

'These people were not soft,' Neil says. 'These people knew, in most cases, they had one chance at a future. And the last people that got on the last RAAF flight out of Kabul, a woman with a three-year-old child, her phone went flat right at the last moment. ADF circled that airport and found them and held the last RAAF evacuation flight to put them on board. That woman and her child are now on their way to rejoin her husband.' Neil's voice trails off. It is raspy as he finishes his interview with me. 'That's what Australians do,' he says.

A female karate instructor, her husband and three children were some of the others Neil helped. Three times they were turned away from approaching the airport. The third time, the Taliban shot at their car. They were convinced to try one last time. Their three-year-old daughter passed out in the moat from dehydration. But they made it through. All survived. They have a new life in Australia.

Neil had a codename for the rescue missions: Operation Dust in the Eyes. The reference was not to the desert sands of Afghanistan but to the human emotion of seeing others facing near-certain disaster and jumping in to help them. There were many tears quietly shed throughout the operation, quickly wiped away as a team of individuals worked frantically and tirelessly to save the women of Afghanistan.

At times like these, national flags and anthems are irrelevant; this is about a shared humanity. This is what sport is all about. This is why I love sport – it is about people, places, culture, politics, power, influence, tragedy and celebration. Sport has it all.

—

'You should write a book.' I've heard it a million times. 'Why?' I always ask.

'Because you're . . .' And then people will add one of a bewildering array of adjectives. 'Scary', 'funny', 'an enigma', 'eclectic', 'a woman of perspicacity'. (Perspicacity? I don't even know what it means.)

'You are such a strong advocate for women,' some say, although I have never thought of myself that way. 'You're a disgrace to women everywhere,' I am often told on social media, because I treat transgender people the same way I'd treat anybody else. I've been told I am a communist, a North Korean sympathiser. More than two decades ago, a newspaper labelled me 'the Holmes wrecker'. Some people still think it's funny to remind me of it. I don't.

Professionally, I've also had all sorts of labels given to me, from 'lightweight' to 'award-winning investigative journalist' – to 'sports reporter' by an ABC who seemed to think sport is only important when there is not enough 'real' news to fill a bulletin. After one lengthy interview with someone at the centre of one of the many sporting sagas I've covered, these two responses summed up the reactions I got: 'Wow, you really went after him, that was great,' and, 'Nice to hear him being given a fair hearing.'

The Eye of the Dragonfly

People see what they want to see and hear what they want to hear. I try hard to see not what I want or expect but what is there, without filters. I try to see through dragonfly eyes – with their 360-degree view as they flit from this place to that. This is the journey I'd like you to have with me in these pages.

At the end of hot days in the Snowy Valleys, where we spend a lot of our time, Stan and I go for a swim in the rock pools at the old goldmine in Adelong. Most days there is an iridescent blue dragonfly that hovers about a foot from me. Dragonflies have been around for about 300 million years. They have seen it all. Native Americans such as the Hopi, Zuni and Navajo believe the insect symbolises maturity and pure water. It seeks to know what's below the surface and beyond the horizon. It strips away negativity and provides hope. For the Japanese, dragonflies symbolise agility, courage and strength. They are often described as the souls of the ancestors. The Chinese associate dragonflies with good luck, prosperity and harmony. They also believe they are linked to the souls of dragons or messengers from the spiritual world. All of this resonates with me. The rock pools I swim in are the same ones my great, great grandfather from Fujian province travelled to. He was a doctor to the thousands of Chinese miners in the area. When I see that blue dragonfly, I think of him. I think of his adventures. I think of my own. And I think of how my journey has helped me to see the world with 360-degree eyes.

This journey-in-a-book will not be conventional. Those who are familiar with my work will know I don't walk down the street in a straight line. I hover here, dart there, join the dots, trying to see the bigger picture in which each of us plays a part. Repetition bores the hell out of me, and I don't tolerate negativity. I'd rather look forward than back, and I relish any opportunity to dive into waters unknown. More and more we are challenged to see the world as a black–white dichotomy. Don't be trapped into believing it. The world is full of colour, even in its darkest hours.

This is not a book about sport; it is a book that uses sport as a lens through which we can interrogate the best and worst of us, because sport is the only international language that is capable of breaking down barriers.

I don't have much to add to the record about being Australia's first female presenter of a national sports program – the ABC's flagship *Grandstand* – and the reaction from what at the time was an overwhelmingly male audience. And I don't believe in revealing other people's secrets – they are not mine to tell. Rather, this is a candid telling of the key people, places, events and ideas that have most influenced me. I hope it'll help you see how I think about the world, and why sport has been central to it.

Sport was a natural fit as a career for me, although somewhat accidental.

As a kid, I was perfectly happy not talking – perhaps not an obvious qualification for a broadcaster. It's not that I didn't like to, I was just happy in silence. I still am today. On the other hand, I was always an observer, viewing life – including my own – from a distance. My mother was also the first to identify another characteristic unusual in my profession: she always told me when I was a kid, 'Don't ever lie, Tracey, because what you think is written all over your face.' I know it. Often, I can tell by the reaction on other people's faces that they can see what I am thinking. After watching some of my coverage of the Vancouver

2010 Winter Olympics, somebody even contacted me to say they'd noticed I wasn't too enamoured with one of the guests I was talking to. They were right. The guest was not my choice but was forced on our coverage. I've tried hard not to be that obvious, but hey, this is me.

Mum did indulge something else that turned out to be a lifelong characteristic. Although my family was not religious at all, she taught me a little goodnight prayer to say as she tucked me in: 'Now I lay me down to sleep,' followed by 'God bless –' and I was supposed to say, 'Mum, Dad and Jodi.' (Jodi is my younger sister.) But my list was a little longer. I blessed the ants and the butterflies, the flowers, the fairies, the angels, the gardener, the ladies selling fruit out of their baskets on the streets, the man on the bus, the waves at the beach – everything I could recall from my world.

Mum would try to interrupt, 'Okay, that's enough –'

'But I haven't finished yet,' I'd say, and keep going.

I have the same approach to my work in sports journalism. A game or match doesn't happen in isolation. It is one point in a long journey that neither starts nor finishes when the whistle is blown. Whenever I can, I like to have a long-form conversation that draws out of my guest a complete story, going to places rarely explored, to gain a thorough understanding of who they are and why. I always hope that at the end of the conversation my voice could just as easily be completely omitted, edited out, documentary style. Former world heavyweight champion and Olympic boxing gold medallist George Foreman once said to me after an interview, 'Hey lady, are you a psychologist? I feel like I've just got off the couch.' Thankfully, he was laughing about it.

A Buddhist monk (whom we will meet again later) introduced me to the term *re-cognising*. Not *recognising* but *re-cognising*: always seeing everything as though for the first time. Over almost four decades, I have looked at our world afresh again and again through the prism of sport. Make no mistake: I am not a sports reporter. I have no interest in scores, injuries and start lists. At tomorrow's press conference for whichever international tennis tournament is being played, you will hear players asked the same five questions that were being asked when Billie Jean King and Margaret Court were playing half a century ago. Round and round on the same boring loop they go. That has never been my thing. I always wanted to go deeper, often through the element of surprise.

Throughout my career, I have resisted the temptation to follow the lead of the loudest voice in the room. I try to look beyond passing bandwagons, to see what's going on behind the scenes, who is pulling the strings, what are the motivations driving the media coverage and the developing narrative. Living, working and raising kids in other countries has given me a front-row seat for some of the world's major political and social shifts. That unique position means my perspective is often at odds with the mainstream, which is trapped in a specific country or a particular sport. I must have been a salmon in a past life, since I've spent most of this one swimming upstream in the telling of a story, against the current of a media narrative. It's often said that we shouldn't mix sport and politics – I think the complete opposite.

People, politics, power, psychology – that's what I love, and there is no better place to see those things played out every way, every day, than in the world of sport. It is dynamic, ever changing, both local and global, frustrating and beautiful. It is an emotion. It is a community and a culture. For some, sport really has replaced religion. It is also a business – and therefore can be the corruption of all these things.

Sport has been a particularly powerful lens through which to examine our attitudes to race and gender, and the media is the perfect vehicle to explore them. Racism is a disease we have not found a cure for, one which still threatens to destabilise our world. On gender, though, we may have turned a corner. When I started in what was a heavily male-dominated sports media world, while there was a degree of resistance (and still is in some parts), most of the experienced, talented men I worked with were happy to give invaluable advice when I asked. Men such as ABC Sports Editor Peter Longman, who was my producer at *Grandstand*, facilitated me exploring new ways of telling sports stories, encouraging me to use my own voice, giving me the space and time to grow my storytelling style, having my back when controversies arose.

And of course, now we are seeing more women's sports on screen. The FIFA Women's World Cup in 2023 got media attention across the board, in a way that had previously been reserved for Men's World Cups only. And I was no longer the only female broadcaster on the coverage: the number of women has grown significantly as former women players now also commentate alongside the men.

For more than a decade, I have mentored young journalists and broadcasters from around the world. Many of them ask how I got here. The answer is simple: chance, a sense of adventure, a need to explore, an interest in all people and all cultures. Plus, I love what I do, which is why I have no problem working 18 hours a day or longer, for weeks on end. My family has grown used to it, and our kids learned from an early age to be self-sufficient; they had to be. I don't look at what I do as a job; it's a lifestyle choice. And it's a choice I'm glad I made.

Part One
First Stories

Dad

Adelong is magical.

It sits at the bottom of the Snowy Mountains, somewhere between the apple-growing town of Batlow, Gundagai's Dog on the Tuckerbox, and the nearest city, Wagga Wagga.

When the sun starts to shift from the north, sliding into the south and turning winter into spring, the creek is clear, cold and full of the melting snow from a hundred or more kilometres away. It makes music as it runs over the rocks where the goldmine used to be. It's where my great, great grandfather and his mates worked back in the 1850s after arriving on a boat from China.

In the autumn, the red, yellow and golden leaves fall from the hundreds of Chinese elms. You can watch them flutter down into the creek, washing downstream and disappearing into who knows where, just like the men who brought the trees here.

The day in 2021 that I returned from the COVID-impacted Tokyo Olympics and was escorted by the Australian Army from Sydney Airport into hotel quarantine at Circular Quay, I got a call saying my dad had had a stroke around 4:00 am and was in intensive care. Before he'd gone to bed, he'd packed his car with his tent, his billy can and his fishing gear, so he could get up early for the drive from Sydney to Adelong, back to the country he loved. He never made that trip.

This morning, I sat by the creek and listened to it for him. My dad, a surfer and sailor, loves the water. He loves the outdoors. He spent little of his life inside. Almost all of my memories of him involve long car trips into the country – in whichever country we were in – to go camping in search of the elusive perfect wave. He and I both like the quiet. We have no need to talk. We can just sit and be.

Right now, it's the spring of 2024, and it's my own bag that is packed and ready for a trip of a different kind that I will make to be with my father. I'm waiting for a call from one of the nurses at the home where my dad lies bedridden as he waits to draw his final breath. They've told me he doesn't have long left. I've come to his place to get what I need before heading four hours back up the road to Sydney to sit with him as his breathing becomes slower and his eyes a little sadder. He's not afraid of dying. He knows there is nothing left to live for. He told his nurses he didn't want any more pills. He just wanted some fruitcake.

Last week, I told his older brother, my uncle Stork, that Dad wouldn't be around much longer, so if he wanted to see him, now would be the time. He and his wife, Sue, made the long drive down from their home on the Gold Coast. They hadn't seen

Dad since before his stroke. The sight of my dad was going to be a shock: everyone remembers the surfer, the sailor, the skier, the tanned, fit, healthy guy who made his living shaping beautiful surfboards and crafting yachts in between his adventures. He'd make enough money to pay the rent, buy the food, put petrol in his second-hand car, and then take off again – over whichever horizon presented itself.

'G'day,' Uncle Stork said.

'G'day,' Dad quietly replied, with only his eyes moving.

'Doesn't look like you'll be heading for a surf any time soon.'

'Nah,' Dad said. 'Not until the swell comes up, anyway.'

The Holmeses are hilarious without ever trying to be. They are ratbags too. Rebels. Hillbillies. What's another good word to describe them? True blue Aussies with Chinese heritage.

My mother is sitting downstairs, suddenly hit with her own grieving for a husband she divorced half my life ago. They'd already been separated for 18 years by the time of the divorce, with barely a word between them in all that time. She had been afraid if she divorced him earlier, he'd ask her to sell the house. It always made me laugh. My dad never wanted anything except to be in the outdoors. What use would he have for half a house?

When they split up, I was 14 and relieved. Since the age of about four, I remember thinking to myself, how did these two end up together? They were both good people but not good for each other. I knew they'd be happier out of each other's orbit. My dad made a camp bed in a garden shed he built at the back of his mate's place. Spooky, as his mate was called, was a hilarious Irish-Aussie married to an incredible South African woman,

Wanda. Dad named his shed Linga Longa and that was home for the next 44 years. A few years back, the neighbours decided to put a pool in the backyard and realised that Linga Longa was partly on their property. Dad had to downsize, losing about a foot off his home and the length of his bed.

Once, after doing the Sydney to Hobart yacht race on the smallest boat in the fleet sometime in the early 2000s, he was sailing back to Sydney but didn't arrive when expected. We hadn't heard from him for a while. Then it was a while longer. Then it was months longer. Seven months later, Dad sailed into Manly. On his return trip from Hobart, the wind had been good and the days were beautiful, so he'd just kept going – up the New South Wales coast, past Queensland, across to the Solomons and an encounter with pirates. He hadn't had a problem, though (with the pirates, anyway), because Dad had a way of relating to people from anywhere and making mates out of strangers, even dangerous types.

I think it's a trait I inherited from him, learned during my early years in South Africa. It was there that I also discovered Dad had no interest in living his life dictated to by a clock or a calendar.

It was there in 1970, when I was around four and my sister was a newborn, I remember seeing Mum crying. It was probably my first memory of seeing her stressed. Dad hadn't come home, and she didn't know where he was. A few weeks later, he walked through the door like nothing had happened: he had been at the surfboard factory shaping boards when someone popped in to tell him how good the swell was about 800 kilometres down the road, so he locked up the factory, hopped into his Kombi van and went surfing for a few weeks. I can understand my mother's stress.

I can also understand my father's wayfaring spirit. Something that annoys both him and me equally is any sense of being anchored or tethered to a place.

When Mum finally decided to register for a divorce and the papers arrived, she put them in her bag, wondering how to get them to Dad without having to see him. The same afternoon, she drove to the mall to pick up some groceries. For the first time in decades, their paths crossed, outside Whitworth's marine and leisure store, where Dad had gone to buy some sailing gear.

'G'day,' he said.

'I've got something for you,' she replied, extracting the divorce papers from her bag and handing them to him.

He unfolded the document, saw what it was, and said, 'I suppose counselling's out the question?'

When she told me the story, I cracked up. That's how the Holmeses are. My mother did not appreciate the humour, even after all those years.

—

Back in the late '70s, when we came back to Australia from years spent living in South Africa and Hawaii, we took a trip down Adelong way to visit my dad's Aunty Daphne, his mother's sister. Mum and Dad decided to take her into Batlow, to the Big Apple, for dinner. My sister, Jodi, and I stayed at Aunty Daph's little cottage. I was about 11; Jodi would've been about seven. Around sunset, there was a knock at the door. When I opened it, there were two men standing there who looked like they'd just come down from the mountains. Big smiles, wrinkled features, a tooth or two missing here and there.

'Are you Darryl's kids?' the older man asked.

'Yes,' I said.

'I'm his father. I'm your grandfather,' replied the older man.

'I'm his half-brother. I'm your half-uncle,' said the other man, beaming from ear to ear.

We'd never met Dad's dad. Didn't even know his name (it was Leonard), didn't even know he was alive. We'd never heard Dad talk about his father. All we knew was that at some point when Dad and his older brother, John (my uncle Stork), and younger brother, Gary, were little, their mum fled with them from the outskirts of Batlow to Manly Beach, in Sydney. Idy (Iris) worked two jobs to keep food on the table, starting early in a newsagency and finishing late after cleaning the Cardinal's Palace, part of St Patrick's Seminary at North Head. The boys ran amok. Cheeky and entrepreneurial.

They decided amongst themselves that school was optional. Don't ask me how, but when my dad was about eight and Uncle Stork about ten, they learned how to make fake coins with a mould. The fake money would turn black after about 24 hours. They'd make their coins overnight, and then in the morning, instead of going to school, they'd catch the ferry to town and hop on the train to Parramatta. On the return trip, they'd get off at as many stations as they could to put their fake coins into cigarette machines. Then they'd place the cigarettes into their shoulder bags to sell at Balgowlah Boys High School once the afternoon bell rang. The real money that had been taped onto the cigarette packages as change would be in their pockets, along with what the boys paid them – a reward after a hard day's work.

They'd saved enough money to head into Kings Cross one afternoon to buy a couple of rifles from a pawn shop. Who sells guns to a couple of ratbag kids who should've been at school? This was Sydney in the early 1950s, and the Holmeses were not only streetwise, they could also tell a good story. Good enough to convince a greedy shop owner that handing over a couple of weapons to minors was okay.

When school holidays rolled around, the boys would go back to Kunama, outside Batlow to be on the farm with Idy's father, Joseph; it was the place they called home. Joseph had married war bride – Alice Selina Trett, a nurse – he met when he was in London recovering from fighting in World War I. He owned a farm by then, but before the war, he worked with his own father down at the Adelong goldmine. In the war, he fought as Joseph Holmes. At the goldmine, he had been known as Joseph Lin, Junior. He and his siblings had changed their name to Holmes so they weren't teased so much at school for being half Chinese. Holmes was the name of their mother's first husband, who had died before she had kids with Joseph Lin, Senior.

When Joseph and Alice had their three children, including my grandmother Idy, their surname was Holmes. When my dad was born, his last name was Colless. Uncle Stork was Leonard John Colless, Junior, named after his father. When my grandmother bailed to Manly with the boys, she told them their name wasn't Colless anymore, it was Holmes. And Uncle Stork was told he wasn't Leonard anymore, either: he would now be known as John.

My sister and I didn't know any of this when the two men appeared at Aunty Daph's door. (In fact, we didn't learn about it until we were into our 50s. And even then, things weren't entirely clear – there was a rumour that our grandfather Leonard wasn't actually a Colless but maybe a Bates or something else entirely.) We certainly had no idea who Leonard Colless was when he introduced himself to us.

'Where is your dad?' Leonard asked.

'He's at the Big Apple,' I said.

'All right, we'll call in there and see him. Get your dad to bring you kids down to the apple cannery where I work, and I'll show you around.'

'Okay.'

My Grandfather and half-uncle drove to the restaurant. As Mum tells it, Aunty Daph started kicking her under the table, and when Mum looked towards the door, she saw two men walking in their direction – and knew immediately the older one must have been Dad's dad. She'd never met him before either. Aunty Daph gave Leonard the evil eye as he approached my father from behind. He put his hand on his son's shoulder, and for the second time that night, introduced himself: 'Darryl, I'm your father.'

My dad was eating soup. He swallowed a spoonful, looked up at his dad and said, 'G'day.' Then he looked back down at the bowl and kept eating. There were a few more introductions and a brief, somewhat strained, conversation before the encounter was over. We never saw them again and the incident was never mentioned.

As we packed up our camping gear and started to go back to Sydney a few days later, we asked Dad if we were going past the apple cannery. 'No,' he said, as he turned up the volume of the Eagles playing 'Hotel California'.

I went back to looking out the window watching the skyline whizz by.

—

My enduring image of Australia is of dead tree trunks, black from bushfires or grey from starvation, with broken branches reaching into the sky. I always thought that when I had time, I would travel these long, empty, winding roads with Dad and collect old tree stumps to make furniture from. He would sand them into shape and resin them, after I had designed where the cuts should be made, where the cushions would go for seats, or the glass would balance for tables. I still see those trees every time I'm on those roads. I will see them tomorrow morning on my way back to be with Dad.

It's him who is grey now. Grey hair. His skin looks grey too. His arms, the muscles wasted, look like the stiff grey branches reaching into the sky. A few days ago, while I was sitting next to Dad as he slept, his eyes half opened and he said, 'The man who came out of the ground has dissolved into nature.'

I think that was Dad describing his final adventure.

Mum

My mother told me that until I was three, she thought I was strange and was going to die.

I was too good, she said, like some kind of an angel. I was quiet; I didn't cry, didn't get angry, could play by myself happily. Then she caught me one day trying to get my tricycle out of my bedroom and into the long hallway in our house on Goble Road, in Morningside, in Durban, South Africa.

I rarely went anywhere without my trike – inside, outside, at the beach. Somewhere in an old box, my mum still has a super-8 movie of me riding it at the beach before Kenny, one of my parents' surfing mates with long blond hair, jumped on it and broke it. As usual, Dad laughed. I remember staring at the trike wondering how it was going to be fixed.

At home, the wooden floor of the hallway, to my child's mind, was as long as one of the dirt roads Dad used to drive down when we were looking for surf or going camping. On my red tricycle,

The Eye of the Dragonfly

I would take myself on imaginary adventures, pretending to do three-point turns, reversing, when necessary. I played make-believe that I was in all sorts of wild and wonderful surroundings as I rode up and down that hallway.

This particular day, for whatever reason, I wasn't riding my trike with its built-in trailer but trying to pull it sideways from my room into the hallway. It was too wide, but I couldn't work that out and persisted. Mum heard me muttering under my breath, each word emphasised with each tug of the trike, 'You. Fucking. Bastard'.

Thank God, she thought, my child is normal. Truth is, I am still that child – just as happy in company or alone, just as happy doing whatever it is I am doing, and occasionally, when all my buttons have been pushed, using all the language skills I have.

Ironically, Mum spent the next 55 years predicting to anyone who would listen that I was on the verge of a mental collapse. She hadn't known Stan long before telling him I needed to see a psychologist because I wasn't dealing with the breakdown I was heading for. To put an end to this ridiculousness, I made an appointment with a Macquarie Street psychologist. He asked me why I was there. I told him. He asked me if I was feeling unusually stressed; I said no. He asked if there was anything I'd like to talk about; I said not particularly. We chatted on for a while and then he said that unless I wanted to make an appointment to come back and chat, he didn't see any need to continue with future sessions. My mum couldn't wait to ask me what he said. When I told her, she got up and walked out of the room to make a cup of tea.

This is the strange relationship my mum and I share. We don't think alike, although we do look alike. My blood pressure is often low, hers is high. When something unexpected happens, her default position is stress, mine is intrigue. Why did that happen? How did that happen? What should I do now? I see challenges that need to be solved; she sees problems that need to be avoided.

Earlier today, Mum told me, 'I'd love to be able to think like you. I'd hate your life, but it would be good to think like you.' This, of course, is code. She wouldn't really like to think like me: she says that because she thinks I don't care enough about things that should matter more, meaning her. If she could think like me, she wouldn't have to care either. But I do care. And in her strange way, she is letting me know she cares too.

Our relationship has had more than its fair share of spiky moments, I'm sure partly because aspects of my character remind her of Dad's. If anyone who knows her reads this chapter, they will be surprised to see her described as tense, because Mum is widely known as Lynne, the cool, happy-go-lucky surfer chick from Manly. It was their love of surfing that brought Mum and Dad together. It was their completely different attitudes to life that drove them apart.

Along with some of her friends, she was one of the original members of the Manly Pacific Board Riders club. An old black-and-white photo shows the crew sitting on the beach wall at Manly. There is Mum, not long turned 18, and there am I, a couple of months old, perched on her lap. Dad, four years older than Mum, was standing next to her. Some of their mates were there too – Midget, Bones, Bubba-Louey, Goody, Baddy, Dummy and Horse. Dad was known as Daz. Mum was known as Gidget. I became known as Pebbles with my blonde hair tied up on top of my head in the style of the Flintstones character.

While Dad shaped and glassed surfboards at the Gordon Woods factory on Harbord Road, just over the hill from Manly, Mum worked at the front counter in the showroom of another manufacturer, Scott Dillon. I slept in a bassinet under the counter. By the time I was two, we were off on our first family adventure, on board the *Galileo* from Sydney to Durban. It was late 1968.

The *Galileo* was originally commissioned to bring Italian immigrants to Australia, returning home via the Cape of Good Hope. It later became a cruise ship, until an engine-room fire in 1999 caused it to sink in the Malacca Strait. All passengers on board were rescued. Luckily, there were no such misadventures on our journey, although Mum suffered terrible motion sickness and spent the two-week journey holed up in the cabin. Plenty of Mum and Dad's friends were heading to South Africa at the time because reports of the wild, uninhabited coastline with large waves posed a challenge too good to resist. Dad's brother, Stork, had already moved to Durban and married his South African wife, my aunty Sue. Their son, Wayne, was still a few years away.

As a bit of a side track here, decades later, while walking through a shopping centre in Sydney, I saw an older lady, about my mum's age, reading a front-page magazine story about a doping saga at Essendon Football Club. I wondered why a woman in Sydney, at her age and potentially not having grown up with Aussie Rules, would be so interested in a very Melbourne story. So I asked her. I introduced myself and said I had been following the story closely and was wondering what she thought about it all. Her answer cracked me up.

'I know who you are, Tracey. You won't remember this, but on the boat to South Africa, your mum was so sick she couldn't look after you, so I did. I have followed your work ever since you began your career in the media.'

Isn't the universe magnificent?

The day we embarked on the *Galileo* for an experience that was to change all our lives, I remember being surrounded by a whole crowd of excited people all a lot taller than me. There was noise on board and noise on the pier way below. I had some streamers like the ones I saw others throwing overboard. I threw mine over too but didn't realise I had to hold on to one end as the other unfurled, twirling down the side of the boat. Dad was laughing, Mum was crying. I thought she was crying because I'd dropped my streamer. I told her it was okay, I had another one, she didn't need to cry. I didn't realise how sad she was to be leaving her family, heading to shores unknown.

From the stories I've heard, Mum was a talented athlete with dreams of competing at the Olympics. She told me having a child (me) put an end to many of her dreams. I can understand how that, too, has added complexity to our relationship: still so young, she was suddenly burdened by a responsibility she had not anticipated. Her older sister, Noelle, her two older brothers, Geoff and Lindsay, and her younger brother, Bruce, were also talented athletes. Their mum and dad, Joy and Noel Webster, were officials in charge of one of the local Little Athletics clubs on Sydney's Northern Beaches.

Noel was a war veteran who didn't talk much. Along with his brothers, all stonemasons, he helped cut the road through to Palm Beach. Many of the stone houses still standing around the Barrenjoey Headland were built by the Websters. Early in his 40s, he was struck down with rheumatoid arthritis. The family moved to Springwood because the doctor recommended the mountain air would be better for him than the salt air.

Joy was an outrageous, loud, give-anything-a-go type of woman who was unafraid of speaking her mind. I have few memories of her because she and my mum were not close, so visits were infrequent. But I do recall one Christmas, when the family gathered at Aunty Noelle and Uncle Peter's place. Their kids were given a mini bike, and Nanny (Joy) was thrilled and decided she wanted to have a ride. She jumped on, revved a little too fiercely, and took off across the lawn and straight up the back fence, falling to the ground. That was Joy.

There is a streak of Joy in me. It was evident in my mum's sister too. Aunty Noelle would give anything a go. She loved life. I used to love school holidays because I'd often get to spend a week or so staying with my cousins Deborah, Linda, Steven and Paul at Aunty Noelle and Uncle Peter's place at Blacktown. Once, I got some sort of a bug and started vomiting through the night. Aunty Noelle had planned to take all us kids to a school holiday showing of *Willy Wonka & the Chocolate Factory* at the local cinema. 'C'mon,' she said to me, 'it'll be good for you to take your mind off being sick,' and off we went.

While Aunty Noelle queued up for tickets, I sat on a bench in the cinema lobby with one of those old hospital-grade grey woollen blankets around my shoulders, vomiting into an empty ice-cream bucket. I was conscious that every other kid who walked through the door said a version of, 'Oh yuck, look at that kid spewing!'

During the quiet bits in the movie, while the audience watched rivers of chocolate being swirled about, there was also the regular interruption of another vomit from me splattering into the ice-cream container. Aunty Noelle would whisper that everything was okay as she wiped my forehead with a cold face cloth she had in a separate bucket of water she'd brought for the purpose. At some point before the movie ended, there was nothing left in me. The shivers started to subside too. 'See,' she said, 'I knew it'd be good for you to get out of the house.'

Aunty Noelle always made me laugh. Later in life, she struggled with chronic diabetes. But did it stop her always ordering an affogato whenever we went out for coffee? No. She was here for an enjoyable time; life was to be lived to the fullest and to hell with the consequences. On her final day before she passed away, I had flown back from working in Melbourne and stopped by the hospital to see her on my way home. When I walked through the door, she was happy to see me and started ripping the drips out of her arm.

'No, you can't do that, Aunty Noelle,' I said.

'Oh no, not you too, Tracey! I didn't expect that from you! Just get these things out of my arm and take me home.'

The nurse came into the room, followed by a lady with a food trolley. Aunty Noelle was immediately distracted. She went straight past the meal to the dessert tray and dived into the ice cream. When I think about my aunty, I can't help but chuckle at how she embraced life, not caring what others thought, forging her own path through whatever challenges were put in front of her.

I imagine that as a kid, her life and that of my mum and their brothers wasn't always easy in a post-war environment. Noel was burdened by his war experiences, and Joy tried to keep up appearances even though money was scarce given her husband's often prolonged medical timeouts from work. They were a struggling working-class family like many others at the time. My mother once told me that her mother's family thought Joy had 'married beneath her'. Mum's family grew up around Dee Why on Sydney's Northern Beaches. A rich aunt and uncle on my grandmother's side, who had no children of their own, were both well-respected artists – Dorothy Reynolds and GK Townshend. They paid for Mum and Noelle to go Queenwood, the exclusive girls' school in Mosman, where their academic and sporting talents were recognised. Mum wanted to be a schoolteacher, but that didn't happen. Instead, she hooked up with Dad, and his adventures became hers.

After returning from overseas, we used to go to visit my mum's aunty Dorothy in Dee Why regularly. Mum would help keep her rainforest-like garden under control as well as clean her cottage, Delmar. When Dorothy became too old and unable to care for herself any longer, Mum helped her move into a nursing home. When she died and left her home to Mum, we moved into Delmar. It wasn't the relief Mum was expecting. Up until that point, we had only ever rented. Dad wasn't a saver, and he wasn't interested in doing anything that might anchor him anywhere. And apart from anything else, in the late 1970s, death duties were still a thing, meaning Mum had to get a substantial bank loan to cover the tax on the valuable land and small wooden cottage. Dad had little to contribute – and even if he had done, I think Mum wanted to do this for herself, proving she could survive without Dad and perhaps giving herself the dose of confidence she needed to kick him out.

Home was not often a happy place when they were both in it. After they finally had their last argument and Mum told Dad not to come back, she worked three jobs to pay off the loan. Jodi and I had both earned scholarships to Pittwater House, a non-denominational private school at Collaroy, where English, maths and sport were single-sex classes, while others were combined. I loved the school and thrived under its experimental system. To help Mum, from our early teens Jodi and I always worked – either on afternoons after school or on weekends at a surf shop in Manly. From the small amount we earned, we paid Mum a percentage for rent. It probably didn't really help her, but it was her way of teaching my sister and me about financial responsibility. With Mum working day and night, often to the point of exhaustion, my default position was responsibility – at home, at school, and anywhere else I found myself. It was a position I was used to. From a young age, and no matter what time of night it was, I would take my little sister out of the house to shield her from the arguments when Dad got home from an evening at the Steyne Hotel in Manly with his mates. I would take her across the road and run down the hill to the public phone box to call the police (we never had a home phone before Delmar). Then we'd hide in the bushes and play whatever game I made up, or I'd tell stories to try and keep Jodi's mind off what was happening at home. I would take her back inside once I saw the cops arrive.

As soon as I finished school, I left home, moving in with a friend, leaving my 13-year-old sister and mum to live their lives together. I think that's why Mum and Jodi are the closest. They also share similar personalities and outlooks. While I stayed in touch with Dad, Jodi didn't. My mum certainly didn't.

Mum met her new partner, Murray, when I was in my 20s. Murray, a Māori, was one of the gentlest people you could ever hope to meet. He was a guardian angel for my mum. When he died suddenly, in early 2023, it left a gaping hole in her life. It seems, no matter what, life for Mum is a struggle.

My mum is a good person. She can, and does, talk to anybody. She has a smile that can light up a room; alternatively, her mood can also quickly cast a shadow over it. She is a force of nature, unaware of her own abilities. She is a complex mix: hyper-confident in appearance, while in reality she can be easily offended and somewhat fragile.

After having two strokes, the second on the one-year anniversary of Murray's death, she decided she wanted to live with Stan and me in Adelong (actually, she wanted to live with Stan). The town is beautiful; our earth-and-wood home looks out to a forest of trees in every direction, and there is a clear, fast-flowing creek on one side. But Mum is not happy. Aside from sporadic moments here and there, I don't think she ever has been. The moment she thinks she's happy, it's as if she feels some sort of guilt or shame, with negative thoughts flooding in.

I love my mum, of course I do. But we can only share short bursts together before something – usually something I say – goes wrong. It's always been that way. Mostly I ignore it. Sometimes I retaliate. But the truth is, her love-hate marriage with my father and the ghosts of lives she didn't get to lead will always haunt our relationship.

In early 2025, while Stan and I were on holidays with our youngest son, Jesse, and his girlfriend Millie, Mum moved out. She didn't tell me, she wanted to surprise me when I got home but I found out anyway. I rang but she didn't answer. I sent her a text asking if what I'd heard was true. She didn't answer the question, but demanded to know, 'WHO told YOU.'

Mum and I are a work in progress. I love you, Mum.

Life Without Borders
Home

My parents were young surfers finding their way in the early days of the sport, when it was still more an anti-establishment counterculture than a semi-professional business. The world was emerging from the Vietnam War. Many of those who fought never returned. Those who did – including friends of my parents – were permanently scarred by what they were forced to do, what they saw, and what they could never unsee.

John Lennon wanted the globe to 'imagine' and 'give peace a chance', while Bob Dylan implored a tambourine man to 'play a song for me'. The Bee Gees were teaching me to contemplate what would happen if there was only one more hour to live, long before I knew it as what the Buddhists call a meditation on death – a very good practice for living in the here and now. Cat Stevens called out the relentlessness of so-called progress by asking, 'Where do the children play?'

These songs were played over and over in whichever VW Kombi Dad had at the time. On our long road trips to camp and surf in places we had not seen before, sometimes I'd be sitting in the front seat with Mum and Dad, and other times I'd be lying on a mattress in the back with a stack of boards as we drove through the night and into the early morning to find deserted surf breaks. There was plenty of time to get lost in the words of these songs while gazing into the night skies or looking out beyond the horizon to the great unknown.

(These hymns of my childhood still resonate. When I was sitting in below-freezing temperatures at the opening ceremony of the Torino 2006 Winter Olympic Games, to the surprise of almost everyone there, Yoko Ono, widow of John Lennon, appeared on stage. 'If one billion people in the world think peace,' she told us, 'we will get peace.' How? 'Remember, each one of us has the power to change the world. Power works in mysterious ways. You don't have to do much. Visualise the domino effect and just start thinking peace. The message will circulate faster than you think. It's time for action. The action is peace.' And then Peter Gabriel sang Lennon's iconic 'Imagine'. It seemed so out of place, yet so wonderful and, ultimately, so Italian – jarring, stylish, beauty triumphant over practicality and logic. And the song has been played at most Olympics since.)

While Dad carved out a career shaping surfboards, Mum put her creativity and sewing ability to work in making beautiful leather clothing. Go-go dancing was a thing then, and some of the teenagers at the beach would get me – not yet seven – up on stage at the go-go contests. It was a bit of fun. My favourite things at the time were my white knee-length lace-up leather boots, my tasselled leather vest, and my two surfboards.

Like the ocean, our lives could be calm and still one minute, turbulent and messy the next. Jodi and I learned to read the weather patterns hovering above the heads of our mum and dad. We learned when to brace ourselves for the storm. We knew when to take cover, and when to re-emerge.

My upbringing was on a beach, somewhere, with people from everywhere, coming and going as they pleased. I was surrounded by people whose lives were a minute-by-minute adventure with a spirit of making do, no matter how much or how little (and it was usually how little) they had. Our youngest years were spent travelling to wherever Dad had heard the surf was good. I once wrote on a piece of paper that if ever I had kids, I wanted them to live in other countries as they grew up, because that was the single biggest determinant in my own childhood that shaped me as an adult. (At this moment, as I write, our three children are holidaying together in Japan after spending many of their childhood years in China and the Middle East.)

There is nothing I love more than exploring. Throw me into a foreign place where I don't speak the language, know nobody and don't know where to go, and I am in heaven. I thrive on new experiences. My husband is so different. He likes predictability, understandable given his childhood growing up in a First Nations family where his father did not know from one week to the next whether he would still be employed. I can't stand predictability. It makes me feel sick. When there is so much out there in the world to experience, why would I want the same thing day in, day out? Early in our married life, Stan would come back home to find I had moved every item of furniture and remodelled the house to the point of it being unrecognisable. 'Oh, no, not again,' he'd say as he opened the door to a place that looked foreign. (Sorry, Stan.)

I am interested in what's ahead – over the horizon, around the corner, down the road. We can all see what is here now. I want to know what's next. On long plane rides, while others watch movies, I am obsessed with the map showing the flight path – watching the contours of the globe, seeing that I am flying over Bucharest or Kyiv or Riyadh, looking out the window to see what it's like down there and to think of all the places I've been to and the many more I have not.

I love Google Maps, but I miss the old street directories. My dad taught me at a very young age how to look up random places and figure out how to get there. I have books of vintage maps, and atlases so large they could break a standard coffee table. Globes, in particular, have always attracted me: the roundness of the planet is so beautiful, how it floats in the universe amongst other planets – the further away you go, the more insignificant it becomes. How insignificant then are we, the lone individuals who walk the earth? Often, as part of my meditation, I imagine going deep inside myself into a single cell, the smallest symbol of life, then slowly pulling back, to a full person; pulling back further to see one person amongst several, amongst many, amongst all; pulling back further, beyond the street, the city, the nation, beyond the earth and into the dark universe. Then I return to myself. Here, now.

When the World Was Black and White
South Africa

Two snapshots of South Africa.

The first: there is an old photograph of me sitting on the ground squinting at the camera while I hold a Zulu baby in my arms. I am about three. Some years later, when I found that black-and-white photo, my mum told me that the Zulu child was the same age as me. The difference in our physical development was stark.

Three-year-old me was happy to spend time playing with another child on one of our pit stops during a camping trip in South Africa. Three-year-old me was not aware of the cruel apartheid regime in the country where we were living, nor of the concept – imposed by the state at the time – that this child and I should be judging each other by the colour of our skin. Three-year-old me was unaware that because of the differences in our colour, I had access to better food, education and medical care. Three-year-old me did not know that by the time we were adults, even though some of the paths we trod together were the same, there would be many more options available only to me because I was white and she was Black.

The second snapshot: George and Lorna were friends of my mum and dad. They were of Greek heritage and ran a local cafe-restaurant that sold beautifully barbecued chickens out of a rotisserie near the front entrance. While the four of them sat having adult conversations, I used to perch myself on one of the tall stools near the bar area, pretending to be the shop manager. Nobody would have been convinced that a white five-year-old with long blonde hair was the boss – certainly not the Black man who, on this particular night, walked in, opened the rotisserie, placed a chicken under his jacket and casually walked out.

Mum, Dad, George and Lorna were laughing about something when I walked over and told them what just happened, thinking I'd be in trouble for not charging the man for his chicken. George and Dad took off, quick as a flash, to see if they could catch the bloke. They did. George asked him what was under his jacket.

'Nothing boss,' the man said, as he opened up his coat to prove it. The chicken fell to the ground; apparently shocked, the man put his hand to his mouth. 'Oh boss! I don't know where it came from,' he said.

When George questioned him further, he said he was hungry and so was his family. George gave him the chicken and told him, 'Next time, just ask – don't steal.' I did not understand why this man and his family were hungry. Why could they not buy food like we did? Why did he call George 'boss' when he didn't even know him? *Boss* was a word I began to hear more and more; it was always said by a Black man in deference to a white man and usually had nothing to do with employment.

Thankfully, given Mum and Dad's Aussie heritage and their egalitarian outlook, not to mention Dad's anti-establishment philosophy common to most surfers back then, the way things were done in South Africa was not the way we did things. Being a Holmes, freewheeling and freethinking is much more appealing than falling into line with the agendas and motives set by others.

Living in South Africa sowed the seeds for what my life would become: one of adventures and new horizons, encounters with people from places I'd heard of and others I had not, and observations leading to questions for which there may be no answers.

—

When Apollo 11 landed on the moon in 1969, hundreds of millions of people watched with a combination of wonder, fear and hope. We had no television – nobody did in South Africa. It had been banned by the Minister for Posts and Telegraphs, Albert Hertzog, who feared it would have a destructive effect 'on children, the less developed, and other races'. What he really meant was that he didn't want South Africa's 80 percent Black majority being educated about political systems in other countries where they would not be ruled by the 20 percent white minority.

I am forever grateful that my mum woke me up in the still dark, early morning in Durban so we could listen to history being made on our scratchy transistor radio perched on the dimly lit kitchen table, broadcasting the commentary from Cape Kennedy (now Cape Canaveral) in Florida.

The countdown to 'Liftoff, we have liftoff' still makes me slightly teary half a century later, thinking of the enormity of what they were doing and yet the calm, measured voice of Jack King, the chief of the public information office at NASA's Kennedy Space Center, who had the job of describing what was happening and being prepared to commentate on anything unexpected.

My young mind being pulled far into space, as though I were walking on that shadowy white ball that I would look at in the sky from my makeshift bed in the back of our Kombi, set me on a path of always looking outward at the possibilities and revelations that lay beyond any horizon. A fascination for journeys into the unknown became my motivating force.

South Africa was isolated in other ways too. Under its apartheid regime – vigorously upheld by its white president, JJ Fouché – 'coloured' people were banned not just from whites-only restaurants, cafes, beaches, parks and hospitals, but also from representing the country in national sports teams. And so the International Olympic Committee banned South Africa prior to the Tokyo 1964 Games. Due to growing pressure from other African nations, the IOC eventually expelled South Africa from the Olympic movement altogether in 1970, meaning their athletes could not compete at the Games, and the country was no longer a member of the organisation, unable to send delegates or representatives to meetings of consequence. The country remained isolated for the next 20 years.

Other sports bodies were slower to join the condemnation of the 'whites only' edict. The Wallabies, Australia's men's rugby union team, toured South Africa in 1969 and saw what was happening. When South Africa then toured Australia in 1970, six Wallabies refused to play against the visiting team. Australian opinion polls showed widespread support for the tour to go ahead, but as it progressed, trade union bans and public protests grew stronger. South Africa's 1971–1972 cricket tour to Australia was cancelled, and the chairman of the Australian Cricket Board, Sir Donald Bradman, stated there would be no more tours with South Africa until its teams were selected on a non-racial basis.

Sport inside South Africa was of course profoundly affected. One of the world's longest-running professional surfing events, the Gunston 500, began in Durban in 1969. My dad competed in that first event, and for many subsequent years shaped the surfboards ridden by many others, including six-time winner and 1977 world surfing champion Shaun Tomson. My mum worked in a surf shop owned by another well-known surfboard manufacturer, Max Wetteland, who along with a couple of other mates, including Shaun Tomson's dad, Ernie, had founded the contest. Max and his wife, Lyn, had a daughter the same age as me. Naturally, Leigh and I became friends.

The 1972 Gunston 500 contest had invited Hawaii's legendary Eddie Aikau, a big wave surfer and lifeguard from the notorious Waimea Bay, to compete. During his short life, Eddie saved more than 500 people from drowning at the Bay, and as a tribute to him, 'the Eddie' contest is staged at the Bay during Christmas–New Year if the surf is big enough, meaning over 6 metres. It's the reason why so many surfers have bumper stickers on their cars saying 'Eddie Would Go.' It takes a particular kind of courage.

When Eddie arrived in South Africa, he was given an 'honorary white visa' because he was competing as an athlete. A stamp in a passport saying he was an honorary white meant nothing at the hotel where all the other international surfers were staying; he was told he had to leave and find alternative accommodation where non-whites were allowed. Originally, he was going to stay with the Tomson family, but a fire in their home meant they were living in a hotel at the time. My mum invited Eddie to come and stay with us instead.

When the contest was over, Eddie added his surfboards to ours, all jammed inside the Kombi, and we set off on yet another surfari through what was then known as the Transkei – a region of the Xhosa-speaking people, distinctive from the Zulu-speaking people in KwaZulu-Natal province, where we lived. The beaches there, on South Africa's Eastern Cape province, were pristine. They had some of the world's best waves and what seemed to be a constant chill blowing, as the winds from the South Atlantic and the Indian Ocean came crashing into each other's path, battling for supremacy.

Mum, always handy with a sewing machine, made sure my sister and I always had the latest fashionable surf gear to wear. My favourite homemade items included my brown tasselled suede jacket and my paisley flared bell-bottom pants. Whenever we stopped on the side of the road for a pee, Dad would get a small fire going and get the billy boiling, and Mum would start trading with locals who came out to see what these strange white people were doing. Not many whites ventured into the Black homelands – surfers were the exception. Mum would trade some of the beautiful clothes she'd made for Jodi and me with the exquisitely patterned thick blankets made by the Africans. Mum would then turn those into one-off-design anoraks, guaranteeing Jodi and I were always warm, no matter how cold the weather was.

Too young to realise it at the time, my experience of South Africa was very different to that of most other white kids. It wasn't until I was old enough to understand politics and ideology that I realised what Eddie's experience of South Africa must have been like. Without my mum and dad, his experience would have been lonely, isolating and depressing.

It was no wonder that when he got back home to Hawaii, his parents wrote to mine saying their son would never be able to thank them enough, and we must accept their invitation to return the favour. It didn't take long for Dad to start planning our next trip. This time, it wouldn't be through the Transkei or to one of our favourite surf spots, Cape St Francis. We gave away the few possessions we had, packed a small bag of clothes each and caught the cheapest flight my parents could find to Hawaii.

It was my first plane trip. I felt like I was one of those astronauts who had only a few years earlier walked on the moon.

—

When FW de Klerk became South Africa's president in 1989, he swiftly started dismantling the hardline approach of previous governments. Anti-apartheid resistance groups had been outlawed as far back as the early 1960s, including the African National Congress (ANC), whose leader, Nelson Mandela, had been given a life sentence in 1962 for his role in establishing its military wing. ('It was only when all else had failed, when all channels of peaceful protest had been barred to us, that the decision was made to embark on violent forms of political struggle,' Mandela noted many years later.) Now, protests were allowed and political prisoners were released, including Nelson Mandela after 27 years of imprisonment, much of it spent in solitary confinement. Working with the government to repeal apartheid law, Mandela and de Klerk were awarded the Nobel Peace Prize in 1993. The following year, Mandela became president of South Africa.

While sport had played a role in isolating his country during apartheid, Mandela now used sport to unite the country and to re-establish its place on the international stage. South Africa's successful hosting of the 1995 Men's Rugby World Cup, which it won, was described as a pivotal moment in the country's history. Sport helped the healing begin.

The governments of South Africa, the USA and the UK had all declared the ANC a terrorist organisation. The USA did not remove Mandela from its terrorism watchlist until 2008, a decade after he'd stepped down as South Africa's first democratically elected president and had become one of the world's most revered leaders.

When I catch the evening news bulletins now, I listen to the language used to describe various world leaders – from the USA's Donald Trump, to Russia's Vladimir Putin, to Ukraine's Volodymyr Zelenskyy, to China's Xi Jinping and others. Will the words we use to describe them now be the same words that will be used to describe them and their places in history in 50 years from now? I doubt it.

There is only one thing I know for sure: things aren't always as they seem. Despite our belief that tomorrow the sun will rise and the sky will be blue, every astronaut who has flown into space has looked back at Earth and seen that it is the small planet itself that is blue; the atmosphere it is floating in is black. That's perspective.

When our youngest son, Jesse, was about three, we were living in Hong Kong. One day, he found some old black-and-white photos. He didn't know who the people were, but the photos really intrigued him.

A few days later, his inquisitiveness got the better of him.

'Mum, were you alive when the world was black and white?'

It's a very good question, one I am still pondering.

Driving Between the Tombstones

Hawaii

My mum learned to drive in an old white VW Beetle whose best days were behind it. It had one seat, the driver's seat. Next to it was placed an old wooden kitchen chair, which my dad sat on. My sister and I stood behind the driver's seat, holding on to the back of it while Dad instructed Mum, driving ever so slowly between the rickety tombstones in the Yee King Tong cemetery.

Living at the bottom of an ancient Chinese graveyard is not every seven-year-old's experience, but it was mine. The family of Eddie Aikau, the surfer who had stayed with us in South Africa, were caretakers of the graveyard and lived in a small collection of houses at the bottom of the burial grounds.

At the top of the property, amongst a grove of trees, was the large white 'bone house'. Many Hawaiians have Chinese heritage, dating back to the arrival of workers during the 1800s, who were employed on the sugar cane and pineapple plantations. For a fee, those of Chinese heritage could be buried at the cemetery, which was built in the late 1880s, and have their bones later dug up and stored in an urn in the bone house until they could be repatriated to their Chinese village of birth, as tradition dictated.

By the time we moved into our own little cabin on the property, most of the Chinese characters on the headstones could not be deciphered and only on a very rare occasion would there be visitors to the bone house. So us kids – including schoolmates who would often take a short cut home through the property – played hide and seek amongst the headstones. If any of us misbehaved, Pops Aikau would threaten us with being locked in the bone house overnight. It usually worked in instantly calming down any kid with a bad attitude.

The Pauoa canal ran behind the property, which was connected to the Pauoa Elementary School by a small footbridge I would use to get to school each day. Eddie's brothers, sister, mum, dad, assorted partners and kids all lived at the cemetery. In front of their houses, there was usually a collection of VW Beetles and Kombis, all packed with surfboards as family and friends came and went according to their work or surfing commitments.

Amongst the trees that separated the houses from the tombstones, they would often dig a hole to bury a pig amongst hot stones – a traditional way of slow-cooking pork in an earth oven for a luau. The luaus were always huge, festive occasions. They hosted one just for us not long after we arrived, with Hawaiians and surfing dignitary coming to meet us out of respect for the Aikaus. In another traditional ceremony, my dad and Eddie made small slits on their wrists to become 'blood brothers', each man wiping his blood onto the wrist of the other.

The Eye of the Dragonfly

Unlike Gordon Road Girls' School in Durban – where I wore a blue beret, white pleated uniform and thin red belt – Pauoa Elementary School did not have a uniform. Most of the locals probably couldn't afford uniforms anyway. On my first day, I was told by the teacher my white thongs – or 'flip-flops', as she called them – were not safe for school because when you ran around the playground somebody could tread on the back of one and trip you up. 'If you don't have enclosed shoes,' she said, 'bare feet would be better.'

The kids in my class were mostly Hawaiians with Portuguese, Chinese and Japanese heritage. We were all different, but all the same because we lived in Hawaii. On weekends, the kids surfed the small waves at Waikiki, the well-known tourist beach. Eddie's brother Clyde had a beach rental service there until he passed away in mid-2025: umbrellas, surfboards, boogie boards, deck-chairs, whatever – all yours for a small hourly fee. You can still get surf lessons there. Some of you might know it. It's just up from the larger-than-life statue of Duke Kahanamoku, Olympic swimming champion, Olympic water polo player, Hollywood actor and the man who introduced surfing to Australia in 1914.

There is a replica of that statue on the rocks at Freshwater Beach in Sydney, where Duke invited a local girl, Isabel Letham, to join him in a display of tandem surfing. Onlookers were enthralled and surfing took off. The board Duke rode in Freshwater is still hanging in the surf club there. That's where we held the service for Dad when he died in late 2024. When some of Dad's old mates and their kids did the traditional paddle out into the ocean to release his ashes, Uncle Stork stood and watched from the beach. I was videoing the moment. My uncle turned to me and said, 'That's exactly where we learned to surf' – I'd had no idea when I organised the service. He and Dad had been given a heavy wooden board by one of the locals, my uncle told me, which they used to hide in the grass at the northern end of the beach so they could paddle it out by the rock pool when wagging school and on days off.

Duke's tandem style is still used 100 years later to teach little kids to surf. My dad taught my sister and I the same way. Jodi was three when we moved to Hawaii, with a shock of black hair and freckles sprinkled across her face. She adapted to the surf scene in Hawaii quickly and lives there today. Half a century ago, she lay on the front of a board with Dad behind her, paddling onto waves at Waikiki. She'd absorbed the local lingo a little too easily: as Dad paddled onto one wave, Jodi yelled out to the dozens of other locals paddling for the same wave, 'Hey, fuck off you guys!'

—

Not far from the rural community where I live now, there is an old Chinese graveyard, much like the one I lived in as a kid. The Chinese workers who came to the area were buried there, with the promise that their bones would be dug up and sent back to their villages when somebody could afford to make the trip home. Workers like my great, great grandfather.

Dr Joseph Lin Su, also recorded in various records as Lim Sue, Dim Sue and Lein Soo, had a chemist in Gundagai. Most likely it wasn't the sort of chemist we visit today, but one specifically for the many Chinese miners and others who travelled here during the gold rush in the 1850s, at the same time other Chinese workers were venturing to the cane and pineapple plantations in Hawaii.

State records show that in 1858 around 10,000 Chinese people (overwhelmingly men) arrived as indentured labour, subject to the Masters and Servants Act. Most of the miners settled in the small but thriving village of Adelong, where one in three people at the time were from China. They also made their homes in the surrounding towns of Batlow, Tumut and Gundagai.

My great, great grandfather lived with a woman named Mary Ellen Sue, who ended up being charged with his attempted murder in 1874. Dr Lin had stumbled upon Mary Ellen drinking with a male patient who was living in his house. When Dr Lin asked what she was doing, Mary Ellen replied that she'd fallen in love with the visitor. The court heard Dr Lin was angered by the news. As he no doubt raised his objections, Mary Ellen reacted by 'attacking him violently with her tongue and eventually seized two knives and stabbed him in the abdomen, across the chest, and in the face', according to the court report in *The Wagga Wagga Advertiser*.

Dr Lin was found by a neighbour collapsed in the street with his innards hanging out, in a pool of blood. On arrival the police presumed he was dead. In the end, the jury found Ms Sue guilty of a lesser charge than attempted murder: 'wounding with intent to do bodily harm'.

A couple of years later, birth registrations show that Dr Joseph Lim Sue fathered Sarah Dim Sue in 1877, Joseph Lim Sue in 1879, and Harry (or Henry), whose birth date is contested. Their mother was Jane Elizabeth Wood. Jane already had eight children to her first husband, William Holmes, who had died in 1875. When Joseph and Elizabeth's children were still quite young, they started using the name Holmes. It was the beginning of my family's Chinese heritage being written out of existence.

It's not surprising they tried to disguise their ancestry given what was happening at the time. Anti-China sentiment was rising in the late 1870s. In 1881, the *Influx of Chinese Restriction Act* was introduced, followed by the repeal of the Act in 1888, then a Royal Commission into Alleged Chinese Gambling and Immorality in 1891. The Royal Commission was fairly complimentary in its conclusion, though, noting the Chinese were, 'a singularly peaceable and generally law-abiding section of the community', with low levels of criminality, and, 'Owing to the exercise of private charity by the well-to-do towards the poor of their own race, they do not depend or rely to any extent upon the benevolent institutions of this country.'

It was not enough to prevent the rise of the Anti-China League in Tumut and Adelong or the introduction of the *Immigration Restriction Act* of 1901, signalling the start of the White Australia policy. As the Chinese had become successful entrepreneurs across logging, farming, market gardens, trucking, laundry services and more, some local business owners felt their own success was being thwarted by the competition. There were plenty of other Australians, though, who stood up for their Chinese neighbours and refused to enforce some of the restrictions being placed on them.

During World War I, my great grandfather, Joseph John Holmes – born Joseph Lim Sue, Junior – signed up to serve. He was 38 years old. He was sent to Bullecourt, in France, which would become the scene of the two deadliest attacks suffered by Australian forces in the entire four-year war. It was there on 11 April and 3 May 1917 that 10,000 Australian soldiers lost their lives. My great grandfather was later awarded the Military Medal for 'acts of gallantry and devotion under fire' for his service as a stretcher-bearer, retrieving injured men from the frontline from dawn to dusk without rest.

Arriving back in Australia, he established a fruit farm in Kunama, on the outskirts of Batlow. He sent money for Alice, his 18-year-old bride from England, whom he met while in London recovering from the war. Against her family's wishes, she sailed for Australia. Little did she know she was heading to an isolated property a thousand miles from anywhere and that she would never see her family again. My grandmother Idy and grandfather Leonard lived in a home on one side of the farm, and it was there that my dad spent most of his childhood being taught by his grandfather all the skills needed to survive in the bush – or anywhere – without relying on a single other person.

Fishing, hunting, camping and making furniture out of fallen trees meant they had little need for anything or anyone else. Grandfather Jack, as they called him, was described as 'hard but fair'. He employed local Aboriginal workers on his farm and gave all the grandkids strict instructions that they were to treat the workers with nothing but respect. He also taught them not to talk much and not to divulge information. Legend has it the tax man once showed up. When he knocked on the farmhouse door and introduced himself, Grandfather Jack reached for something behind the half-opened door.

'Did anyone see you arrive?'

'No,' said the tax man.

'Then nobody will ever know if you left,' Grandfather Jack said to him as he revealed his rifle. The dollar signs in the tax man's eyes quickly dissolved as fear took hold.

'My advice to you,' Grandfather Jack said, 'is to turn around, walk away, and don't ever come back.'

The tax man cleverly took his advice.

One of my dad's cousins still lives up there in Kunama. Uncle Denny exhibits the same traits as my dad, his brothers and his cousins, no doubt learned from their grandfather: words aren't wasted. They are laconic, with a wickedly dry sense of humour and an ability to appear so distant yet be so aware of all that is happening around them.

I never met Grandfather Jack. He died three years before I was born, but if it wasn't for him, my life would've been very different. When my dad was just a small boy, his estranged father, Leonard Colless, kidnapped him from the farm. Grandfather Jack tracked Leonard down with his rifle, no doubt gave him a similar message to the one he'd given the tax man, and took my dad back to the farm. To prevent Leonard returning to the home he had once shared with Idy and the kids, Grandfather Jack burned it to the ground.

The next time my dad saw his father was about 30 years later, the night I answered the door at his aunty's cottage in Kunama.

Part Two
Life Stories

The ABC and Me

Women in Sport 1989 to FIFA Women's World Cup 2023

In 1989, I started a two-year traineeship as an ABC Broadcast Specialist, working in news and sport.

How I got there was another story of the universe working in interesting ways.

After finishing high school and spending some time contemplating whether I wanted to be a marine biologist, an ASIO spy or several options in between, I decided to enrol in a public relations course at TAFE, knowing the skills I learned there could be applied to whatever I decided to do longer term.

As luck would have it, my teacher was one of the most irrepressible people I have ever met: Kim McKay. For more than a decade Kim has been the CEO of the Australian Museum. Prior to that, she co-founded the hugely successful Clean Up Australia and Clean Up the World campaigns, held senior positions at National Geographic and Discovery channels in the USA, and authored five books. When I met her, she had just become partner of one of Sydney's leading boutique PR firms, Harfield McKay, with clients ranging from construction companies to sports events. After only a couple of weeks studying part-time with Kim, she offered me a job.

You won't believe this, but at the same time I started working at Harfield McKay, one of the biggest surfing events on the Australian calendar at the time employed the company to promote the event through the Australian and international media. It was a match made in heaven. I knew everything about surfing and most of the surfers competing, plus I was familiar with most of the media, having worked as a media liaison officer for local and regional surfing events during high school.

One thing led to another. After a couple of years, I left Harfield McKay to work on surfing full time, including travelling to some of the overseas events, filing reports to Australian Associated Press (AAP) and various radio stations, plus facilitating TV networks' requests for interviews with the champions of the day.

The year before Australia's bicentenary celebrating 200 years since the arrival of the First Fleet, I got a call from Kim. The Australian Bicentennial Authority (ABA) needed somebody to do the PR and handle media for the packed Sport '88 program – a schedule of 1,500 events throughout 1988 ranging from regional thong throwing and boomerang championships through to the prestigious women's Cricket World Cup, and the four-nations men's football Gold Cup, featuring world number one team Brazil, reigning FIFA World Cup champions Argentina, reigning Asian Cup champions Saudi Arabia, and host nation Australia. Kim told me she'd recommended me for the job. It was an incredibly busy, exciting, rewarding year, although

The Eye of the Dragonfly

I look back on the bicentenary with a mixture of thoughts these days.

When I started at the ABA, I was 21. Although I had been formed by my experiences in South Africa and Hawaii, and had always been surrounded by surfers from everywhere, my knowledge of race relations in my own country was lacking. It was not something we were ever taught at school and, to be frank, few people from Sydney's Northern Beaches had ever met an Indigenous person. Through surfing, I did, but it was not really talked about, because in the waves, everyone was equal – not judged by their colour. One of my closest friends on tour, Robbie Page, never spoke about his Dunghutti heritage, but these days he's an elder for all Indigenous surfers, having risen through the rankings to be one of the world's best, winning the prestigious Hawaiian Pipeline Masters in 1988. He now speaks much more openly about his Indigenous heritage and his connection to this land and its water. In 2008, he won the World Masters title in Peru, becoming the first surfer ever to win a world title while competing under the Aboriginal flag.

When I think now about the billions of dollars spent during the 1988 party celebrating the arrival of convicts to settle on stolen land, I feel incredibly embarrassed that my knowledge of Australia's history was so lopsided.

On Australia Day, 26 January 1988, more than 40,000 people marched through Sydney calling for Aboriginal land rights. It was known as the Long March for Justice, Freedom and Hope. One of the organisers was Linda Burney, who in 2022 would become Australia's first Indigenous female Minister for Indigenous Australians under Prime Minister Anthony Albanese.

While I did my thing as part of the small Sport '88 team – which included the News Corp journalist Steve Warnock, who came on to help cover the extraordinarily large program of events – the waves of the universe kept rolling. I spent much of my time filing reports for any news organisation that could not get to an event themselves, doing plenty of interviews with both local and international media about what had become a large celebration of multicultural Australia, while Steve introduced me to plenty of his mates, who were all old-school, hard-nosed journos who were good at sniffing out stories. The full-on year gave me an instant introduction to every sports organisation in Australia, from smallest to largest, as our team helped them plan and promote their events on the world stage, while Steve was giving me a condensed course in old style journalism in how to draw out the real stories from behind the scenes.

At the end of 1988, I got a call from one of the men I'd been interviewed by many times during the year, ABC's legendary Aussie Rules and boxing commentator (amongst many other things) George Grljusich. He was a former Aussie Rules player in Western Australia, known as a man who did not suffer fools (and who usually put every female he ever met into the fools basket). George told me the ABC was about to do job interviews for its highly coveted Broadcast Specialist trainee program. If I was interested and applied, he told me, I might get in.

Thousands of people applied, I was told, but I was lucky enough to make the shortlist for interviews. I got through a second round of interviews and was offered one of only two positions. This is one of many examples where I feel I've never fought to ride a wave but have enjoyed riding the wave that found me.

The Eye of the Dragonfly

Each weekend, in the early days, I'd help the producers find guests for the sports program that ran from morning till night each Saturday and Sunday, covering everything that moved – as long as it was men. Occasionally, there'd be some women's netball squeezed in, maybe even hockey, cricket or soccer.

I took it upon myself, in my spare time, to record some interviews with women who worked in sport for a weekly 15-minute segment that I called, creatively, 'Women in Sport'. Those days we had to record our phone interviews on old reel-to-reel tapes. Editing out glitches or mistakes in the interview required a special white pencil to mark the tape, a razor to cut it, and some slim white tape to splice the cut. It was a delicate process which I loved. It was like surgery for audio, the aim being to leave as small a scar as possible. If edited audio tape could be evaluated for scar tissue, I reckon I'd be in the running for the plastic surgery award, because my edits were so clean.

After I'd been splicing for about six months and had become highly proficient, a new member of staff joined us – a male commentator from regional New South Wales. This bloke had a penchant for alcoholic beverages during lunch. He often took lunch at morning-tea time. One afternoon, as he did his best to walk in a straight line into my office, he told me to come into one of the edit booths and he'd teach me how to cut-edit taped interviews. He proceeded to butcher several interviews, cutting the tape in the wrong places so that when they were played back there were entire words missing from sentences. It was hilarious! I learned there will always be a bloke who presumes he knows how to do things better than the female in the room, because, well, how could a female be as good? It was one incident of many which taught me that to stay in the race with the leading pack of men, it was a good idea to work harder, research more, arrive earlier and leave later. This became my work pattern and remains so till today.

After adding to the many contacts I'd made during the bicentenary and building up some knowledge about the women's sports scene, I remember presenting my first Women in Sport 'program' to the weekend sports producer, Peter Hoban. I leaned over his legs, which were outstretched on his work desk, to hand him the silver container protecting the audio tape inside.

'What's this?' he asked.

'It's a new weekly program that will run for about fifteen minutes with three or four interviews about women in sport.'

He unhooked his hands from behind his head, took the tape and snapped his legs back under the desk.

'Oh. Right.'

I turned around and walked back to my office, imagining what sort of conversation he was now having with the other two (male) broadcasters in the room. My guess is they imagined after a few weeks I would tire of seeking out news and interviews and Women in Sport would die a quick death. What they hadn't yet recognised in their junior colleague was a boundless well of energy, a certain stubbornness and a refusal to give up, like a dog with a bone. My commitment to seeking out new stories, and new ways of telling them, would have appeared like a lightning bolt arriving in an otherwise regular round of social golf amongst friends.

Unlike the seasoned broadcasters I worked with, I knew little of professional broadcasting, the strict protocols around news reporting, or the skills and techniques involved in extracting information using a range of interview styles – from the short, sharp news-gathering interview to a more relaxed feature taking the interviewee to places and depths they may never have previously gone. The energy I brought to the ABC Sports department, and my willingness to learn, meant the accomplished broadcasters I worked with were almost always willing to impart the wisdom of their experiences whenever I asked, including sharing some of their most valuable contacts – which can make or break careers. To each of the men I worked with in those early days I owe an enormous debt of gratitude, men whose voices were as recognisable as the sports they covered – Norman May, Alan Marks, David Morrow, Jim Maxwell, Peter Longman, Peter Wilkins, George Grljusich, Tim Lane, Gerry Collins and many others. Writing that sentence makes me wonder how long it is going to be until a future male sports broadcaster and journalist can say he was mentored entirely by women. Or even better, when gender becomes irrelevant, so junior men and women will be mentored by an equal mix of both.

Even in 2023, when I resigned from the ABC (for a third time in four decades), there were too many conversations in which men asked other men for their thoughts on an editorial decision regarding a story one of the women in the room had been working on. There were men who constantly asked the women in the department to chase contacts, find footage, or answer queries – as though the women were there to help the men, when the women were sometimes more experienced and almost always harder working than the blokes asking them for favours. Some wheels turn slowly. The male-heavy mindset in sports broadcasting is a particularly rusty wheel, with a few shiny new spokes added for show.

While I was learning the craft at ABC Radio, Karen Tighe was beating a similar path at ABC Television. Every now and then, I would be called across to fill in on a television shift, and from those early days, Karen and I forged a lasting friendship. We are so different in personality and style, but both of us see the humour in life's often challenging experiences. We are like two sides of the same coin, and we are often in awe at how lucky we have been to have stumbled into make a living out of talking to the world's most results-driven, committed and positive people – sometimes simple, sometimes complex, but always intriguing. Having become Australia's first female host of a national sports program in the early 1990s, I resigned in 1996 to work with the Sydney 2000 Olympics organising committee. It was such a special moment to have Karen named as my replacement on *Grandstand*.

—

Even when I ended my relationship with the ABC in 2023, I was still proposing projects that took them by surprise. Despite a 25-year connection, most never really knew what to make of me or the work I did. That might be a little harsh. The managers in the early years were probably more attuned to me and my work than many of those in the role in the later years. I don't know what it says about management today that they cannot see it's a waste of time and space to dress up day-old results as a sports segment when anyone interested in a result was either at the match or had the result in an instant on their phone. I am constantly stopped by people in the street who tell me they have no interest in sport but thank me for making it interesting and relevant via the stories I tell.

I rejoined the ABC in 2014, after more than a decade living and working in Hong Kong, Beijing and the Middle East. I was already an Olympic veteran, having covered five Summer and three Winter Games. Most journalists are lucky to cover one. I was known in Olympic circles, had excellent contacts who respected my work, and understood the Olympic movement and its member sports better than anyone in Australian media. Yet the ABC did not think I would add value to their coverage of Sochi 2014, Rio 2016, or PyeongChang 2018. For each of those Games, I took leave without pay and joined my old colleagues at CCTV (China Central Television), now known as CGTN (China Global Television Network). I actually enjoyed being part of their coverage much more than working for an Australian network, because they took a global perspective, unlike the Australian media, whose coverage I find mindlessly parochial and gold-medal-centric. I have always thought Australian audiences are denied so many fantastic stories because of the Australian media's narrow gaze. As a consumer, I have often wondered whether Australian networks are aware that there are other nations competing.

The Tokyo 2020 Olympics were the first I covered for the ABC during my third stint at the organisation. In my early days, I had covered Barcelona 1992 and anchored the coverage for Atlanta 1996, and I returned for a cameo at Beijing 2008 because of my intimate knowledge of China and its aspirations in hosting the Games. During my time overseas, I had also been one of the anchors of Foxtel's award-winning coverage for both the Vancouver 2010 Winter Olympics and the London 2012 Summer Games. When Tokyo rolled around, a year late because of COVID, I went as a writer for ABC online, a position I was most grateful for, since I was not selected by my own department, ABC News (radio and television).

Prior to Tokyo, I emailed the chair of the ABC board, Ita Buttrose, suggesting the ABC should consider bidding for the free-to-air rights for the FIFA Women's World Cup 2023. I knew it would generate huge interest not just for followers of the Matildas but for Australians from everywhere, who would also cheer on teams from nations they or their forebears had migrated from. She invited me up to her office for a pleasant cup of tea, asked me a few questions, told me her granddaughter played football and adored the Matildas, and asked me to send her a one-page brief as a follow-up.

I never heard back.

I had decided to go straight to the top because I knew the lack of interest in sport from many in the several layers of management that sat between me and her. Gone were the heady days when the ABC was a national leader in sports coverage. The phenomenal growth in broadcast rights fees meant the taxpayer-funded ABC could no longer afford the biggest events, and the sports department became a shadow of its former self. The FIFA Women's World Cup, however, had not reached the epic value of most other major events, and it could still be justified as a worthy investment by the national broadcaster, which has a charter and mandate to, 'contribute to national Australian identity and reflect cultural diversity.' It is almost impossible to imagine an event that encapsulates that requirement more perfectly than the FIFA Women's World Cup.

But the ABC let it slide through to its competitors.

In mid-2021, it was announced that Optus had secured the rights, and in October 2022, the Seven Network was announced as the free-to-air partner. Both broadcasters should be congratulated for their coverage, but I still believe it was an opportunity missed by the ABC.

Early in the World Cup year, having returned from covering the FIFA Men's World Cup in 2022 in Qatar, I wrote another proposal. This time, it was a detailed coverage plan, working around not having any rights. I sent it to my direct boss, James Coventry, the head of the sports department at ABC News, as one of my last contributions to the ABC, since I had already resigned. I wrote that I would like to coordinate the ABC's multi-platform delivery of the Women's World Cup by mentoring many of the young, talented multicultural women at the ABC to deliver a spectacular female-led coverage showcasing the ABC's diversity. He liked my proposal but told me he would put Amanda Shalala in charge, asking me to brief her on how I saw the proposal working. I could be part of the reporting team, he said. I hadn't wanted to be on air during the coverage – it was time for the next generation. I was disappointed, even momentarily angry.

Having worked in and out of the ABC for the best part of three decades, I thought I'd earned the right to oversee the coverage I had designed – including a daily podcast, daily television previews and reviews, live crosses for radio and television, a weekly update show, the 7:00 pm nightly news packages and crosses into the late-night program *The World*. All of this was to be done despite the ABC not being a rights holder, which would make coverage more difficult – but it would be very much in keeping with what I believed the national broadcaster should be doing for events of such significance.

Over the years, I had put in a ridiculous amount of unpaid time at the ABC, often working into the early hours but never failing to arrive back in the morning after minimal sleep. Most of my work involved events and press conferences that often took place in time zones unfavourable to Australia, but I did my best never to miss them. Not only did this give the ABC content for their radio, TV and digital platforms, it also kept the ABC's name on the international radar, ahead of many other Australian organisations who rarely had anybody attend the virtual press conferences.

Willingly I gave my time to mentor many of the young journalists that came through the ABC's doors, including almost all of those from diverse backgrounds. Amanda Shalala had been one of my mentees early on in her career, so it was a pleasure to work with her on one of the world's biggest events and to see her go on to be appointed James Coventry's deputy sports editor for news.

The World Cup itself was an exhilarating, exciting and exhausting month. The best part of being on the frontline was interacting with fans who spanned multiple generations across the nation. I had a front-row seat watching people come together, putting aside their differences and much of the negativity in the world in order to celebrate something good. This is the beauty of a job like mine, and it is the beauty of sport. It is that unquantifiable element which, by its nature, is not represented in any economic or academic ledger.

The Eye of the Dragonfly

Many of the 2023 Matildas named Sydney Olympic gold-medal athlete Cathy Freeman as their inspiration to become elite athletes themselves. In another 20 years, it will be the names of today's Matildas who will be recalled as that generation's inspiration.

To have had a career that has coincided with the growth of women's sport from being played in virtually empty stadiums with little media coverage to drawing capacity crowds and global coverage is to have witnessed one of the great social and cultural shifts of our time. For that I am grateful to every colleague whom I have worked alongside, every senior journalist from whom I have learned, each of my bosses who supported me (and I know it wasn't always easy, because of my sheer determination and vision), and most important, to all those who come next. It is the journalists of tomorrow who must find new ways of storytelling in a fractured world and an equally fractured media landscape. If I could impart one thing, it would be this: when you know the story is worth more, resist the pressure to water it down – fight for what you know is right.

As I mentioned earlier, I had already resigned when I submitted my proposal for the World Cup coverage. James Coventry, with a little help from my husband, convinced me to stay, knowing it would be an historic event, as would the next Olympics, in Paris in 2024. I am not often talked out of decisions I make. I could count the times on one hand. I agreed to stay, but only lasted until the end of the World Cup year. The Paris Olympics I would do on my own terms.

An Improbable Introduction to F1

I'm not sure how you'd describe it, but every now and then a certain spirit takes hold of me – a spirit of defiance? A fighting spirit? An adamant spirit? An 'I will not be swayed' spirit? Maybe it's a combination of all four. One time this spirit took hold of me was in Portugal, September 1990, during my second year at the ABC.

My sister, Jodi, inherited Mum's competitive sporting gene. I was competitive too, but it was an internal competitiveness that rarely required a voice. It was a mindset I recognised in my father. When triggered, the colour in my eyes strengthens and those opposite me recognise I am not in the mood to be tested.

Before my sister moved into sports management, she was a pro surfer. In 1990, when she headed off to contests in France, Spain and Portugal, I took some of my holiday leave and joined her. The contest in Portugal ended up being delayed because there was literally no surf for a few days. Reading the English-language edition of the local paper over my morning coffee, I saw that the Portuguese F1 Grand Prix was being staged on the coming weekend. Immediately, the thought struck me: I have to go. Not as a spectator, though – I'm going to get an accreditation and join the media contingent.

How naive.

I caught the bus to the world-famous Autódromo do Estoril track and found the media office, where journalists and commentators could pick up their accreditations.

'Hello, my name's Tracey Holmes. I am from the ABC. I'm here to pick up the accreditation for me and my camera person.'

The front-desk staff member searched and then regretfully informed me there were no passes.

'Well, there must be some mistake,' I said. 'I've travelled from Australia. It's a very long way to come.'

'I'm sorry. There is nothing I can do.'

'That's okay,' I replied, feeling the spirit take hold. 'I'll wait here until somebody who *can* help arrives. Or you can phone my boss in Australia and explain why I won't be sending any interviews back.'

There I sat. Ten minutes went by, 15 minutes, 20 minutes. Eventually, the poor woman on the front desk made a call to someone and had a conversation in Portuguese, and five minutes later, the head of media marched through the door.

'Can I help you?' he asked.

'Yes, there has been some mistake. My two accreditations are not here, and I'm not leaving until I have them.'

'Follow me,' he said as he charged towards his office.

After he sat behind his desk, a short interview of sorts ensued, with a barrage of questions: who are you, where are you from, why are you here, what type of reports will you do?

Five minutes later, he pulled two 'Access All Areas' passes from his top drawer. It was all I could do to keep a straight face. I could not believe my luck. Then he grabbed a permanent marker and began crossing out certain areas: pit lane, one-on-one interview area, access to team trailers. By the time he'd finished, all that was left was an entry pass with some access to press conferences. But hey, beggars can't be choosers, right? Jodi and I were in!

Back on the bus to our beachside accommodation, with the two passes hanging around my neck on flashy F1 lanyards, I took the seat I have preferred since high school: back corner, giving me full view of everyone coming and going. It was about a half-hour ride, so I figured I had time to take my nail polish off. (What I carry in my bag would amaze you.) As the bus hit a bump, a drop of nail polish remover fell onto one of the passes. Quickly wiping it off so as not to damage our entry tickets, I noticed that the only thing damaged was the permanent marker. It wiped right off. Now I was chuckling out loud. With my tissue, I carefully removed the permanent marker from the other pass, and suddenly, Jodi and I had full access to pit lane and all the behind-the-scenes buzz of F1.

I did not waste the opportunity. On Thursday, when all the drivers arrived to test their cars and get in some early practice sessions ahead of Sunday's race, Jodi (with a borrowed camera and a ridiculous hanky tied around her throat because she thought it made her look like a professional) and I headed to the track, with our best 'we belong here' casual expressions plastered on our faces.

The Eye of the Dragonfly

The areas behind pit lane are an absolute hive of high-powered, high-octane activity, all the teams housed in their trailers and the mechanics in the garages, furiously at work setting up the cars, tweaking this and that, huddled over computers in team meetings with managers and drivers. It was an incredible introduction to the high-tech engineering world that is F1.

You thought a capacity football crowd at the MCG or Wembley or Maracanã was good? There is nothing like pit lane at an F1 Grand Prix. It makes your bones shake and your brain rattle inside your head. Each time one of the drivers pulled out to burn around the track, testing whatever fine-tuning had just been done, it felt like a thunderstorm was coming out of the ground beneath our feet.

The superstar driver of the time was Brazil's Ayrton Senna. He had already won a world title in 1988 and would win his second in 1990. He was an absolute hero to all my Brazilian surfing friends. So Jodi and I made a beeline to the McLaren trailer and requested an interview. We were told to come back in half an hour, when Senna would be on one of his breaks. (To all the budding journalists and sports commentators out there: access like this doesn't exist today, but do not let me deter you – where there is a will, there is a way!)

While I recorded an interview on my ABC-issued Sony recorder, Jodi was snapping away from all sorts of angles. Just as the interview finished, Senna's teammate, Gerhard Berger, arrived. Did he have time for an interview too? Yes, he did! We tried to get the grumpy French champion Alain Prost, but he waved us away. We did manage a doorstop with England's Nigel Mansell and the notoriously reserved McLaren team boss,

Sir Ron Dennis. He was the mastermind of the team, winning seven consecutive championships, three of them with Senna.

On the day of the actual race, the Portuguese swell arrived, meaning the surf contest was back on and I'd lost my camera person. I chose to support Jodi (plus I didn't want to push my luck).

My unexpected introduction to the world of F1 had me hooked. When I got back to the ABC and presented my bosses with a series of interviews they would never have otherwise obtained, I convinced them to broadcast *Grandstand* from pit lane at future Australian F1 Grands Prix. Wearing a legitimate accreditation pass, hosting the ABC's sport program from above the roar of the engines was an annual highlight. I got to know several of the drivers and the CEO of the Australian Grand Prix, Mal Hemmerling, who would go on to become my boss for a short time at the Sydney 2000 Olympic Games organising committee.

My last interview with Senna was after he won the Australian Grand Prix in November 1993. Six months later, I woke around 4:00 am to listen to the overnight sports news from BBC and heard the devastating news that he had died in an horrendous crash at the San Marino Grand Prix. Senna was well known for his advocacy of driver safety, often speaking up when others felt they could not, and he had been anxious about regulation changes to the cars for the 1994 season. The day before the San Marino race, rookie Austrian driver Roland Ratzenberger died when his car crashed during qualifying. Twenty-four hours later, F1 had lost one of its greatest drivers.

Going into work that day, knowing this would be the story that dominated the news, I listened back to my interview with Senna. There had been only three races since. I had not realised it before, but I was struck to hear Senna answering in past tense, telling me about how he'd like to be remembered and what he saw as his legacy. On this particular day, it was like hearing someone speaking from the grave.

Grandstand

My bosses at the ABC took a gamble when they appointed me as the host of the national sports program *Grandstand* in the early 1990s. It was back in the days when ABC Radio dominated the sports media landscape because it still fought to own the rights to AFL, NRL, the Olympics and many other major events. That we had a team of commentators in every major city and a number of regional centres made it impossible for any other network to match the service and coverage we could provide.

The larger-than-life Tasmanian Neville Oliver was head of sport, the master planner and strategic guru Alan Marks was executive producer of national sport, and Peter Longman, who would go on to become head of sport, was the executive producer of *Grandstand*. Peter was the man who had to deal with the troops on the ground – refereeing all the battles over which staff members would get to cover which big events, whether states could break away from national coverage to do something that might have been of more interest locally, and even having final say over the many thought bubbles I came up with on any given day, such as the idea to broadcast two hours of the show from a hill in the middle of nowhere because the national skydiving championships were being held there.

I'm sure Longy thought most of my ideas were mad (because they were), but he'd always listen before giving me all the reasons why not, while I'd plead passionately with all the reasons of why we could and should, and then at the end of some verbal volleying and plenty of laughs, he'd make his decision. I won some, I lost some. Many years later, after he'd retired, someone at work questioned me about being a team player. Of course I was a team player, I argued, but that means making the best decision for our audience, not the best decision for one of your mates. Afterwards, I rang Longy to see whether he thought I was a good team player in the years that I was on his team. 'Of course you were, Holmesy,' he said, 'as long as all the decisions went your way.' Yep. I can handle that.

One of the segments I introduced to *Grandstand* was a weekly half-hour interview called the 'Hall of Fame'. We'd approach some of the biggest names in the world of sport – athletes, administrators, members of the royal family who had been involved in sport, IOC presidents and pretty much anybody who had a fascinating story to tell.

Before the 1990s, there were few fully professionalised sports. Athletes did not have long careers, because they couldn't afford to. Sponsorships were not the norm, prize money was non-existent in many sports, and there was no social media to drive personal branding. The segment was hugely popular because the interviews were less about sport and more about life. People who'd previously had no interest in sport were touched by human stories they could relate to.

I remember interviewing American tennis legend Arthur Ashe, one of the most gracious people you could ever hope to meet. He was the first Black man to win Wimbledon, as well as the Australian and US Open tournaments. He thought his greatest personal achievement was publishing a three-volume series, *A Hard Road to Glory: A History of the African-American Athlete*. It had taken him and a team of researchers six years to put together. After his playing days, he became a commentator and writer for publications including *Time* magazine and the *Washington Post*. He lived a life of service and giving back to the community.

Towards the end of 1992, when I interviewed him for the 'Hall of Fame', he was 49 but had only a few months left to live. It was believed that during one of several heart surgeries, he was given a transfusion of HIV-infected blood, and with no treatment in those days, he faced certain death from AIDS. I asked whether he ever thought, why me? No, he said, because if it wasn't him, it would have been someone else, and he wouldn't have wished that on anyone. With death so near, I asked what he had to look forward to. 'I hope I make it to my daughter's next birthday.'

The simplest observations can touch us all deeply. It is the reason why I work so hard at preparing for my interviews and hope my guest trusts me enough to share something so incredibly personal.

—

The Eye of the Dragonfly

The modern cliché says it takes 10,000 hours of practice to become an expert in something. I'd like to think I started developing my interview skills while competing in the Australian Surfing Scholastic titles, contests I never wanted to compete in (thanks, Mum!) where I'd sit out the back behind the breaking waves and talk to my opponents, deliberately not catching a wave so I would be eliminated. I might not have ever won a trophy, but each time I paddled back to the shore, I had gained further experience in talking to anyone about anything.

Depending on what you're trying to achieve, there are many ways to interview. The short, sharp, straight-to-the-point style for news programs with time limits; the doorstop when time for the interview is brief; the breaking news interview to try and establish some of the facts around an event that has just happened; the 'lead you down the garden path' style resulting in a gotcha moment; or the long-form, conversational interview hoping to tap into something unique that listeners or viewers may not have heard before. Long form is the style of interview I most enjoy, and the one I used in the 'Hall of Fame' interviews.

I spend a lot of time researching the guest – not just what they've had to say previously but what others have had to say about them. I think about what makes them interesting or what they might be interested in, other than the obvious topic of sport. I imagine the interview in my head: I think about where the conversation will go depending on the responses to my questions, and I wonder what the key might be to unlock something deeper inside. Often, I won't even ask the most obvious thing, because the guest will have answered that a thousand times before and can probably answer without the need to think. I want them to think. I want them to go somewhere different.

Any rugby league fan will know of Wayne Bennett, arguably the greatest coach of all time with his seven championships across multiple clubs spanning decades, his mentorship of other coaches, his innovation in the game and his sixth-sense ability to inspire his players individually. Anyone who has ever watched a media interview with Wayne Bennett will also know that he is notoriously difficult. He doesn't like or trust the media generally and has mastered the art of one-word answers. Not a great CV for a half-hour interview.

But I've always been intrigued by Wayne's Midas touch. He is more psychologist than football coach. He's been a Queensland cop. Of his three children, two have had lifelong disabilities, which he's rarely spoken about. He's a complex character, and it's that complexity that makes him interesting to me. One of the early pieces of wisdom I was taught was: if you are interested in your topic, others will find it interesting. For some time, I had been wondering why so many in the media steered clear of him while every player he'd ever coached would walk over hot coals for him. I thought I may as well put in a request with his club, and I was surprised when the Brisbane Broncos rang me back to say Wayne had agreed. He even volunteered to venture into Brisbane's ABC studio.

A couple of weeks before the interview, I was sitting on my balcony in my quiet street on Sydney's Northern Beaches. One of my neighbours, a man in his 80s, was always out hosing his garden at this time of the afternoon. I'd come to realise it was around the time his disabled son would be dropped off after his shift at a factory. I could sometimes hear their conversation, the dad asking his son how his day was, if he was tired, that he should go in and have a cool drink and put the telly on. His son would thank his dad, who kept hosing for a little while longer. I could see that his dad was thinking about something serious and wasn't yet ready to head inside.

Early on in my interview with Wayne, I retold the story of my neighbour and said that I thought what he was thinking about was what will happen to his son when he is no longer there. Wayne's eyes had been watering while I told him the story of my neighbour, and when I stopped, he audibly gulped, sucking in a mouthful of air. Through tears, and in a voice cracking with emotion, he said he knew what my neighbour was going through. As the parent of a disabled child, it is the first and last thing you think about every day of your life, he said, questioning what happens when you're gone. This lived experience plays a part in his relationship to every one of his players. It was a window into his soul.

—

My ABC training (oh how I wish they would bring back traineeships!) included learning how to do live commentary. My first lead commentary role was a sink or swim moment, completely unplanned, as I got to call the final stages of the 1991 World Netball Championship final between Australia and defending champions New Zealand, widely recognised as one of the greatest netball games ever played.

David Morrow, who was inducted into the National Rugby League Hall of Fame in 2024, was the ABC's NRL chief commentator at the time. He was going 'around the grounds', as it's called, during a break in play to get updates from commentators at all the other live sporting venues. I was at the netball and, after giving a quick score and saying that the match was electric given the two teams were going goal for goal, I crossed back to David, who said, 'Well that's more exciting than anything happening here, stay with it.'

An intercept pass in the last second meant Australia beat the Silver Ferns by a single goal. The capacity crowd at the Sydney Entertainment Centre erupted, and the Australian players jumped all over each other before collapsing in a heap on the floor like they were in a mosh pit. I remember trying to describe the scene as fully as possible while not wasting any words, knowing I had to get back to what the audience considered to be the main game, the rugby league. Once the initial mayhem had died down and I did indeed cross back to David, I heard his voice crack. He had become emotional just listening to the commentary. It was one of those moments that sticks with you forever.

Netball, at the time, was Australia's most popular women's sport in the media. Prime Minister Bob Hawke, a well-known sports enthusiast, described it as the best sporting contest he had seen. The team and its coach, Joyce Brown, were awarded the Medal of the Order of Australia in 1992, and in 2012 were all inducted into the Sport Australia Hall of Fame.

One of the players – the best goalkeeper in the world at the time, Keeley Devery – went on to become a top producer at Fox Sports, overseeing the first decade of what was the hugely popular weekly program *The Back Page*, hosted by Mike Gibson and comedian Billy Birmingham. I was the only female weekly panellist on the show and inevitably found myself on the other side of every argument with *Sydney Morning Herald* columnist and former Australian Wallaby Peter FitzSimons. Traditional sports viewers loved Fitzy giving it to me, while others loved me taking him on. After a decade together on the show, Fitzy and I were offered a gig together by the owner of the number one rating radio station 2GB, John Singleton. Fitzy was keen. I was on holiday in Hawaii at the time with Stan and his youngest son then, Dylan. I was about to fall pregnant and my life was heading in a completely different direction, so I turned it down. Fitzy and I remain friends to this day, but he still reminds me of the opportunity missed a quarter of a century ago.

—

For nearly a decade, I would set my alarm for 3:00 am most weekdays to get into the ABC to compile and present the sports news on the morning bulletins. After 9:00 am, I was free to start planning, researching and lining up guests for the weekend *Grandstand* program. My working week was Thursday to Monday; for years, like everyone who works in sport, I did not have a weekend off.

On one rare occasion that I did, I was at Clareville on Sydney's Northern Beaches inspecting houses to rent. It was the summer of 1994; bushfires were raging across a quarter of the state. To my north, the Central Coast Leagues Club had become a campground for thousands of people who'd been evacuated from their homes. Smoke was also filling the skies from fires to the south, with homes already lost from the Sutherland Shire to Chatswood and Turramurra. While standing on the balcony of one house, I looked across the bay in the direction of Ku-ring-gai Chase National Park. I watched orange smoke rising from behind the hills, darkening the sky at an increasing rate. I could smell the fire coming. Then flames became visible at the top of the peak.

I rang in to *Grandstand*, and Longy put me to air with host Mike McCann. I described the scene in front of me, as flames were blown down the hillside towards the small communities at the bottom of the national park.

Most people are not aware that the best live-action commentators in the world are radio-trained sports commentators. They are usually the only ones practised in calmly describing all types of frenetic events as they unfold, aware of what's happening on the periphery while keeping up with the action, which can change from moment to moment – whether it's a ball, a car or a bushfire. They need to paint full pictures, unable to rely on the vision television commentators work with. Remaining calm under pressure and describing live action is not the same as filing a one-minute news story with the advantage of preparing a written script and recording it. There is no script when events are unfolding quickly in front of your eyes. You must step into the moment and become the conduit between the event and the audience.

A regular listener to *Grandstand* phoned in to the program to say he was nearby and could pick me up in his tinnie at the nearby wharf to take me closer to the action. I was given his number. Fifteen minutes later, we were bouncing across the Pittwater swell, heading into what was now a thick, orange haze, the type that burns your eyes. As the devastation unfolded in front of me, I was kept on air. There were occasional momentary breaks so that sports action could be updated between the reporting. Some of my colleagues headed to other areas where they could give eye-witness accounts. I saw people leaving their homes, sitting on the end of the pier, some who'd packed a suitcase or bag, others with nothing, wondering how much of their homes and belongings would be destroyed. It was devastating to describe. Longy told me the ABC's Sydney station manager, Peter Wall, had phoned in because his brother lived in the small national park community I was describing. He asked if I could see whether his house was safe. Sadly, it wasn't. Peter's brother was one of the people sitting at the edge of the wharf.

Grandstand's coverage of the fires all over New South Wales that weekend was extraordinary, and it won the New York Festivals Radio Award for best live commentary. After that, the ABC established its emergency coverage plans, which now operate across the nation in times of fire, flood or any other crisis – although they missed what is, in my view, the significant opportunity to include sports commentators as part of the plan.

—

While I love the commentary opportunities I've had, it is interviewing I love best. One-on-one conversations with people who have experienced the ultimate highs and lows, or who have wrestled with complex life experiences, providing insights that can take us deep into their world, allowing us to see new or different perspectives – it's those conversations that drive me.

When the athletic track was finally laid at Stadium Australia for the Sydney 2000 Olympic Games, the Channel 7 program I presented, *The Games*, confirmed an interview with perhaps the one Australian who would bear more pressure than any other once the Games began: 400-metre world champion Cathy Freeman, a Kuku-Yalanji and Birri Gubba woman from North Queensland.

In trying to put myself in her shoes before our interview, I thought about pressure and inspiration. I wondered what it would mean to get a sneak preview of the Olympic track before anybody else had seen it. Would that give her an advantage over her rivals? Would it make her feel more at home on the big day? The plan was that I would start the interview with Cathy while we walked down the tunnel, leading from what would be the athletes' waiting area out onto the track. As we emerged, our producers would surprise Cathy by replaying her world championship win earlier in the year on the largest high-definition screen in the world, which had recently been erected at the end of the track. The commentary would be turned up to reverberate around the empty 110,000-seat venue. As we emerged from the darkness into the light and the video started, Cathy sank to her knees, watching her history-making moment in silence, daring to dream of another in less than a year's time.

On the night of Cathy's 400-metre final at the Games, Stan and I were lucky to be sitting amongst the crowd, thanks to Sydney Lord Mayor Frank Sartor, who had gifted us two of his own tickets. I remember the chills up and down my spine as Cathy ran around the back straight, with the crowd's raucous support pushing her on, stride after magnificent stride. As she crossed the finish line, she collapsed onto the track as she did on the day of our interview. Only, this time, it was different. This time, she was Olympic champion in front of a stadium full of homegrown supporters.

Years later, when interviewing her onstage at a function in Hong Kong, I asked her what was going through her mind as she sat on the track that September night. 'Between you and me,' she said, in front of almost a thousand people in the room, 'I thought, what a fucking relief.'

Pelé

Before Cristiano Ronaldo, before Lionel Messi, and before Diego Maradona, there was the greatest footballer of all time, a Brazilian legend who set the footballing world on fire while earning three FIFA World Cup titles.

At the height of his fame, Edson Arantes do Nascimento was – like Jesus, Mohammed and Buddha – known by a single name: Pelé. It was said that the name meant the 'black pearl' and illustrated the rarity of his footballing ability. (Sadly untrue; his nickname had no such meaning.) In Brazil, he was dubbed 'O Rei', the king. He also learned later in life that in Hebrew, *pele* means 'miracle'. As far as nicknames go, he had a fine selection to choose from.

I had travelled to Brazil in the late 1980s and spent time in Pelé's home city. Few would otherwise have heard of it, but Santos had previously held quite a place in world affairs. It was where international coffee prices were once negotiated, according to its coffee museum. Now its main attraction is a 5-kilometre-long white sand beach full of surfers, beach volleyballers and beach football players enjoying its tropical climate year-round.

I should point out that at the time, I knew little about football, even though at my local fish and chip shop in Manly I was often served by its owner, the legendary Joe Alagich, a former Socceroo, whose family was synonymous with the rise of football in this country. His cousin, Dianne Alagich, was capped 86 times for the Matildas. In my first news report for the ABC, in 1989, I described a goal being scored by 'a headbutt'. Luckily, I learned quickly, and I set about filling in the enormous gaps in my football knowledge before I was tested again. Ignorance framed in a more positive light could be described as innocence. And for those rare individuals who cannot escape their fame anywhere on the globe, meeting someone with little understanding of their fame is a unique experience, as I discovered.

In 1990, a luxurious, two-volume hardback publication called *The Pelé Albums* was released, containing a lot of material from Pelé's own collections, some of which had not been previously seen. As part of the launch, Pelé planned a worldwide tour, including a visit to Australia. I had recently started the 'Hall of Fame' interviews on *Grandstand*, and somehow I found the number of the agent coordinating Pelé's tour to Australia. She told me his agenda had been booked out months in advance and there was absolutely no time for a one-on-one interview, but I'd be welcome to travel to Western Sydney to join a five-minute all-in doorstop.

I decided to take a chance. The night before I journeyed west, I took a closer look at Pelé's itinerary. I noticed that after the doorstop he'd be travelling back to the city of Sydney for another appointment, presumably in the luxury of a hire car. I rang the agent again. I told her how I'd been to Santos, knew of the city's extraordinary love for the footballing star, and even had a copy of a record he once released, with its hit track 'My World Is a Ball'. How about after the doorstop, I ride in the back of the limo with Pelé, record my interview and get him to sing one of his famous songs from his 1977 album? She said she'd run it by him.

A day later, I walked into the office, my little Sony recorder in hand, with a 40-minute interview with Pelé – enough for a two-part series – complete with him singing his hit song from the back of a car. All I remember was my boss laughing, shaking his head and saying, not for the first or last time, 'Holmesy'.

Two years later, I was at my desk at the ABC in Ultimo planning the weekend *Grandstand* show when my phone rang.

'Hello, is this Tracey Holmes?' a thickly accented man asked.

'Yes.'

'I am from *Pelé* magazine. I know you interviewed him, and I would like to get some thoughts about what you thought of him for an article we are writing giving opinions from around the world.'

The story was fishy, but the voice – I'd heard it before.

'Pelé! It's you!'

He started laughing at the other end of the line. He was coming to Australia and would like to invite me and a couple of friends to dinner in Manly – a quiet dinner, he said, no fuss, nobody needs to know, especially not the media. He asked me to pick the restaurant and name the time. Done.

—

Pelé was not dissimilar to Messi, Ronaldo or Maradona. All of them were born into families that struggled economically, which might have been the root of their genius with a football. Playing from their earliest days with kids of all ages on rocky dirt roads, barefoot, kicking anything that could be made to resemble a round ball, honing their hand-eye coordination and subconsciously teaching themselves how to master the geometry of the game and the peculiarities of a ball's aerodynamics. Pelé's early days were spent playing soccer with an old sock stuffed with rags since he could not afford a ball.

All four champions learned their craft through grit and determination, beating those who were older and bigger than them, refining their reflexes, and most of all, filling them with a love of the game. They achieved every young player's dream, rising from humble streets to the top of the world's most recognised sport. But they all found that fame is a tangled web, one which renders escape impossible – perhaps none more than Pelé.

As Pelé's fame grew, his reluctance to speak out against racism, torture and injustice meant he had his critics. Some will tell you he remained politically neutral; others will point to his willingness to lend his fame to the military dictatorship that ruled Brazil from 1964 to 1985. During the 1970 FIFA World Cup, which Brazil went on to win, Pelé's image was used on propaganda posters declaring, 'Brazil, you love it or leave it.' And then when Brazil had left-leaning governments, Pelé would appear at their side. Everyone wanted a piece of him, and he appeared too willing to give it.

In a 2021 Netflix documentary, Pelé said he knew political opponents were being tortured during the military dictatorship and that, 'At that time, I would have preferred not to be Pelé.' The criticism he received for being the regime's puppet in the 1970 FIFA World Cup was perhaps the reason he refused to play in a fifth World Cup in 1974. That decision, in turn, resulted in him being labelled in some quarters as a traitor.

Pelé loved the money his fame brought him. Who could blame him? Far beyond being the face of a regime in 1970, he became a global ambassador for football, Pepsi, Mastercard and numerous other products. When he signed with the New York Cosmos football club in 1975, the struggling football league in the USA took off. Pelé was joined by several other global stars at the time, making Cosmos a glamour team that saw football move from sport to entertainment – a model now being copied in Saudi Arabia as it aims to establish a league supported and celebrated at home while earning recognition internationally.

Winning in sport delivers a peculiar type of fame. Being recognised globally for something you do with your hands or your feet has somehow come to mean you need to have a view on each global complexity. Worse is when that fame makes you think you should deliver those views. The media was the first to amplify this tendency; social media has seen it blow out exponentially. Pelé was one of the world's first successful conversions from athlete to brand, therefore one of the first to understand that politics swirled all about, and that the price for money and fame might be a piece of your soul.

As Australian critic and broadcaster Clive James wrote in his book *Fame in the 20th Century*, fame has a life of its own. I often wonder how many people made famous through sport would hand it all back to be able to play the games they love, with those they choose to be with, and head home to be with only those they love.

In 2022, a year before he died, Pelé described himself as, 'neither a superman nor a miracle worker . . . just a normal person who was given the gift of playing football by God'.

Pelé. The king, the black pearl, the miracle. Pelé, a normal person at the mercy of an almighty gift.

Managing the Media
Sydney 2000

They say the most traumatic things in life are break-ups, marriage, changing jobs, having kids and moving. Try doing it all of it within a year. I can laugh now.

In the lead-up to the Sydney 2000 Olympic Games, I worked at the organising committee, SOCOG, as the media information manager. Seven days and nights a week, the media could contact me from anywhere in the world with their questions – from mundane sports questions, to whatever political controversy was bubbling away, to the concern about the endangered green and golden bell frogs who lived in the waterways near the Olympic construction zone in Homebush (an underpass was built so they could avoid traffic as they travelled from one habitat to another), to one American journalist's repetitive questions about Ross River fever and why we weren't concerned about athletes potentially being infected with it from mosquito bites and dying while at the village. Seriously. I have never heard of anyone in Sydney dying from Ross River fever. I had two mobile phones and a pager so if a journo needed to contact me, they could leave messages on three separate devices. None of them ever stopped pinging.

I remember my first day at SOCOG, catching the Manly ferry to work with Simon Balderstone, a general manager in the CEO's office and former advisor to prime ministers Bob Hawke and Paul Keating. Splashed across the front page of the newspapers was a headline regarding whatever the latest scandal happened to be. We were heading straight to a press conference for a marketing announcement at which Olympics Minister and President of SOCOG Michael Knight was to appear.

Knight and I knew each other because I'd interviewed him a couple of times on *Grandstand*. The conversations weren't incredibly friendly but were always respectful, even though it was probably through gritted teeth. When I arrived at the SOCOG press conference, the minister walked in my direction, book-ending me between himself and a parked car.

'Welcome to the job,' he said with that political smile designed to fool a camera in case someone was recording the moment, but without hiding the intent of his message from me. 'You might think that as media information manager your job is to help the media. It's not.'

I don't recall much else of the conversation, other than I did not agree.

It was the start of a sometimes testy relationship. At one point, Knight's media staff requested weekly meetings with me so we could be across each other's briefs. I quickly figured out it was a fishing expedition on their part to know what I was up to, as if I was harbouring secrets. That's never been my game.

(Interestingly, there are a lot of people I've come across in my time who do play those games. Their suspicion often reveals their own motives.) The meetings with the minister's staff were a waste of time for me, so I told them I wouldn't be attending anymore but they should feel free to let me know if there was anything they needed help with.

Another warning I was given when I first arrived was that the Olympics editor for *The Sydney Morning Herald*, Matthew Moore, was 'real trouble'. What I saw was a journalist good at doing at his job. One thing that amazes me to this day is that despite constantly dealing with the media, there are many people inside sports organisations who either don't understand how the media operates or, despite understanding it, create an environment of mistrust and secrecy, which can only end badly. To be fair, there are also some journos who believe sports governing bodies can never be trusted and only ever do bad things.

I made it my intention to get to know all the Olympic reporters, to help where I could, and to explain why I couldn't on other occasions, so they knew I was never trying to bury a story or control the narrative. There is a fundamental principle in the sports-media relationship: if you have to hide something, then most likely it should be exposed. If it can't be exposed because of privacy issues or commercial in-confidence, as much transparency as can be offered should be offered. By briefing the media on such situations, you help them understand why some things can't be out in the open at a time of their liking. Moore told the ABC in an interview in 1999 that he was often attacked for being negative and suggested that if the organisers were less secretive, he wouldn't have to write the stories he did.

We had a great media team at SOCOG. Former ABC journalist and current affairs host Richard Palfreyman was my immediate boss and the man responsible for employing me. Quite quickly I learned the most frequent words uttered by Richard were, 'Jesus, Trace'. As soon as I heard those words, I knew I'd be getting a tap on the shoulder from Sue Graham, our incredibly efficient team manager, asking me to please go and see Richard in his office. All three of us remain friends to this day. What unfolded was some discussion or other about something I'd said or done to piss off the minister or his office. I usually interpreted that to mean I'd done my job as media information manager. Clearly my interpretation of the position – and I'd say the interpretation most of the media used – was at odds with the minister's.

As D-day approached, the organisation grew, and a former editor of *The Sydney Morning Herald*, Milton Cockburn, was put into a newly created position above Richard. He was a decent man who realised pretty quickly that running an Olympic Games organising committee came with some unique and conflicting challenges, with plenty of egos pulling strings from the sidelines. Navigating the daily politics was like trying to complete a 3D sudoku puzzle in real time.

The other members of our early team included Reg Gratton, an old-style newspaper and wires man; Nicole Reynolds, who became my assistant; and two media specialists whose paths crossed with mine before the Games and continue to do so to this day, Scott Crebbin and Steve Dettre.

Steve, Scott and Nicole were excellent team members whom I could rely on totally when needed. They were professional, supportive, knew the ropes and always did their utmost.

Reg and I, in the early days, would often find ourselves still at our desks late into the evening, finishing off whatever needed to be done before starting again early the next morning. A bottle of red would magically appear from one of his bottom drawers, and we could finally put our feet up on the desk and our hands behind our head, and have a good old laugh at what we'd seen play out on a local stage with global interest that only an Olympic Games can provide.

It was around Easter time in 1998, after I'd returned from a couple of Olympic meetings in London and Lausanne, that I decided staying at SOCOG was not for me. Despite the fact I loved my job and, even more so, loved the staff who were putting together what would become widely regarded as the greatest Games ever, I felt that the organisation and the Games themselves were being used for political gain, and I would not play those games. I had got to work around 6:00 am, and as I sat down at my desk, intending to deal with the numerous requests that demanded my time, I typed a resignation letter instead and placed it on Milton's desk.

After he arrived and read it, Milton called me into his office. As I walked in, his head was in his hands, and he said he'd spent the weekend wondering how we were all going to get through this Olympic cycle given the mounting political games; however, he said, I should reconsider. I told him I wasn't interested in being used in such a way. About an hour later, I was summoned to the office of Sandy Hollway, the remarkable CEO and former public servant who knew how to navigate political waters expertly. I admired Sandy greatly, while recognising I could never be like him.

We sat down for a cup of tea so he could discuss my resignation with me. A couple of minutes into the chat, his phone rang. He answered on speakerphone. 'What's that bitch gone and done now?' is what I swear I heard. Sandy took it off speakerphone to quickly finish the call. I never asked who was on the other end of the line. I didn't need to.

Sandy knew the media liked me, and I them – for the most part, there was a mutual respect for the jobs we each did. Sandy was instructed to offer me a pay rise or whatever it took for me not to resign. I suggested he could offer to pay me all the money in the world, but I wouldn't accept it. I was not prepared to be a political stooge. I said I was standing by my notice. For the time being, my resignation would remain private.

So when I arrived at work the next day, I was surprised to see all the camera crews, radio reporters and newspaper journos gathered outside the building. When they turned their cameras on me, I realised my resignation had been made public by others who would no doubt spin it to their advantage. It shouldn't have surprised me that as I tried to swipe my card to enter the building, it was rejected. My access had already been cancelled. Whoever had orchestrated this didn't get to control the entire narrative, though. One cartoonist drew Michael Knight driving an Olympic bus with me sprawled across the front. Another, with the Olympic rings looking like cogs, had Michael Knight winding them with a lever as an image of me, with my high heels and handbag, slid towards the point where the serrated edges were about to slice me in in half. I have always thought cartoonists are the best journalists. They nail the story with great humour.

—

The Eye of the Dragonfly

I am not somebody who ever looks back with regret. I loved working at SOCOG. It gave me an insight into the complex nature of organising the equivalent of dozens of world championships concurrently, all in one place, and the absolute need for political, corporate and public goodwill. I got to work more closely with IOC members and staff, most of whom I had known as a journalist before joining the organising committee – but I got to work with them on a different level. One man I was particularly fond of was Fekrou Kidane, a pioneering journalist from Ethiopia, whose legacy included a strengthening of ties between the IOC and the UN, including projects around the Olympic Truce, the promotion of women in sport, and the environment.

Kidane was appointed by IOC President Juan Antonio Samaranch in 1990 as an adviser on developing countries and the issue of apartheid in South Africa. In 1992, he was promoted to IOC Director of the Executive Office of the President. It was in this capacity that he asked to meet with me during one of the visits of the IOC's Olympic Coordination Commission for Sydney. The most senior Olympic officials fly into future Olympic cities to go through every detail and receive updates on all matters to do with the hosting of the Games. They cover the lot: transport, marketing, merchandise, accommodation, ticketing, athlete services, you name it.

When I arrived for our meeting, Mr Kidane invited me into his temporary office at the hotel where the commission was meeting. He had a deeply concerned look on his face. After some pleasantries, he said, 'The IOC has some concerns.' I wasn't sure where this was heading but was aware he had asked me to come alone. I asked what the problem was.

'We have noticed whenever we come to town, we do not see any of your Aboriginal people, other than the ones that have been organised for specific meetings. Where are they being moved to?'

The IOC wasn't the first or the last to ask me this. Many visitors to Australia are keen to know more of Australia's First Nations peoples, because their art and culture are recognised globally. Numerous tourism advertisements and international promotions feature Indigenous people. When overseas visitors arrive, they are surprised that our streets, restaurants and hotspots seem almost devoid of Indigenous people.

At the Atlanta Olympics in 1996, the Games immediately before Sydney, it became a matter of huge concern that in Olympifying the city, low-income neighbourhoods housing mostly African American families had been gentrified, with the local population evicted so others could move in. Homeless people were jailed. The IOC wanted to make sure Sydney had not embarked on a similar project. I offered to connect him with First Nations elders from Sydney who could give him a thorough briefing, while also explaining Australia's Indigenous people make up around 3 percent of the total population, unlike many black populations in other countries, such as the USA. Fekrou was one of many Olympic officials I stayed in touch with after my SOCOG days.

—

While I might have been done with SOCOG, the Sydney Olympics weren't done with me.

About 48 hours after my resignation, Mr Football (Les Murray) called me to ask whether I would like to join the SBS team for its national coverage of the France 1998 FIFA Men's World Cup. I thought about it for about half a second and said, 'Yes, I will.' While in France with Les and his sidekick, former Socceroo captain Johnny Warren, I was approached by the Seven Network, who had the rights to broadcast the Olympics. They asked to meet when I returned from France: they'd like to offer me a job as their Olympic face for Sydney 2000. Though I had never had any desire to work in commercial television and had rejected numerous offers previously, this time I couldn't refuse.

I love the Olympics for all their complexities. It is the only time the world is together in a single place to celebrate and commiserate with thousands of people striving for excellence. The Seven Network's offer meant I could still be involved with the greatest show on earth, in my hometown, a once-in-a-lifetime opportunity.

But if the Sydney Olympics weren't done with me, nor was the agitation that surrounded them: maybe being inside the machine of one of these mega-events inevitably meant you either turned into a cog or got your fingers jammed fighting the machine. It might not surprise you which of those happened to me.

Channel 7 had planned a big announcement about me joining the network to play a prominent role in their Olympic coverage. It would take place at a gala event in front of all their sponsors and advertisers. The network's legendary commentator Bruce McAvaney was to make the announcement, invite me onstage and conduct an interview. Not being someone who particularly enjoys a fuss being made over me, it was one of those moments where my mother was probably more excited than I was.

I stood next to Bruce in front of the mic – he had that natural twinkle in his eye that makes him so appealing to so many – and he asked me something about how I saw my role. When I answered that I wanted to do what he did, meaning apply myself wholeheartedly to sharing Olympic stories with as many people as possible, I swear I saw a chill flicker in his eye. Maybe he misinterpreted my meaning. Maybe he thought I was after his job. I wasn't. I have never seen myself doing what somebody else is doing, only doing what I do. I have always felt that Bruce was guarded with me from that day on. He was never anything but cordial to me in person, yet I learned quickly that asking Bruce for his thoughts or advice was only ever going to get a brief response.

Channel 7's *The Games Show* began as a weekly update on all things Olympic, designed to introduce audiences to some of the athletes hoping to compete in Sydney and to provide the network's Olympic sponsors an advertising platform. Originally my co-host was former Olympic swimming gold medallist and well-known larrikin Neil Brooks. I enjoyed working with Neil, although you never knew if he was going to turn up on any particular day and what level of hangover he might be suffering. I was sad when he left, leaving me to host the show on my own.

At the same time, I was heavily involved in the promotional activities for the network, my face was on the back and side of thousands of public transport buses, and I was hosting a couple of other programs, including the *Tracey Holmes Show* (a half-hour interview program with some of the world's best-known sports identities) on Seven's startup pay TV channel. I was busy, but that's how I like it.

Funnily enough, despite being on TV, I am not a TV watcher. Maybe that's why I have never shared in the over-the-top adoration of people who work in the industry. It is just another job. Nobody who works in TV is flying to the moon and back. None of us are solving homelessness, poverty or cancer. None of us are ending war.

One day, I was sitting at the staff canteen with one of the producers of *The Games*, when I saw the host of the network's current affairs show, *Today Tonight*, walk by. I'd seen him before, but he always kept to himself and had a way of looking that said, 'Leave me alone, I'm busy.' I said to my lunch companion, 'That's Stan Grant, isn't it? He's pretty good looking, isn't he?'

As he walked by, I called out, 'Hey, Stan.'

'Oh no, don't,' said my colleague.

'We've just voted you the best-looking guy here,' I said.

'Oh, thanks.' He laughed as he kept walking with his bagged sandwich.

Stan was embarrassed, my colleague was embarrassed, I didn't think much more of it.

A couple of months later, I was told I had to go and get some publicity shots done with the Olympic torch because I would be going to cover the lighting of the flame at ancient Olympia. I didn't know Stan would also be sent. The photos were taken without much discussion between us.

On the day of our departure for Greece, I met the team at the airport. Stan had ensured he wasn't seated with the rest of us, preferring to keep to himself and read from the pile of books he was travelling with. During one of the stopovers, I wandered over to him to ask what he was reading. So began one of our many discussions about philosophy, psychology, history and everything else that makes the world tick. Those conversations continue to this day. Forget the irrelevant part, Stan's looks; I'd fallen for his mind.

(A quarter of a century later and having travelled the world together with the three boys – John, Dylan and Jesse – we are still having those conversations. Stan still travels with an overnight bag that weighs a tonne, filled with the half-dozen or more books he reads concurrently.)

As it turned out, it was more than the Olympic flame that was lit in Greece.

We told our Channel 7 bosses that we were moving in together. We said that while it carried sadness, given the end of Stan's marriage to Karla and the inevitable challenges for his three kids – Lowanna, John and Dylan – we were convinced that in the long run we were doing the right thing and that our relationship would work. The Seven Network was not happy. The next day, our relationship was leaked to the media.

We were stalked constantly by paparazzi. Photographers would hide out in our neighbour's yard, trying to take photos over the fence through our bathroom window. We were run off the road. At one point, I swear photos of us knocked Tom Cruise and Nicole Kidman off newspaper front pages and magazine covers. *The Daily Telegraph* even ran a poll asking readers whether they supported us. What does that tell you? When else have you seen a poll asking whether a couple – who had ended other relationships so they could be together – had the support of the public? But apparently our relationship was different.

I had a call from a senior Seven person. I was told, 'We all like Stan, but they are not like us.'

I was confused. 'Who's us?'

Meeting after meeting was called with what seemed like everybody in the organisation who had the word *manager* or *executive* in their title. The NSW Station Manager called us into his office and told Stan, 'It might be time you go back to your tribe.' This toing and froing went on for weeks. There was a full-day publicity photo shoot planned for all the Seven staff who would be working on the Olympic Games coverage. It was clear plenty of my colleagues had suddenly decided I was poison to be around. They kept a wide berth. Many of these former colleagues reached out afterwards to tell me that in private they had defended me and Stan. Yeah, sure.

The support I did receive was from some of Australia's greatest Olympians, including Dawn Fraser, Murray Rose, Herb Elliott and Ron Clarke. The Lithgow Flash, Marjorie Jackson, who went on to become governor of South Australia, said to me at the publicity shoot that if Stan and I wanted a quiet weekend away, we would be welcome at her place. I booked tickets. The airline happened to be an Olympic sponsor, and somehow the head of Seven's sport and games coverage was alerted to the fact that Stan and I would be heading to Adelaide. It was after 11:00 pm when he rang me at home, waking the kids – Lowanna, John and Dylan who lived with us during the week. He told me that Stan and I were not to travel together, and if we did, he would make sure the papers photographed us, piling further hell on our relationship. I suggested he was my boss, not my father, and I would do what I wanted with whom I wanted on my weekend off. We flew to Adelaide. A News Corp photographer was there to greet us. Our photos appeared not long after, with the associated over-hyped scandalous tone we had come to expect.

When it was clear Stan and I would not be dissuaded from continuing our relationship, Kerry Stokes invited us to separate meetings at his North Sydney office. He told me that until the Olympics were over, Stan and I were to be separated. For the next few months, he was going to send me to the USA, 'where you can sit there and do interviews with Marion Jones and all the other American Olympic stars'. I told him I had no intention of sitting out the next few months in the USA, and if that was what he was planning, he could have my resignation there and then. He said, 'You'd never give up a job in television.' I told him I just did. As I made my way to the door, he suggested that if I went to see a lawyer, he would make sure I never worked in television again. I let him know that's exactly where I was heading. Stan's meeting went much the same way.

Despite Stan and I being two of the highest-profile presenters at the network whom they had invested in heavily, Kerry Stokes had decided the two of us together were bad for business. That's okay. We decided his business was one we needn't to be a part of. The lawyer we chose to represent us was awesome. Having both resigned Stan and I thought that chapter of our lives was over. We woke up the next morning to headlines saying Seven had sacked us.

—

Because I'd grown up in numerous locations with friends of every colour and nationality, my perceived reality of Australia was somewhat distorted. I knew there was racism but had no idea how pervasive and ever-present it was. From the newspaper poll asking whether the public supported us, to shop assistants who spoke to Stan's family members like they were inhuman, I had a rude awakening.

Two of Stan's nieces joined me on a trip to a bread shop on Sydney's Northern Beaches one morning so I could buy some rolls for lunch. I gave my order, and the shop assistant put the items on the counter, Stan's nieces picked them up.

'Put them down!' the shop assistant yelled. 'Those are not yours.'

I informed her the two girls were with me. She didn't apologise. She certainly blushed.

Later the same day, we went to a coffee shop overlooking the water at Palm Beach. Along with Stan's sister-in-law, who is also Indigenous, I went to place our order. After the waitress asked what I wanted, I ordered and then looked across to Stan's sister-in-law so she could add her family's order.

'I didn't ask you,' the assistant said.

For the second time that day, I said, 'She's with me.'

After many years outside Australia, where the boys went to school in Hong Kong, Beijing, Abu Dhabi and Dubai, they came back to Australia to do their HSC. Jesse, our youngest, had been in an advanced maths class at one of the most incredible schools on the planet, the Western Academy of Beijing. Back here, without testing, he was put into the lowest maths class in his year. When I queried the decision, I was told the school had learned through experience that Indigenous kids didn't really like maths and weren't very good at it. That was just one example of many such experiences that revealed a level of judgement our family received based purely on race.

Despite being fee-paying parents, our boys were often scolded with, 'Be careful, son. Your scholarship could end.' It was a way of controlling the small number of Indigenous kids more ruthlessly than their counterparts. Once it became better known that our boys were not on an Indigenous scholarship, they were then told they couldn't attend the Aboriginal boys' barbecue on Friday nights. Somehow, Aboriginality was defined by means testing.

We had imagined things might have changed in the decade or more that we were away. Sadly not. Stan and I both resigned from the ABC in 2023 after he was subjected to the most appalling racism week in, week out, with the ABC offering little to no support. All of this played out during the referendum asking Australians whether they would say 'yes' to recognising Indigenous people in the nation's constitution. During the lead-up to the vote, David Adler – the co-founder of ADVANCE (a right-wing political movement) and president of the Australian Jewish Association – repeatedly raised the colour of my husband's skin. It took off on social media. I was bombarded with messages accusing Stan of artificially darkening his skin. I still frequently get messages referring to 'Tan Grant'. It's no wonder the ABC did not know how to support Stan through this. As the racism review into the ABC in 2024 revealed, it is endemic there.

This type of racism has been unrelenting during our marriage, and I know throughout Stan's life. It is cruel and hurtful, and yet we know there are far more good people who have supported us – both at work and in the public. During the worst of it, Stan and I went out to get our morning coffee. We were really touched to see people had put signs up on telegraph poles throughout the suburb with the hashtag, *#IStandWithStan*. Similar signs were put on notice boards and outside elevator shafts at the ABC. Whenever they were pulled down, they would miraculously reappear by the next morning.

After the FIFA Women's World Cup in 2023, I took time out to travel with Stan while he was doing some work in Denmark. It was a much-needed respite.

While there, I emailed one of the news executives and told him I would volunteer for one of the redundancies that were being handed out. He refused. So I resigned, giving one month's notice. Four weeks later I went in to edit the last edition of my weekly one-hour sports politics program, *The Ticket*. While in the studio, I recorded a short video saying how excited I was to be covering my 14th Olympic Games in Paris 2024, although it wouldn't be for the ABC since I was finishing up in a couple of days' time. I posted it to social media.

About an hour later, I got a strange message from the head of news suggesting we talk before I made any decision. But the decision was already made, and he knew it. When I showed the message to one of my colleagues, she asked whether I had forgotten to tell him I was resigning.

'Why is he mentioning this now?' she asked.

'Because,' I said, 'I reckon News Corp has reported it – it's the only thing management responds to.' She went on to news.com.au, and there it was: Stan Grant's wife, Tracey Holmes, has resigned from the ABC.

—

After Stan left Seven, he wrote his first book and was offered a job at CNN, and I had our son Jesse. He was six weeks old when we moved to Hong Kong for Stan's job, with his two older brothers joining us as soon as we found a home to settle in to. That was the year of relationships ending, a new one beginning, resigning from our jobs not knowing where the next ones would come from, becoming parents together, and moving to a foreign land. What a year.

Thank you, Seven. Without you, I wouldn't be married to Stan, the most extraordinary person I've ever met, with whom I've had a 25-year conversation that is nowhere near reaching its conclusion, and I wouldn't have shared a thousand adventures around the world with him and three beautiful boys – along with our collection of stray animals we seem to adopt everywhere we go.

Living Like Locals
China: Part One

Shortly after we arrived in Hong Kong, Stan's new colleagues decided a great way to get to know him would be to invite us on a day-long hike through a national park, stopping for meals at some of the ancient little villages dotted along the way. At 6:00 am, we set out from CNN International at Quarry Bay, with Jesse strapped into a pouch on my chest, for an 18-hour cross-country hike. It was a fabulous introduction to the real Hong Kong, not the tourist version of shopping, traffic and neon lights.

Six weeks after having a caesarean following a 24-hour labour, my life had changed significantly. Stan took turns carrying Jesse when he slept, then he'd hand him back to me for feeding. I'd sit on a rock or a stump while Jesse fed, then I'd catch up with the group, who had walked ahead. I wondered whether I was doing the right thing with a six-week-old baby, but as Stan reminded me, mothers had been giving birth and travelling around the countryside for thousands of years. He had a point.

We found an apartment at Kornhill, a 15-minute brisk walk up the hill from CNN. While Stan worked, I explored – back streets, train rides, bus tours – and attended a cultural immersion course. On weekends, I'd take Stan to some of the places I'd discovered, usually involving a hike. It didn't take me long to find my kind of place: Shek O, a fishing hamlet at the bottom of a national park, where locals lived a relaxed life in shorts and thongs, and the few expat residents who lived there (as I found out later) were mostly journalists looking to opt out of the hustle and bustle of the city to give their kids a relaxed beach lifestyle with Hong Kong locals. It was an amazing place full of amazing people.

There was only one road into the village, leading to a beachside carpark and a roundabout so drivers could turn and take the same road back out. Shooting off from the main road was one road up to the headland and back. All other 'streets' were narrow walkways wide enough for a single person only, which twisted and turned between two- and three-storey houses that had been built over time without approval. If someone walked through the village to hop on the number 9 bus from Shek O to Shau Kei Wan station to get the train into the CBD, the locals would often ask, 'Are you going to Hong Kong today?' They thought of themselves as a different place entirely.

When Stan suggested we move from Kornhill to Shek O, I was thrilled. He asked me to organise whatever we needed in order to rent a place there. The next weekend, we caught the number 9 bus, sitting at the front of the double-decker to take in the sights of the national park on the left of us while on the right was a drop down to the ocean and the small fishing villages dotted here and there. As we disembarked with kids in tow, Stan asked, 'Is there a real estate agent meeting us?'

Shek O can be described as off-grid. No police station, no ambulance, no health clinic, no banks, no real estate agents. It is run by locals who want nothing to do with authority. I told Stan that if we stood on the roundabout, I was convinced someone would come along and rent us a place. He thought I was mad and told me so. As we stood on the roundabout debating the merits of my strategy, a grey-haired Chinese man started walking towards us. 'Stan,' he said, with a big smile, 'what are you doing here?'

Bill was a CNN cameraman who lived in Shek O. His cousin, a well-known artist and village identity named Ray Yip, owned most of the places for rent in the village, and there were a few vacant. Bill rang Ray, and within an hour we had a new home. It's funny how the universe has a rhythm you can occasionally tap into, letting its flow take you where you'd like to go. The older kids spent the next three-and-a-half years surfing, rock climbing and playing beach footy with their friends in the village, and more formalised rugby once a week on the beautifully kept fields at Stanley Fort, the local base of mainland China's People's Liberation Army. Friends we made there are still close friends today.

The village operated on cash only. Sometimes, through the night, another floor would be added on to a dwelling, giving the local landowners another room or two to rent. The local shop, the Fuk Lee store, remarkably had one of everything. Whatever you needed – a can of something, an electronic device, kids party balloons, you name it – it was there. Around the corner was the Black Sheep restaurant, and opposite that was a hole in the wall containing an oven and a couple of enormous soup pots. From there you could get the best duck soup on the island. Usually, after a duck soup with the boys on Saturdays, we'd pay a visit to the local village temple at the end of the lane, a stone's throw away, so the boys could light their incense and meditate on whatever was important to them at that time. The temple was built by the local fisherman in 1891, who dedicated it to the goddess of the ocean, Tin Hau.

Our local coffee shop, actually the street-level entrance to a residence upstairs, was run by Lulu. She liked to wear tight knee-length denim shorts, ankle socks and high heels. She was always friendly and well groomed. She'd been a ballroom dancer of note, according to village folklore. Lulu's coffee was Hong Kong style: black tea mixed with black coffee with a larger-than-usual dash of Carnation evaporated milk. It was thick, rich and bitter. I was hooked. We'd meet our friends down there on Sunday mornings. It had a bare concrete floor and a couple of round Chinese-restaurant-style tables with an assorted collection of chairs and stools tucked under them. Kids would sit at one table with bowls of noodles or orders of French toast before they all took off to play some game or other on the beach. The adults sat at the other table enjoying the same breakfast offerings and endless cups of Lulu's coffee, watching the day visitors pour out of the number 9 bus that pulled up every 20 minutes or so. The visitors were mostly Chinese people from other parts of Hong Kong, coming to enjoy the beach and the barbecue pits built into the sand at one end of the beach.

Everyone who came into the village had to drive or walk past Lulu's, which was about three doors up from the roundabout.

The Eye of the Dragonfly

Inevitably, everybody who left would also have to pass Lulu's. She knew everyone and all their business.

Living in Shek O was like living in one of the random lands that would appear at the top of the ladder in Enid Blyton's *Magic Faraway Tree*, a favourite book of mine out of all the ones Mum used to read to me when I was a little kid. It was a fabulous community where locals and expats shared in each other's families' births, deaths and marriages, and an interesting assortment of other affairs. During Chinese New Year, a performing arts company specialising in Beijing Opera would set up an elaborate bamboo-pole stage in the beach carpark and perform for free each night for the locals. The kids were allowed to go backstage, watching the performers put on their intricate stage make-up and costumes. It was the most fabulous cultural immersion.

—

Soon after arriving in Hong Kong, I took Jesse for one of his baby boosters. I had no idea that in China children were expected to have several more vaccinations than in Australia. While I sat in the waiting room with a lot of Chinese families, a young woman came in, introduced herself to me and asked if I would visit her office down the hall after Jesse's medical appointment. I agreed. She ran a small school teaching English to Chinese toddlers and to older kids after school. She said because she was Chinese, the parents were reluctant to sign up their kids – they wanted a native English speaker. She asked if I would do a class or two each week, and that became my first job in Hong Kong. What an introduction to the expectations of Chinese parents. Even the two-year-olds I taught required monthly report cards and tests. The children were phenomenal – incredibly attentive, so well-behaved, respectful and hardworking.

The parents of one of my grade 6 students was so impressed with the development of their son's English that they asked if I would tutor him privately. Spending time with a Hong Kong family inside their own home, I learned more from them than I was probably teaching their son, whom I will call Jason, one of the most popular English names for Chinese males in Hong Kong. Aside from his English tutoring twice a week after school, he played trombone with the Hong Kong Youth Symphony Orchestra, practiced piano at a high level and did advanced Chinese calligraphy, all of which contributed to him winning an international student award that he had to travel to England to accept. This kid worked incredibly hard. I convinced his initially reluctant parents to let me take Jason outdoors for our classes so we could practise English in real-life settings. We ventured to the large headquarters of the Hong Kong Central Library in Causeway Bay and signed him up to a membership, exposing him to a whole new world of stories; we bought tickets to travel on the MTR (Hong Kong's underground metro); and he ordered for us both in a coffee shop. Sometimes we just sat on the bay, describing the life of the harbour as ferries and other boats jetted in and out.

I also started working part time for RTHK (Radio Television Hong Kong). While I continued tutoring Jason, I stopped teaching at the little school, as they had built up their clientele and gained the trust of the parents. Through RTHK, I met the officials who ran the Hong Kong Olympic Committee. I volunteered to help in their media department one day a week.

The Eye of the Dragonfly

At one stage, I had to organise a press conference at which one of the dignitaries attending was none other than the Australian Olympic Committee president, John Coates. What a shock he got when he walked into the room and saw me. The sports world is incredibly small, with many of the same people rotating from sport to sport, committee to committee, with seemingly no exit point. It takes me back to the Eagles and their 'Hotel California' – you can check out any time you like, but you can never leave.

It was my experience at the Hong Kong Olympic Committee that got me fascinated in China's 'one country, two systems' policy, which Hong Kong operated under. The IOC recognised an Olympic committee in mainland China, as well as another in Hong Kong, and a third in Taiwan – an example of a complex reality being negotiated for a mutual benefit. I was intrigued by China's three Olympic committees and the years of discussions it took to reach such a compromise. The background to it is a study in high-level politics, diplomacy, and the ability for sports politicians to negotiate outcomes that others can't.

China first competed at the Olympics in 1932 as the Republic of China. After China's civil war, the representatives of the Republic of China and its Olympic committee, along with millions of other people, fled to Taiwan in 1949. Initially, the IOC continued to recognise the same officials they had already established relations with, meaning the athletes in the Republic of China team came exclusively from Taiwan.

Back on the mainland, the People's Republic of China, as it became known, established its own Olympic committee and over a couple of decades successfully argued that the Republic of China team was not representative of most Chinese people. Initially, they refused to compete while the team from Taiwan was referred to as the team from China. It wasn't until 1979 that a deal was brokered that saw the Taiwanese-based Olympic team become Chinese Taipei, freeing up the People's Republic of China to become 'China' at the games.

Hong Kong's story is different. It was governed by the British from the end of the first Opium War in 1842. As a British colony, it established its own Olympic committee in 1950, which was renamed the Sports Federation and Olympic Committee of Hong Kong, China in 1997, when Britain handed back the territory to the People's Republic of China following the end of its 99-year lease. The IOC, and China, guaranteed the Hong Kong athletes could continue to be represented under their own flag as part of the 'one country, two systems' policy.

One person who was actively involved in the work that led up to this incredible outcome was one of Australia's early and unsung IOC members, David McKenzie, who was murdered in 1981 in a Honolulu bathhouse. His murder remains unsolved.

—

After three years in Hong Kong, we moved to the outskirts of Beijing. It was Christmas day, and snowing, although the entire family almost arrived in bare feet.

Having young kids around the house when a team of removalists poured in ready to pack 300 boxes worth of belongings was not ideal. Luckily, from our Shek O home it was only a short walk to the beach, so I took the boys down there to have a swim and run around while the packers did their thing.

The Eye of the Dragonfly

When we got home, they'd done such a good job of packing that they'd boxed and taken everything, including our shoes that we'd left by the front door which we were to wear to the train station later that day to board the 'Polar Express'. If you've been to Hong Kong you'll know that bare feet are not the done thing. We jumped in the car for the twenty-minute trip to Stanley markets to buy us all a new pair of shoes. Every time I hear the old hit song from Paolo Nutini, about putting new shoes on and suddenly everything being all right, it makes me chuckle.

Our journey from hot, humid, coastal Hong Kong to a wintery Beijing with its chilly winds blowing from the neighbouring Gobi Desert, and the snow fall painting the city white, was a 24-hour trip starting on Christmas Eve. The boys had their own sleeper where we hung their Christmas stockings. In the middle of the night Stan and I snuck in while they slept to fill them with presents for their new home. We spent the day watching the changing landscape as the train chugged on through numerous provinces, some highly congested, others barren, sometimes fields with a single farmer and his ox, other times a distant Buddhist temple rising above the trees.

I had already travelled to Beijing about a month earlier to make sure the house we'd rented had a Christmas tree surrounded by another few presents – this time a bike for each of the kids so they could explore their new surrounds. Buying the tree was an interesting prospect. Christmas wasn't really celebrated at the time although there were a couple of shopping malls that catered to expats who did. I found a stall at one of the centres that had on display three or four different sized trees that had been decorated for show. In my mixture of English and sign language the Chinese man running the stall picked up the tree I pointed to as he guessed it was the one I wanted. I thought he'd hand me a box to take home and erect. Instead, he lay the exhibited tree down on its side (it was about two metres tall) and started wrapping it in glad wrap. I had no idea what was going on. Then he took it outside to my waiting taxi and tied it to the roof! A ready-made tree – no problem! We had plenty of fun getting used to the different way things were done.

Again, we chose not to live where the other expats conglomerated: we found a place that was entirely Chinese. Barely anyone could speak English. When we live somewhere, we like to experience it as the locals experience it. As much as possible, we wanted our kids to make friends with local kids. It meant language and cultural differences had to be learned quickly – Mandarin was very different to Cantonese, the diet was much spicier in the capital, and although it was a city with a population almost as large as Australia's, Beijing was still very underdeveloped in parts. Living entirely amongst the locals gave my husband and I invaluable insights in our reporting and gave our children an understanding of China that cannot be read in a book or taught in a classroom.

There were no ATMs where we lived – none that accepted international cards, anyway. Taxi drivers did not have access to anything like Google Maps, and in a city as large as Beijing, where construction was booming ahead of the 2008 Olympics, not even old-fashioned street directories were of any use. People used to love to say that 75 percent of the world's cranes were operating in Beijing at the time. Food items were bought fresh from the market. Packaged goods at the small supermarket were all Chinese, so until we learned to recognise the packaging, it was trial and error to see whether the product inside was actually related to the picture on the outside. It didn't always turn out to be that way. Each time we ventured outdoors, we were on another journey of discovery.

Market shopping was an exercise in bartering. We learned how to say numbers in Mandarin before we learned any other vocabulary. The kids became experts in the process. Until the age of seven, foreign kids could be enrolled at the local Chinese school. That meant only Jesse, at three, qualified. The older boys were first enrolled at the newly established Australian International School on the outskirts of the city, near a weekend retreat called Xie Dao (Crab Island), which was just taking off with some of the locals, who increasingly had more spending money and free time.

Xie Dao had a wave-pool machine, beach volleyball courts, fishing ponds and barbecue pits. There were young boys in Hawaiian shirts sitting on top of lifeguard chairs, although I'm not sure they were actually qualified. One time I took our boys to Xie Dao to go fishing. It wasn't like my memories of fishing with my dad when I was a kid.

I remember on one camping trip at Cape St Francis, South Africa, doing some rock fishing. I was four or five. Dad and I had climbed around the rocks at the end of the beach. In my young mind, the rocks were huge, like ones you might see at the bottom of a collapsed cliff face along much of the Australian coastline. In reality, they were probably relatively small and much flatter. Having set me up with my makeshift bamboo fishing rod, which

Dad had made, he told me he'd forgotten something but he'd be back soon. With hindsight, I reckon he just went around the corner so he could pee.

No sooner had he disappeared from view, I felt a fish tugging on my line. I was thrilled to pull it in. But as it lay flapping on the hot rock, I got simultaneously sad and scared. Sad that I was the cause of this fish dying, and scared that it was flapping so violently that it was going to jump up and attack me. I decided I had no option but to jump across to the next rock, so I dropped my rod and took a massive leap. I made it but slipped on landing and slid on my stomach down the jagged oyster shells on the rock. Right then, Dad reappeared to carefully wipe the broken shells out of the cut in my side, with the damp edge of our towel. The scar is still there today.

So, back to Xie Dao with my own kids. Stan was away on one of his many long trips for CNN, probably in a war zone somewhere. Included in the entry price was a fishing line for each of the three boys, tiny little fold-out stools that locals in China are so good at squatting on, and bait. The idea was you could catch fish and barbecue them for lunch. When it was obvious the boys weren't as handy with a fishing pole as I had been at their age (wink, wink), I suggested we leave our stools and rods and head over to buy some of the tasty Xinjiang meat sticks that were a favourite.

When we returned five minutes later, there was a family (mum, dad, kid) sitting in our seats, fishing with our rods. When I told them politely that they belonged to us and asked them to move, they had no reaction at all, as though ignoring us would make us go away. Chinese people do not like public confrontations;

they do not like to lose face. I respect that, so I tried again to explain what was clearly a misunderstanding – but still, nothing. My few words of Chinese, with my monotone Aussie accent, wasn't cutting through. In frustration I got a little louder. All the other people sitting around the pond were pretending not to notice. They were looking at us – until we looked at them, and then they quickly looked back at the pond. Having no success, I walked over to the management desk to let them know, but before I could explain, the family of three (which was most Chinese families in the era of the one-child policy) had jumped off our seats and disappeared into the crowd.

Behind our apartment in Shi Dai Zhuangyuan, on the 100-kilometre-long fifth ring road that encircles the city, sat an old amusement park that looked like it hadn't operated for decades. There were some dodgem-style cars that you could race around a circular metal track, something called a pirate ship with a large boat-like swing, a merry-go-round featuring monkeys clanging cymbals and playing drums, and a few other indescribable rides. Beyond the park there were only dirt roads leading to small *hutong*s (laneways) leading through small old Chinese villages that usually had only a communal tap and little to no electricity.

We came to learn that the operators of the theme park had passed away. Their children, who had now grown up and had children of their own, lived at the theme park, but there was nobody who could afford to pay to ride. They cranked up a couple of the rides for our kids every so often. Jesse still has a dimple-like scar when he smiles, because his head slammed into the steering wheel of his dodgem car after Dylan hit him at pace from behind.

We drew the line at one cultural experience, though. Our neighbour knocked on our door one day and, through a combination of her few words of English and small Mandarin phrases she thought I'd understand, mixed with sign language, invited us to a kids' movie night that coming Friday at the community centre. She told me to bring a cushion for each of the kids to sit on. When we arrived, there was a large white sheet hung at the far end of the room, and an elderly man was feeding an old reel-to-reel movie into a projector. The kids sat on their pillows amongst all the other kids, ours being the only foreigners there. As the lights dimmed, the rattling projector beamed an old black-and-white movie onto the sheet.

The movie started with a line of people being marched up a hill. Their forms were more or less silhouetted against the sky, outlined against the arc of a bare landscape. Then the camera angle changed. It revealed a line of tanks rumbling towards the people. The tanks opened fire, and the bodies began to fall. All the kids in the community hall started cheering. It was a propaganda movie. The Chinese military was destroying their enemy. I tapped the boys on their shoulders, told them to pick up their pillows, we were leaving.

Another Move, Another World

Al Worood means 'the rose'. It was the name of the school recommended to us for our two younger sons, Dylan and Jesse, ahead of our 2007 move to Abu Dhabi, in the United Arab Emirates. The eldest, John, who was already in high school, would stay in Sydney to board at St Joseph's College.

Back in Sydney for a few months, ahead of CNN's official opening of its first Middle East hub in Abu Dhabi's newly established twofour54 media free zone, we made a weekly trip to our local pizza restaurant, which was run by a beautiful Jordanian family we had come to know quite well. The wife had previously been a teacher at Al Worood Academy and spoke highly of it. We did some research and saw it had been rated as one of the best local schools delivering all its classes in English.

But in the time between our Jordanian friend teaching there and us making the move, standards had begun to slip. A few years after we left, the school was shut down altogether after the tragic death of a kindergarten student who had been accidentally locked in a bus overnight without food or water.

On the first day of school, the boys were confronted in the playground by some of the locals.

'Israeli?' they asked.

'No, Aussie, Australian,' our boys replied.

A scuffle ensued because many of the kids had never heard of Australia and thought 'Aussie' sounded like 'Israeli' in a foreign accent. Apparently, there were really only two nationalities that mattered. Dylan was in grade 6 at the time, a star athlete, with hands as powerful and quick as any of the great boxers. He knew how to handle himself and protect his brother, who was four years his junior. Not that Jesse didn't know how to handle himself but it was good to know someone had his back. The other students always thought twice before messing with our boys again.

When they arrived home from school, Jesse's school shirt, starched white with a red rose logo, was covered in brown stains.

'It's from the coffee we drank while we were playing soccer at lunchtime,' he said. Coffee?! He was seven. The kids could buy small shots of Arabic coffee from their canteen. Who could blame them? The addition of a dash of cardamom in the thick, rich shot of black coffee had me hooked too. This wouldn't be the only 'norm' in the Middle East.

One of the things we had to get used to was explaining where we lived. Houses weren't numbered, and some streets were not named. Directions to our place involved a passage that went something like this: *Heading west, turn right off Sultan bin Zayed the First Street between 29th and 31st Streets, turn right on Al*

The Eye of the Dragonfly

Hamlah Street, go past the mosque on the left, then opposite the juice bar you will see a white villa with a red door.

I noticed that mostly it was the fathers who dropped their kids at school and picked them up in the afternoon, or sometimes the kids' personal drivers. During the hottest months, it could be upwards of 40 degrees Celsius outside, so I drove our kids to school too. In heat like that, the soles of your shoes would start to melt on the tarred roads and after 30 seconds you'd be drenched – heading into chilled air-conditioned classrooms in wet clothes was not a good idea. Occasionally, after I'd done the drop-off, some of the fathers would follow me in their cars to see where I was going – there were not a lot of expats in our area, so I was a novelty once word got round. It did astound me, though, when the odd one followed me all the way to work at Dubai Eye, 140 kilometres away.

Jesse always adapted quickly. Seeing what locals wore and how they behaved, he would do the same. Unbeknown to Stan and me, he enrolled in Islamic studies. The first I knew of it was when his teacher phoned me to say what a good student he was, currently top of the class. Apparently, you are exempt from Islamic studies in Abu Dhabi if you are not Muslim, but Jesse said he was. Even though he was only seven, he knew something of most religions, telling me once, 'Why do people fight about God? Every religion wants you to be the best person you can be.'

There was a kid in Jesse's class who was constantly mucking up. One day, the teacher turned to the class and demanded to know who had just shouted out, and this kid pointed to Jesse. As the new boy, he was an easy target. The teacher sent him outside for what we came to realise was the standard punishment: standing with your face against the hallway wall, arms outstretched above your head, on one leg. There was a hallway monitor, so if anyone dropped their lifted leg or let their arms slide downward, they would be slapped across their butt with a ruler. When I raised this with other parents, they mostly laughed and couldn't see the problem. I guess it worked in one regard: having suffered that punishment once, you wouldn't chance having to go through it again.

One of Dylan's best mates from school was surprised when he found out Dylan didn't have his own fleet of cars and a personal driver to chauffeur him around. When we invited Ahmed back to our place after school one day, he was surprised to find out we were walking the three blocks: Ahmed had never pressed a pedestrian crossing button before. As we got to know him better, some of the oddities began to make sense. He'd been kidnapped as a three-year-old and held for ransom. From that day on, his parents made sure he was never alone. Even when we walked, his driver and usually a nanny would follow along slowly in whichever car Ahmed had asked them to use that day.

Foreigners are usually impacted early on by the overt display of wealth in Abu Dhabi. After some time getting to know the people and their history, it does not seem so confronting. I had always wanted to read and write Arabic – along with Sanskrit, I think Arabic characters are the most beautiful in the world, each an artwork in itself – so I started lessons. The language classes I had with my teacher, who was from Syria, also served to teach me about Islamic culture and the history of the region.

The discovery of oil by the British in the 1960s turned the UAE incredibly rich, incredibly quickly. (Prior to oil, the region made its money from pearl diving, an industry that died out with Japan's invention of cultured pearls.) The UAE is an alliance of seven emirates on the Arabian Peninsula that formed in 1971 after the British announced they were withdrawing from the Persian Gulf. Two men who were crucial in setting the foundations for what is the UAE today were Sheikh Zayed bin Sultan al Nahyan of Abu Dhabi (described as the founding father) and Sheikh Rashid bin Saeed al Maktoum of Dubai (called the co-founder). Both men are widely respected inside the UAE for their commitment to their people. Oil money was used to transform the region through the building of schools, a healthcare system envied by most other countries in the world, tourism and industry hubs, and irrigation for the inland desert. The sons of both men remain in charge today. The president is Sheikh Zayed's third son, Sheikh Mohamed, and the prime minister is Sheikh Rashid's son, Sheikh Mohammed.

On a ranking of 181 countries, the UAE sits in 12th place in terms of GDP per population. In a total population of around 10,500,000, Emiratis account for around 11 percent. The country's oil wealth is distributed amongst the Emiratis through free education (including sending Emiratis to overseas universities), free health care, government support to establish businesses, subsidised fuel, tax-free income, interest-free loans, the provision of land, and generous pensions for retirees and widows. Not all Emiratis enjoy the same wealth or development but nearly all live comfortable lives, especially compared to just over 50 years ago, when the British would ration their bread and tea, which were considered luxuries at a time when most people lived in basic homes built from palm trees, without water or electricity.

This rapid change also has a lot to do with what we in the West see as the region's flaws: its treatment of foreign workers, its lack of human rights and democratic values, and its lack of a free press. While recognising these flaws, we also need to see them through the eye of the dragonfly, a 360-degree perspective. These phenomena didn't emerge from nothing; they are a consequence of history, including the role the West played, intertwined with the region's own cultural and religious values.

While criticism of other countries is often valid, I am wary of pointing fingers when we have work to do in our own backyard. Our growing epidemic of homelessness and the inability to close the gap between Indigenous and non-Indigenous citizens in our country concerns me. Our recent history of detaining refugees like prisoners, then paying third countries to take them is inhumane. It strikes me as hypocritical that the people we lock up are not so different to many of the workers who have built what the UAE is today, able to support their families and educate their children with salaries they could not earn in their own countries – nor ours – despite the strict, even harsh, conditions in the Gulf. Of course, one does not excuse the other. People often accuse me of whataboutism. I agree with them. Whataboutism points to the hypocrisy at play, and hypocrisy is a deception. It is negative and harmful. Not recognising our own flaws while scrutinising another's does not sit comfortably with me.

In mid-2025 the Australian government still maintains offshore detention centres. Even asylum seekers who are granted temporary protection visas in Australia are often unable to work legally, leaving them open to exploitation.

The Eye of the Dragonfly

The Asylum Seeker Resource Centre's 2024 report, 'Cruelty by Design: The health crisis in offshore detention', describes living conditions in offshore detention facilities as 'inhumane' and, 'akin to torture'. Inadequate medical care has 'led to morbidity and mortality'.

I don't have the answers to solve the world's problems, but living in other places amongst people of other cultures has helped me understand that there is far more to any story than the political ideology we are fed from one side or the other.

It's no surprise that when we moved back to Australia, we moved to Auburn, in Sydney, because that's where we (our sons included) could find our favourite food on every corner: Xinjiang stew from China's predominantly Muslim region, barbecue pork and rice from the Cantonese region, spicy lamb curry from Afghanistan, and biryani, so common in most South Asian regions.

We lived in a semidetached house, sharing a driveway with our Muslim neighbours, the Zouds, from Lebanon. Without fail, whenever they noticed Stan and I were late home from work, they would give our boys freshly cooked meals fit for a king. I remember frequently getting home after 11:00 pm, and within ten minutes, there would be a knock at the door from one of our neighbours bringing me a tray of all my favourite dishes, 'Just in case you didn't get dinner tonight'. Our kids became friends with their kids; every birthday, wedding or celebration of Eid after Ramadan was another invitation for our family to join theirs. Our experiences with our Muslim neighbours both in Australia and overseas enriched all our lives greatly.

This is not to say we saw everything through rose-coloured glasses. One year in Abu Dhabi, the boys and I saw Stan for a total of seven weeks as he constantly flew into the region's hotspots, where war, terrorism and tragedy raged, all of it politically driven. Our one-on-one experience has often been completely at odds with what we see and read in our media. By focusing only on the worst of the region, we completely ignore the best of its people.

Meeting My Monk
China: Part Two

He is not *my* monk, of course, but that's how I've always referred to Gen Kelsang Tonglam, a Buddhist monk I met on the street in Shek O – initially through a case of mistaken identity. As time always reveals, it was the universe working in miraculous ways.

Back in 1999, I watched what would become one of my all-time favourite films, *The Cup*. It's the story of two football-obsessed Tibetan boys studying at a Bhutanese monastery who try to convince their abbot to rent a satellite dish and television set so they can watch the final of the 1998 FIFA World Cup. That World Cup was my first as a journalist, and it had been magnificent in so many ways: France was magnificent, the SBS team was magnificent, the football crowds were magnificent (hooligans aside – more on that to come), and the atmosphere inside the stadiums was magnificent.

The film also resonated with me because it portrayed a clash of realities, bringing the meditative and physical worlds together.

It might surprise you to learn that journalism involves similar disciplines.

Like many old-style journalists, I try to observe what is playing out in front of me and not only describe it but draw out its meaning for people who are not there. (I say 'old-style' journalists because today too many have fallen into the trap of thinking the story is about them – the 'look at me' Instagram reporters.) If you can observe an event with a type of meditative detachment, distancing your own emotions from the event and the people involved, you are able to see it with a different kind of clarity. It makes you question the reality of what is unfolding. Is it momentary or significant? Will its effects be long-lasting? Will it change anything substantially? Is it just a frenzy brought on by hype? Is there something deeper at play?

Over the years, I have learned to remove myself, sometimes almost to the point of feeling as though I am not physically present at all, in order to witness truthfully what is happening, without my own emotions or judgements tainting my perceptions.

This is what the young monks had to wrestle with in *The Cup*. What was important and why was it important? The film's setting in the Himalayas is beautiful, its Dzongkha language script is rhythmic, and its message is simple, profound, and hilarious – just like life.

Stan rang me one day from the CNN studio to tell me he'd been asked to do a feature interview with the director of *The Cup*, Khyentse Norbu, a Bhutanese lama. About a week after the interview, we were heading into Hong Kong to do some shopping. As we drove down the steep hill from the headland where we lived, we saw a monk in traditional robes in deep conversation with a

The Eye of the Dragonfly

woman as they walked up the hill. Stan said, 'That's him, that's the monk who made *The Cup*!' He stopped the car; I jumped out and ran over to him.

Beaming, I held out my hand to shake his and to tell him how much I loved his film. A large smile spread across his face as he shook my hand and thanked me, then asked, 'Which film?'

It wasn't Khyentse Norbu; it was a monk named Kelsang Tonglam. After an apology, a laugh and an explanation, we stood on the side of the road chatting for at least 20 minutes. It was as though we had a lifetime of conversations to catch up on, even though he'd never seen or heard of *The Cup*. He and his friend were in Shek O to see if there was a place where he could run a retreat for some students from his Buddhist centre. He continued on his journey and we drove into town, our two paths going their separate ways.

About ten days later, I was standing at the kitchen sink – most unusually, because it is the room in the house where I spend the least time – looking out the window as I washed the dishes. Suddenly, a tall man in Buddhist robes reared up on the other side of the glass, startling me, in the same way my presence startled him. It was Tonglam again. He had been bent down patting our kittens, who were warming themselves in the sun against the wall.

'Oh, it's you,' we both said at the same time.

'I'd better come in,' Tonglam said. 'I think this is supposed to be.'

Stan and I started going to meditation classes at Tonglam's centre, and later, I took Buddhist vows. I knew when we moved to Beijing in 2004 that I was going to miss Tonglam's teachings, but the students at the centre were incredibly diligent in recording weekly lessons onto CDs and regularly posting them to me.

—

After we'd spent a couple of years in the Middle East and had returned to Beijing, Stan was in a pretty bad way. A decade of unrelenting travelling and storytelling from the world's worst catastrophes had taken a massive toll. He wasn't sleeping and he didn't take days off. He had been chased and detained in China, come face to face with the Taliban, had reported the devastation of the Boxing Day tsunami in Sri Lanka, spent time doing live crosses from war zones in Iraq and Afghanistan, dodged bullets on the Kashmir border between Pakistan and India, and witnessed firsthand the devastation of suicide bombers in Israel.

Frankly, I feared Stan was going to end his own life. Because his moods were so volatile, the kids were wary around him on the rare occasions that he was home. I was reluctant to say much, knowing the smallest thing could send him into a rage. His eyes were completely bloodshot, and I'd noticed how the soul behind his pupils was fading back into a distance I can only describe as the dark tunnel to a cave.

I'd seen that look before. During the late 1970s, when my sister and I were young and my mum used to work a night shift, a 16-year-old boy who lived down the road and whose family we knew well would come to babysit us. Over time, I saw Darren's soul retreating behind his eyes. One day, he walked onto the busy main road in front of an oncoming bus and ended his life.

During the 1990s, it was a colleague of mine on the ABC TV sports show *Ballzup* whom I witnessed heading to a dark place. Peter Jackson had played rugby league for numerous clubs in Australia and England. He was a tall, strapping centre, with cheeky eyes that twinkled and a smile that could light up a room in a flash. He was a naturally gifted storyteller who always left audiences in stitches. Alongside Lex Marinos, the actor and director who hosted the show, Jacko kept the program rocketing along, while I, together with former rugby union player Brett Papworth, were the boring straight shooters (sorry, Pappie, but we were) trying to keep the show on track.

In 1997, aged only 33, Jacko overdosed alone in a motel room. It was only then that the stories of him being sexually abused as a young teenager by his boarding-school house master were made public. His friend and former coach Wayne Bennett said at the time, 'He was so gifted, so much ability and . . . then the devil would come along.'

There have been others, too, whom I watched retreat inside themselves before opting out of life on this planet.

When I looked at Stan's eyes, I could see him heading to the same dark place. I knew better than to raise it with him, because he would just explode, and then for the next three days at least we'd all be walking on eggshells. The phrase 'if looks could kill' was coined by someone who must have experienced what the kids and I went through at those times.

I went online and searched for the most respected psychologist with a specialty in journalism and post-traumatic stress disorder. I didn't even know if such a person existed. He did: Dr Anthony Feinstein, a physician and professor of psychiatry at the University of Toronto. Once I explained there was no way I could get Stan to entertain the idea of seeking help, we devised a strategy – an emergency plan, if you like – and documented what I would need to do on the day that would inevitably arrive.

That day came when Stan rang me from a rooftop in Mongolia. He said he couldn't take it anymore and he wanted to say goodbye. My emergency strategy went from being parked in the back of my mind to hitting 100 kilometres per hour in a split second. I rang the producer who was with Stan and told him to get to Stan immediately, not ask questions, stay by his side and escort him onto a plane back to Beijing. I emailed Dr Feinstein and the psychologists he had found for me in Beijing and Australia, who were all on standby.

Stan was a shell of himself when he returned. He looked like a man needing resuscitation, but for the first time, I saw a vulnerability that I'd never seen in him before. Sadly, he had to hit this point before he would let anyone help. Our older two boys were back in Australia, boarding at St Joseph's College, and Jesse was still with us in Beijing. I phoned the parents of one of our closest friends and asked them if they could please look after him for a week or so because of a family emergency. Without question, they did.

I will be forever grateful to them for the care they gave Jesse without ever prying. There are some unique challenges living in countries where everyone is a stranger and nobody is family. You quickly build relationships with families from everywhere, all based on your kids' friendships. To this day, Jesse remains friends with his schoolmates from Israel, Kazakhstan, Denmark, France, South Africa and Hong Kong. I explained to the two older boys, Dylan and John, that Dad was unwell, but he was okay and he'd be coming home for a while. They understood. For years, I had

The Eye of the Dragonfly

always told them during Stan's moments of fury that this was not the real Stan, and they needed to understand what was making him behave this way.

I flew to Sydney with Stan and spent a few days with him as he established a relationship with his psychologist and took plenty of time to rest, trying to emerge from his state of deep sadness. It's as though all the trauma and tragedy he had seen around the world had been trapped inside his mind, slowly poisoning him. Thankfully, that bubble had burst, and while it wasn't pleasant or easy, the healing had begun. A healing that has continued every day since.

Against their advice, I told his doctors I was heading back to China, because at this point, Jesse needed me more than Stan. What they didn't know then, but what I did, is that Stan had the most remarkable ability to separate his own emotional mind from his logical brain to understand what the doctors were explaining to him. In that regard, Stan's best way of treating himself was to spend time with himself.

In many ways, I have always felt like a distraction for Stan. When he doesn't want to deal with something, he spends time talking to me. I did not want to be that distraction at this critical time. He really needed to observe himself up close. His best mate, fellow journalist Mark Bannerman, and his journalist wife, Sharon O'Neill, lived around the corner and agreed to stay in daily touch with Stan, whether it be for a coffee or a meal. I knew he was supported by those who would understand.

When I got back to Beijing, there was an email waiting for me. Tonglam was in Beijing for a short time, and he'd like to catch up. Here was the universe again, wrapping its arms around

Stan and me when we needed it most. Tonglam and I walked through the forest that ran across the back of our compound and along a stormwater canal, to a small restaurant tucked into the trees, which I knew served the best bamboo shoots in Beijing. It mustn't have been easy for Tonglam to get into Beijing – the officials are wary of outside Buddhists, and any type of religious teacher. Knowing that Stan and I were under constant surveillance, it was obvious that Tonglam would be too.

There is only one way I can explain what Tonglam's presence was like. When a storm has cleared over an ocean, with the black clouds in the distance near the horizon, the wind often turns offshore. The raging ocean subsides. The surface of the water is smoothed, and the planet is at peace.

Buddhism has taught me that storms will always rage, but from inside you can find that calm, where the raging winds and waters can be separated and rebalanced.

Why the universe should shine on me the way it has, by bringing both Stan and Tonglam into my life, is a constant source of wonder. I feel an overwhelming sense of gratitude.

The Ticket

Coming back to the ABC in 2014, I was liberated from the small but influential bubble that global sport is.

The manager of NewsRadio, Helen Thomas, oversaw a small but committed staff delivering a 24/7 domestic and international news service. I have long argued every ABC employee should serve a stint at NewsRadio to understand what it is to produce cutting-edge coverage on the tightest of timelines and the smallest production teams in the entire ABC. We also had the smallest budget. We consistently rated equal to, if not higher than, Radio National, with a fraction of their resources. Ours was a niche audience, but as in the world of sport, it was an influential one: politicians, CEOs and decision-makers who relied on being across what was happening hour by hour.

I began hosting the evening show. Because it had a good time slot for connecting with international guests, we focused on world affairs – from Trump's first run at the presidency and his subsequent election, to Boko Haram's kidnapping of hundreds of Kenyan schoolgirls, to the disappearance of Malaysia Airlines jet MH370. We were active domestically too: I was NewsRadio's first reporter on the scene at the Lindt Cafe siege in Sydney's Martin Place. Other experiences that stick in my mind are doing live coverage on budget night with former treasurer John Hewson and hosting NewsRadio's only-ever talkback program, *Q&A Extra*, with guest presenters such as former Justice of the High Court of Australia, the honourable Michael Kirby.

So when Helen asked me to start a one-hour weekend sports program to replace one that had folded because the host left, I declined the offer. I felt like it would pull me backwards. Helen kept asking, and I kept declining. Finally, I said I'd do it, on one condition: that it wouldn't be just another results show. It would be a serious hour looking at the biggest issues in sport, both at home and overseas. *And* I still wanted to do regular programming. Helen agreed. I was kept on usual programming and given a producer one day a week for an in-depth one-hour show called *The Ticket*. (Stan came up with the name because the program was a front-row seat to the games being played behind the scenes.) Due to cutbacks, I ended up losing my producer and resorted to making the show by interviewing guests at midnight and editing after I'd finished my regular shift. But the program took on a life of its own.

Breaking stories became a regular feature. More than once, I was told by a sporting official how relieved their staff were on a Monday morning if they'd not heard about their sport on that week's program. The real strength of the show lay in its ability to delve into the biggest stories. I provided interviews with key people from as many sides of a story as possible, so the audience could both understand the complexities involved and be free to make up their own mind.

Stan woke me early on a March morning in 2018 when news was breaking out of South Africa about a cheating scandal involving the Australian men's cricket team – an episode that would go on to grip the nation under the soubriquet 'Sandpapergate', after the substance secretly used to rough up a cricket ball and give Australian bowlers an advantage. It was still dark outside, but I showered and dressed in under ten minutes, and made my way into the studio, calling contacts in South Africa and elsewhere as I drove, lining up interviews. I knew this story was going to be explosive, because it involved the Australian men's cricket team – former prime minister John Howard once described the captaincy of the men's team as the second-most important job in the country (after his own, of course). Captain Steve Smith was about to find out what happens when the reputation of such a position takes a battering.

While the International Cricket Council (ICC) gave the team relatively minor penalties – including a fine, the loss of points and a one-match suspension – the ferocity of the reaction at home, particularly to the idea that Australians had been *caught* cheating, meant a much heavier penalty was inevitable. Prime Minister Malcolm Turnbull decided the nation had been so embarrassed that Smith had to be removed as captain, and he phoned the chairman of Cricket Australia (CA), David Peever, to let him know. Smith, Vice-Captain David Warner, and the young Western Australian opening batsman who had been caught on camera roughing up the ball, Cameron Bancroft, were stood down and sent home pending a further CA investigation.

All three were found to be in breach of Cricket Australia's detailed code of behaviour, which could include, but was not limited to: actions that could bring the sport into disrepute, behaviour against the spirit of the sport, and actions that were unbecoming of a representative. (Sport is full of language that allows officials whatever interpretation they feel the times dictate.) Smith was given a one-year suspension and 100 hours of voluntary service in community cricket, and he was told he would only ever be allowed to captain again if the fans and the playing group accepted it. Warner, who was found guilty of masterminding the plan, was also suspended for a year and ordered to do community service, but he was told he would never have a leadership role again. Bancroft, the player instructed to cheat, was given a nine-month suspension and was also required to complete voluntary service in community cricket.

Time heals all wounds, they say, and several years on from Sandpapergate, all three players have continued with their cricket careers. Steve Smith has even gone on to captain Australia again. Although many cricket fans have softened their views, all three players know that whenever their names are mentioned, recollections of the saga are never far from people's minds.

Whether time has healed all the wounds in the biggest scandal *The Ticket* covered – the so-called Blackest Day in Sport – is open to debate.

On 7 February 2013, the federal Labor government released details of an Australian Crime Commission report alleging deep ties between professional sport and crime gangs. The CEOs of the country's highest-profile sports – cricket and all four footy codes – played an unwitting role in politicising the report's release by agreeing to stand onstage at the press conference behind Minister for Sport Kate Lundy and Minister for Justice Jason Clare.

There is nothing new about there being links between some athletes who will push beyond what is ethically acceptable in their pursuit of victory and criminal gangs involved in the supply of performance-enhancing and illicit drugs. Crime gangs are also behind some of the match-fixing dramas we hear about. But the way Parliament House was handling 'the Blackest Day' story implicated all sports and all athletes, casting a dark shadow globally over the professional reputation Australian sport had enjoyed.

Most in the media jumped on the bandwagon with their shock-and-awe reporting.

To my mind, the report contained a lot of hearsay and possibilities but was rather short on evidence. Predominantly, it was Michael Warner from the *Herald Sun*, Chip Le Grand at *The Australian* and I who remained sceptical of the extent of the allegations, how the genuine allegations were being investigated, and who was being pilloried so that blame could be assigned as quickly as possible, allowing all others to move on unscathed. The public humiliation for many of the players and coaches who were implicated was life changing; careers were cut short, lifelong friendships ended, and marriages failed as the saga dragged into a second year without resolution or justice.

The AFL's Essendon Football Club arguably carried the heaviest burden. They (and to a lesser extent, the NRL's Cronulla Sharks) were singled out from a number of clubs who'd used a controversial supplements program overseen by sports scientist Stephen Dank. Dank would later be banned for life from all sport. Essendon was kicked out of the finals series, fined $2 million and stripped of draft picks for the following season. The club's chairman, David Evans, had a physical breakdown; CEO Ian Robson resigned; and coach James Hird was suspended for 12 months. They, along with respected club doctor Bruce Reid, football manager Danny Corcoran and the club itself were charged with bringing the sport into disrepute. Throughout it all, the players, coach and club doctor maintained their innocence and gave evidence supporting the lengths they had gone to so as to establish what they were doing was within the sport's anti-doping rules. Dr Reid took his case to the Supreme Court, prompting the AFL to drop its charges against him.

Essendon's 34 players were provisionally suspended while the anti-doping AFL tribunal began a hearing in December 2014. In March 2015, all players were cleared: the tribunal, chaired by experienced barrister David Grace KC, ruled there was insufficient evidence to prove the players were administered with a banned substance. Then in May 2015, the World Anti-Doping Agency (WADA), appealed these findings in the Swiss-based Court of Arbitration for Sport (CAS). By January 2016 – almost three full years since the Blackest Day – the CAS ruled that all 34 players were guilty of doping, handing them all backdated two-year suspensions.

Despite there being no positive tests, plenty of evidence the players had asked for assurances from the club that the supplements they were being given were legal, and confusion over whether the supplement recommended by the sport scientist was actually banned at all, WADA successfully argued the 'strands in the cable' legal approach rather than the 'links in the chain' approach used by the AFL tribunal. The 'strands in the cable' argument relied on a collection of circumstantial evidence deemed to be sufficient in this case. Unlike courts of law, sports anti-doping organisations assume guilt and require the athletes to prove their innocence. Some of the players found guilty of being injected with a banned substance had never actually had injections. In the 'links in the chain' approach, the chain of evidence broke at this point. Using the 'strands in the cable' approach, it did not.

The Ticket did numerous hour-long features on the saga, including interviews with the sports scientist at the heart of the scandal, the club president, the AFL anti-doping tribunal chair, the Australian Anti-Doping Authority (ASADA), WADA, Minister for Sport Peter Dutton, Essendon players, international doping experts and lawyers. Club coach James Hird – who, unlike the players, was never implicated by ASADA and was targeted only by the AFL – did not do any substantial interviews during the period. I flew to Melbourne numerous times to meet with him and to cover the story broadly, and when in 2016 he agreed to give his one and only extensive interview, it was with me. It was agreed it would be done live for the ABC News channel, in front of an audience at The Ethics Centre in Sydney. He did not ask me what I was going to ask, and I did not offer to provide him with the questions.

And there were dozens of questions. The live audience was surprised at his honesty and at elements of the story they had not been aware of throughout the media onslaught, and they found his at times emotional responses to be genuine. The live broadcast, on a Sunday night, gave the station its second-highest rating since inception; only a federal election had garnered more viewers.

Given I have never been an AFL reporter, so to speak, many in the vast AFL-accredited Melbourne media wrote stories rubbishing the interview, which was to be expected as it was their beat. Until the doping saga, Hird had been the golden-haired child of Essendon and a superstar of the AFL generally. Why would he choose to speak to me, a Sydney-based journalist with little interest in the day-to-day AFL season? Perhaps that was the very reason: unlike some of the Melbourne-based media, I had never trotted out the AFL line. I just ask the questions and let the audience make up its mind.

(Incidentally, the head of ABC News sent a congratulatory note to everyone who'd worked on the live coverage – the director in the studio, the camera operators at The Ethics Centre and numerous others – without mentioning me. When I went to see him about it, he told me the interview had been panned by Melbourne media and that I probably didn't have a future at the ABC. It made me wonder who had called him to complain. As I turned to leave his office, I made a promise with myself that I would remain at the ABC as long as it took to outlast him. I tend not to break my promises; this time was no different.)

The Ticket went on to win numerous awards, including Sport Australia's Best Coverage of the Business of Sport and several international awards from the International Sports Press Association. Each year, the IOC names one person from each of the five continents as the winner of the Women and Sport Award, and in 2021, I was honoured to be the recipient for Oceania. Then, in 2022, I was given the Lifetime Achievement Award by the Australian Sports Commission. I am grateful for the honours – but to be honest, a journalist can only do their work if those at the heart of a story are prepared to trust them and talk to them. My heart goes out in gratitude to every single person who has trusted me with their story, knowing that while I might not always see it in the way they do, I will respect them and give them a fair hearing.

Having said all of that, I also played a key role in what must be the worst hour of live-sports coverage in the history of television. I mean it.

Working at CCTV (China Central Television) when we lived in Beijing provided me with an insight into how the vast nation of a billion-and-a-half people adored sport in all its guises. I worked with a (mostly) fabulous team at *Sports Scene*, and I had numerous experiences that offered priceless and precious memories. One thing I loved about the job was to expect the unexpected. One day, I arrived as usual just after 8:00 am to prepare for a day of presenting three different editions of the daily sports program. After I put my bag in the office and before I headed to make-up, the director for the day said, 'Oh, you'll be on air at 10:00 am for the live coverage.' Live coverage of what? Apparently, an air show was being put on by a visiting group of Russian acrobatic pilots, one of whom was a woman. Oh! But I don't know anything about aerial acrobatics or air shows! Never mind: there was an expert coming, and he could provide commentary if I just led him throughout the program. I madly scrambled to find out about the visiting team, the planes used in such performances, the geography of the mountainous province where the show was taking place, and any other things that would help me not look like an absolute fool on air.

When the expert commentator arrived, I told him how glad I was to meet him, as I shook his rather sweaty, shaking hand. He was nervous.

'Don't worry,' I said, 'I will lead, and you provide the expert comments.' I asked him how he became an expert in air shows.

'I'm not,' he told me. 'I'm an expert in English, and they needed someone for the program who could speak English.'

Oh my God, now I had sweaty hands! Okay. Let's just go with it; I'll use all the techniques I learned in my ABC commentary training.

In the short promo break between the news headlines and our one-hour live show, we positioned ourselves behind the desk in the studio. I noticed on the monitor that the event footage projected above my shoulder for viewers looked like a white box of smoke.

'What's that image?' I asked. The director said it was cloudy and rainy in the region, and the air show was delayed because of the dangerous white-out.

'How long is the delay expected to last?' I asked.

'We don't know.'

Then the on-air light came on, and there we were, me and a guest who spoke English and knew nothing about acrobatic air shows, for our live coverage of an event that wasn't happening. The white-out remained for the duration of our program, the air show was cancelled, and I spent the hour praying *nobody* was watching CCTV that day.

Part Three

World Stories

The Olympic Flame
Atlanta 1996

Each time the Olympic flame is extinguished at a closing ceremony, it is a moment of melancholy. It is literally the lights being turned off after a two-week party in which most of the globe has participated, just as you've started to think we could live like this forever – celebrating with the winners, commiserating with the losers, recognising the effort everybody has put in, and feeling good about being part of the human race where everyone has done their best. I know that's a pipedream, but not to have that somewhere in the back of your mind is to give in to mundanity – or worse, to the negativity hyper-inflated by our nonstop media world.

When the flame is lit, with it comes the promise of what lies ahead: extreme displays of human beings' physical, mental and spiritual limits. That one flame burns through the duration of the Games – a single light beckoning us into this part-myth, part-human construct that is the greatest show on earth.

What else inspires billions of people to tune in once every four years?

And yet the Olympic flame itself emerged out of a dark period in modern history. It was introduced in the 1936 Berlin Olympics, which were carefully stage-managed to celebrate Adolph Hitler's Nazi ideology.

When the IOC awarded Berlin the 1936 Games, Carl Diem became the secretary-general of the Berlin Organising Committee, appointed only days before the Nazis came to power in 1933. Diem was an athlete of note himself, had reported for German media from three Olympic Games in the early 1900s, and had been Chef de Mission for German teams to the Games in Amsterdam in 1928 and Los Angeles in 1932. Diem was described by his detractors as a 'white Jew' because of the number of Jews he had taught at the German College of Physical Education (the world's first sports university), which he'd founded. Under the Nazis, he lost all his positions except with the Berlin Organising Committee, since it was argued to Hitler that the country may lose the Games without the knowledgeable and well-respected Diem at its helm.

Diem was an expert in the history of the ancient Games, a passion he shared with his friend Baron Pierre de Coubertin. When de Coubertin revived those Games in Athens in 1896, the start of the modern Olympics, there was no lighting of the flame in ancient Olympia, no global torch relay, and no cauldron burning for the duration of the Games as there is now. Those elements – some of the most recognised, if not revered, symbols in sport – were designed as part of the opening ceremony by Diem, described by the International Society of Sports Historians as one who 'sparkled with ideas'. These ceremonial elements were as successful then as they are today. Diem's creations suited the propaganda arm of Hitler's Nazi regime, built on symbolism and marketing.

Diem was never a member of the Nazi party, but that didn't save his reputation after the war. Seen as a collaborator, he was the target of violent criticism. And the Olympic stadium in Berlin had an even harsher fate. In *Nazi Games: The Olympics of 1936*, David Clay Large documents how in April 1945, 'SS execution squads shot more than two hundred "traitors" at this site, many of them young boys,' just before Red Army soldiers captured the stadium. Then, 'Three days later, the Hitler Youth brigades in the area were ordered to take back the stadium at all costs. The boys did manage briefly to dislodge the Russians but lost more than two thousand dead in the process. A few days later Berlin surrendered to the Soviets.'

Large turns to Diem's autobiography to describe what the former Olympic Games boss saw when he walked into the stadium a few days after the surrender.

'The field where the Olympic youth had once assembled, the buildings and monumental grounds that had once delighted the world, had become a deadly battlefield, revealing nothing but sickening remains and gruesome debris wherever one looked.'

—

I have twice run with the Olympic Torch – during the Sydney 2000 Olympic relay and again on the day of the opening ceremony at the Paris 2024 Olympics. Both times, and indeed every time I've watched the cauldron being lit, I have felt conflicted. In the building of its myth, it has come to represent the oneness of humanity, yet its foundations were used as propaganda for the evil Nazi regime.

One of my clearest memories is of Cathy Freeman, the Kuku-Yalanji and Birri Gubba woman who lit the cauldron in Sydney for the 2000 Games – particularly the long pause as she stood in the water fountain waiting for the cauldron to rise, the momentary technical glitch that felt like minutes, before the spontaneous cheer from the 110,000-strong crowd filled the emptiness around the Olympic stadium.

But it was the lighting of the cauldron four years earlier, in Atlanta 1996, that perhaps touched me the deepest.

A couple of days before the opening ceremony, I saw a small boy on the side of the street amongst a throng of people who had gathered early to get their view of the flame as the relay ran through their town.

'I've been lined up here with my parents for a couple of hours,' the boy, who looked about 12, told an American camera crew. 'But we're not going anywhere. I want to be here when the torch goes by – not that I'll be able to see it, because I'm blind, but I'll feel the Olympic spirit go by,' he said.

That hit me like a brick. What is this thing we call the Olympic spirit? What are we searching for that makes us attach such meaning to these sporting symbols?

Later, as the opening ceremony drew towards the big moment at the Centennial Olympic Stadium, nobody knew who the final torch bearer would be – traditionally, the secret is only revealed in the darkness of the arena, to a collective gasp. Olympic champion swimmer Janet Evans made the final lap of the track with the flame before the spotlight revealed the final recipient, former Olympic and world boxing champion Muhammad Ali.

A torrent of emotion ran through every person in the arena, and I'm sure the many more watching on their television sets at home. That emotion was not just in response to Ali's sporting achievements – arguably the greatest boxer of all time, Ali won an Olympic gold medal at the Rome 1960 Games before turning professional. The greatness of the man who stood in front of us also came from his remarkable charisma, his word-artistry, his political conviction as a conscientious objector to the Vietnam War, his controversial conversion to Islam and his growing activism. The sportsman was great, but the whole human being was greater.

Shortly after returning home from his successful Olympic campaign in 1960, Ali and a friend were denied entry into a diner in Ohio because of the colour of his skin. An urban myth arose that he threw his gold medal into the Ohio river in disgust. (While it's true he was denied entry to the diner, he'd apparently lost his medal elsewhere.) In Atlanta, the IOC did something it rarely does: during half-time of the men's basketball final between the USA and Yugoslavia, it presented Ali with a new gold medal to replace the one he'd lost. The medal presentation was also kept secret from the crowd. I was seated in the broadcast stand that night for *ABC Grandstand*. When the Olympic presentation anthem began and the arena announcer informed the spectators what was about to take place, the reaction was electric. Once IOC President Juan Antonio Samaranch hung the gold medal around Ali's neck, the crowd went wild. While the cameras were still flashing, the US men's basketball team – boasting some of the best players of all time, including Shaquille O'Neal, Reggie Miller and Charles Barkley – ran onto the court to hug and congratulate Ali. They were men reduced to boys in front of their hero. As the American team peeled away, Yugoslavia's team made its way over to Ali, each player offering their own congratulations to the man whose star power did not stop at national borders. Each new moment brought a new wave of cheering from the spectators. Even writing this makes my eyes water.

As Ali stood at the opening ceremony with the torch held aloft in his right hand – his left hand shaking uncontrollably by his side, revealing the Parkinson's disease that had been growing since his late 30s – he slowly turned around, as if to gaze into the eyes of every single person in the stadium. His face, expressionless because of his illness, belied the depth of emotion that must have been flowing through him. What a moment in history I am witnessing, I thought: the man who can no longer talk is saying so much by saying nothing at all.

Pressure
France 1998

At the FIFA Men's World Cup in France 1998, my cameraman and I became the hoolicam crew.

This was an era when thugs used the cover of football to turn up for a fight. In the lead-up to the World Cup, senior personnel from the gendarmes, Scotland Yard and other European national security forces had all been busy trying to prevent as many known thugs as possible from entering the country to stir up trouble. But still, it seemed wherever we went, the hooligans turned up too. I was in Marseille when three days of rioting marred England's opening match against Tunisia. Then I was in Saint-Etiénne the night England was defeated by Argentina in the quarterfinal and got caught in the middle of another hooligan rampage that smashed up shops and parked cars.

While I was sitting in the Saint-Etiénne town square one afternoon, a plain-clothes policeman arrived to take in the scene. It was hot and tense but quiet – as though the trouble was sitting there, lurking in the shadows, and we were all waiting for a sign that all hell was about to break loose. The man walked up to me, introduced himself as a football fan and asked what was going on. I told him he looked like a cop in plain clothes. He acted shocked but eventually confessed. We kept in touch while my cameraman and I were in town. On one occasion, he warned us we should move somewhere safer; trouble was coming. On another, he took us up onto a rooftop for a bird's-eye view of the rioters, who were planning to come around the corner. He left me and my cameraman up there with the police spotters. Right on cue, it happened just as his intelligence had told him. In news-gathering terminology, we got 'great pictures' of a horrible situation.

We didn't always manage to keep a safe distance. Another night, my cameraman had his camera smashed and his face bruised, and he was knocked to the ground. A large English thug confronted and threatened me before somebody else got his attention. A lady who had been walking in the street with two young kids was understandably freaking out as the rioting amplified around us. She held one child, and I grabbed the other and left my cameraman to fend for himself while we raced down to an accreditation-only area, where some of the outside broadcast trucks were parked. I flashed my credentials, and thankfully security let me and the lady with kids in. I bashed on the door of the nearest van, which happened to contain an Argentinian TV crew, and asked them to please take in the lady and her kids until the mayhem dissipated. Then I went back to find my cameraman.

While these brushes with violence stand out in my memories of France 1998, there's another moment I think about more often.

The Eye of the Dragonfly

At a press conference with the impressive Paraguayan team captain and one of the best goalkeepers in the world, José Luis Chilavert, someone asked how his team was dealing with the pressure of its upcoming round-of-16 encounter against the hosts, France. Chilavert was eating an apple at the time. He stopped munching, glared at the man who asked the question, and paused. Finally, he answered.

'Pressure? How are we dealing with the pressure? This is a World Cup. It is about a game of football. I will tell you what pressure is – not being able to afford food for your children. Don't ever think playing football is pressure. Save your thoughts for those families.'

The best moments in sport have the power to take us to someplace else, touching something deep within us along the way. These are the moments that force us to confront a bigger world, our place in it, and to contemplate what is truly significant.

The Loneliest Games
Tokyo 2020

Dear Tokyo,

It's incredibly difficult to know the right thing to say as the 2020 Olympic Games come to a close.

Is it, 'Thank you, Tokyo,' for all that you've done?

Is it 'Sorry we have imposed,' when you really didn't want us here?[1]

Is it 'Congratulations' for the incredible success you have had on the medal tally and for staging the Games so successfully during the enormously challenging times of a global pandemic?

Should we instead say no words at all but, as I have seen good friends do in the past, just bow to each other respectfully, hold back the tears, and quietly take our leave?

---

1 Covid caused the Tokyo Olympics to be postponed a year, and they were held with as much isolation as possible: without crowds; with each nation in a separate part of the village; and with a majority of Japanese wishing they weren't there at all.

The Eye of the Dragonfly

There are no words in your language or mine that can adequately express the two weeks you have provided and we have experienced.

Perhaps the right word is tied up somewhere in the reactions of many of the athletes from 206 countries who have at the same time cried with joy and disappointment, who are all at once feeling exhilarated and exhausted, who want to run victory laps but have nothing left physically, mentally or emotionally to be able to pick themselves up off the running track, the judo mat, the boxing ring, the volleyball court and every other venue that enabled the possibility for dreams to be realised.

You have thrown a party and excused yourself from attending, but we understand why.

This illness that creeps around corners threatens us. It makes us fear each other in a way that has affected all our lives differently – weddings have been cancelled, funerals held without families, borders closed and businesses ceased.

Despite being able to fly to the moon and access the world over the internet, we are experiencing a modern version of the medieval drawbridge: once it is raised, you cannot enter; once inside, you cannot leave.

It's had an incredible impact on the athletes at the Games.

Being prevented from mixing with other nations, as is generally the done thing at an Olympics, competitors have instead gotten to know their own countrymen and women better, in a way that has not been experienced before.

Perhaps it's why Australia has had its best Games ever if we are to combine the medal tally with the things that really count: personal bests, personal effort, cohesion, mateship, friendship, support and understanding – and that's just here in Japan at the athletes' village.

If we also include the moments of national celebration that have distracted our people from their COVID concerns, you can increase the positive impact of these Games tenfold. No, make that a hundredfold, based purely on hearsay.

When our runner Peter Bol crossed the finish line in your national stadium, he brought with him an entire section of the Australian community, to walk through a door called 'the mainstream' for the marathon of life and for generations to come.

When your young skateboarders won three of the four categories in the new Olympic sport and our own Keegan Palmer won the other, together we were written into the history books as 'the first ever' for a sport that many ridiculed before the Games but have since come to admire, teaching us that while tradition should be valued, modernity should not be discounted.

When the greatest gymnast of all time, American Simone Biles, withdrew from her event because she was struggling with her mental health, you enabled a global discussion on the strength required to recognise weakness.

When Quinn was part of a gold-medal-winning Canadian football team and Laurel Hubbard failed to successfully lift a weight for New Zealand, you showed us that the difference between winning and losing is irrelevant when the result is recognition that transgender people are welcome too.

When Qatar's Mutaz Essa Barshim and Italy's Gianmarco Tamberi, friends off the field and rivals on it, were permitted to share victory in the men's high jump, we learned there is something better than Olympic gold: the ability to share equally by refusing the temptation for personal glory.

When the Australian Kookaburras, competing at what should have been a good-luck venue – the Oi Stadium – lost a gold medal to Belgium after a penalty shootout, we saw elation and devastation sitting together in front of the world's press. You showed us that there is no such thing as a single side to any story and that the world experiences the same story in many different ways.

When paddler Jessica Fox lost a final everybody had already awarded to her, we were all reminded there is nothing certain in life. Two days later, to see her return and fight for what she believed was hers taught us something else: don't let defeat beat you.

When bronze-medal-winning lightweight boxer Harry Garside fronted up to take on two-time Cuban world champion Andy Cruz and was outclassed by a better fighter on the day, his lesson was one for us all.

'I'm just learning to be a good human, and I think the good athlete will come after that. I'm not there yet. I've got some stuff I need to change and fix, but I'm trying my best to be better every day,' he said.

'I'm pushing myself, and I'm looking inside every day through every experience and saying, "What am I doing right, and what am I doing wrong? What can I do better?"

'I'd rather be known as a good human than a good athlete, for sure.'

And when the Australian men's basketball team finally broke through for an Olympic medal in Tokyo 2020, it was the realisation of a dream that began in Tokyo 1964. The team's belief in one another and their ability to rise again after too many fourth-place finishes is the kind of resilience we know you understand.

Tokyo, as we prepare for the final events and for the Olympic flame to be extinguished, know this . . .

Despite unrivalled challenges and enormous costs, through a superhuman effort, you have delivered the world an Olympic Games like no other.

It is for you to decide their place in your history and whether it was an experience worth having, but what the world has seen is that sometimes, even at an Olympics, it is not the gold that counts but the legacy of change.

You have shown us a window through which we see that by our own efforts we can help drive positive change that makes each of us individually, and the world collectively, better.

Thank you for having us.

Sorry to impose.

Congratulations on your success.

Sayonara, Tokyo.

Welcome to My Country
Qatar 2022

The girl at the immigration counter is slouched in her chair, not happy to be working at 4:00 am on what should be a day off. Pesky visitors, she seems to be thinking. Why would they fly in on a Friday? She looks at me like I'm being disrespectful by arriving on their day of prayer. I put my passport on the counter as millions of inbound passengers do at airports all over the world every day of every year, waiting for immigration staff with their uniforms and their stamps to permit entry – some of them are pleasant, plenty are not. Every now and then, they can be downright awful, no matter what their nationality.

Today's young staffer is indifferent. Her abaya-covered elbow is resting on the arm of the chair she is leaning back in. She doesn't reach for my passport; instead, she makes eye contact with me and opens her hand without lifting her elbow from the chair, where it seems to be glued. She doesn't respond to my 'Good morning' either. She is waiting for me to pick up my passport, reach over the counter and place it in her hand. This is her having a little power trip, because she can. This type of insolence I have seen at other airports, but generally not from the women and not in Qatar. Perhaps they are sick of the tourists now after staging one of the world's great parties in 2022, surprised that so many of the invited guests came here only to say negative things about them and their country, despite the hospitality they offered.

Locals still are struggling to understand why the Western media spent a decade or more criticising Qatar's bid but turned up anyway. It seems all they really wanted was to trash the joint in their newspaper columns and television broadcasts, although they never gave up the opportunity to attend the world-class matches for free thanks to their fancy FIFA accreditations.

It's mid-April 2025. Two-and-a-half years since little, tiny Qatar did what many thought was impossible: hosting one of the world's biggest sporting events, the World Cup. I am on a stopover from London. My flight to Sydney won't leave until 8:00 pm. This gives me a chance to go and visit some of the old sites to see how they look and feel now that the party is over.

The air temperature is 37 degrees. You drip while you walk. But I love the Qatari sun. I love the water even more; it's a perfect 28 degrees today, according to my submerged watch as I cool off at the beach. I had no time to dive into the turquoise waters during the World Cup, which felt like a crime. These waters pull at my soul like a magnet. I don't *want* to dive into these waters, I *must*. For me, it's the most beautiful water in the world.

It is this water, with its famous pearls, that brought traders with slaves to the region long before gas and oil were discovered.

The Eye of the Dragonfly

The traditional dhow boats with their thick white sails and beautifully crafted wooden hulls were home to those who kept the pearl industry alive. This water has simultaneously carried workers, adventurers, pirates and warships.

Today, as I dry off under the shade of a cabana and read *Hillbilly Elegy*, the memoir of the man who would become America's vice president, JD Vance, the Friday call to prayer rings out from several mosques around me. I look out to the horizon. The solemnity of the prayers and the peace of the sea belie the mayhem of the Israel-Gaza war not so far away. How can such a beautiful desert landscape surrounded by this calming water be the canvas on which so much trauma in the region can be written? Just across the strait is Iran, and beyond it, Afghanistan. Behind me is Saudi Arabia, and to the south of me is Yemen. Fanning out above Saudi Arabia is Iraq, Syria, Jordan, Israel, Gaza and Lebanon. All of these countries are too familiar with the politics of war. Maybe this is why the Qataris have developed a reputation as regional negotiators. They are like the Switzerland of the Middle East, sandwiched between religious and ideological fault lines they have to navigate for survival.

—

It was 2022, three days before the start of the most controversial FIFA Men's World Cup in history.

After 12 years of sustained criticism in Western media regarding human rights abuses in the small Gulf nation of Qatar, billions of people were about to tune in to the football world's mecca. It was the sport's quadrennial month-long tournament that hundreds of nations had tried to qualify for, with only

32 making it, including – at the very last minute – Australia's Socceroos.

As usual, on a Thursday night, local Qatari families were sitting out on picnic rugs, eating, laughing, celebrating the end of their working week. Others were strolling along the Corniche promenade, catching the light sea breeze cooling down the air from a daytime high of 30 degrees to a pleasant 23. That's where I was. I had come down to do a live cross to the ABC's breakfast program. I was standing amongst the dozens of tall silver poles, each bearing the flag of one of the many nations represented at the FIFA World Cup, designed to make visitors from everywhere feel welcome amongst all the locals by the water.

I was my own camera operator, using my iPhone, during the month-long assignment. As I started to pack up my tripod after the live cross, a local woman approached me while her husband and two children stood a little way behind. She handed me a white box with a handmade sweet inside.

'Welcome to my country,' she said in her Qatari accent, from behind her black veil.

'Thank you,' I said with a smile. 'That's very kind of you.'

She hovered, as if she wanted to talk more, so I asked if these were her children with her husband. 'Yes,' she said. I asked whether she'd do an interview with me. 'Yes,' she said.

Having lived in the Middle East previously, I knew how special this family time was in the cool of the night, with picnic blankets for coffee-sipping adults, kids running around being kids, others pulling out their prayer mats and facing Mecca to perform their prostrations. Nobody was drunk. Nobody was belligerent. Kids were safe as they ran this way and that.

Most women in Qatar wear a hijab, with their faces exposed. Few wear the more conservative niqab revealing only their eyes, which was worn by this young woman. I sensed she was both friendly and a little hesitant. 'How will this stranger from the West respond to me?' she must have been thinking.

As soon as we started chatting, it was obvious from the warmth in her voice and the smile on my face that neither of us needed to be concerned about the other.

I asked her what she thought of the world coming to her country. Her answer has stuck with me years later, for its spirit of generosity. She told me how happy she was to welcome people from everywhere.

'I hope they will understand us more. I am so proud of my government for banning alcohol. I have never seen a drunk person. I did not want my daughters to be exposed to drunk people. My family would not have been able to come out like this if there would be drunk people around. I hope everybody enjoys our hospitality and goes home with good feelings about our country and our people.'

Her voice was young but strong; her happiness at having the world in her country was evident and genuine. It was a lovely interview with a local perspective, one that was almost absent from mainstream media coverage from Qatar. Sadly, the ABC decided not to use the interview. I've often wondered why. Were they intimidated by the black niqab? Did it show a welcoming, friendly side of Qatar that went against the tide of most other reporting? Were they so stuck on their anti-Qatar agenda that they could not, or would not, see beyond politics and into the minds and lives of the ordinary people on the street?

Earlier that day, the Emir of Qatar, Sheikh Tamim bin Hamad al Thani, had decided to ban the sale of alcohol at football venues, meaning it could only be bought at licensed World Cup Fan Festival sites and the international hotels where tourists usually drink. The decision sparked another round of condemnation and angst in the foreign media, who suggested there would be hell to pay with fans unable to drink while they watched football in the venues.

It was also reported that FIFA's alcohol sponsor, Budweiser, would be fuming at the $75 million investment they had made. As it turned out, there was little fuss. (Later, I was told Qatari officials had asked the beer brand how much they had invested and expected to make during the tournament, then wrote them a cheque for the entire amount. I have not verified that story, but none of the parties involved has denied it, as far as I know.)

The controversy around Qatar had started more than a decade earlier, the moment they were announced by FIFA as the 2022 event hosts. The shock of those in the room who were from competing bid committees, including Australia and the USA, was evident on their faces. Only moments before, England had also been surprised to lose its bid for the 2018 World Cup to Russia. Australia spent more than $40 million on its bid. At crunch time, that investment delivered only a single vote.

Almost immediately, allegations of bribery were reported in mainstream media across the Western world. It became a daily volley of he said, she said – allegations from the West, refuted by Qatar. In the end, FIFA suggested it would re-run the vote if corruption of the bid process was proven. They commissioned US lawyer Michael Garcia to investigate.

—

The Eye of the Dragonfly

One year before the vote to determine who would host the 2022 World Cup, the head of the Qatari bid, Sheikh Mohammed bin Hamad bin Khalifa al Thani, who was the son of the Emir, was flying into Dubai to conduct a series of one-on-one briefings with international media. CNN rang me because I did occasional freelance work with them, and asked if I would go along with one of their cameramen to film a story.

The first thing that struck me was how relaxed and friendly Sheikh Mohammed was. The cameraman and I had been casually lounging in a waiting area of the hotel where the briefings were to take place when a young Qatari came and sat in one of the chairs closest to us and engaged us in conversation. Eventually, he asked what we were doing there, and we replied we'd come for a briefing on Qatar's World Cup bid.

'Well, should we start then?' he asked with a huge smile.

This was Sheikh Mohammed. I should have recognised him – he became quite famous in the region as the athlete on horseback who lit the flame at the opening ceremony of the 2006 Asian Games. Those Games were one event on the ever-growing list of events the Qatari monarchy staged as they built towards their grand vision of one day hosting the biggest events of all: the FIFA Men's World Cup and the Olympic Games.

Most people don't realise that Qatar's World Cup did not come out of the blue but was part of the ruling family's vision of what their nation could become. The World Cup was not the final destination in their plan either, but a stepping stone as Qatar also built its international reputation across numerous other areas: creating the world's best airline, Qatar Airways; building the Al Jazeera international news network to rival CNN and the BBC;

and becoming the location of choice for high-level diplomatic meetings and negotiations between East and West, including between politically opposed groups such as the US government and the Taliban. Many years later, when the Taliban took over Afghanistan after the US withdrawal, it was Qatar that helped evacuate many of the women athletes as they sought refuge in countries such as Australia, the UK and Canada.

The Asian Games were not unfamiliar to me. I had spent time in Qatar working at the lead-up event, the 2005 West Asian Games. I was part of a team put together by Infostrada Sports (now known as Gracenote), which was commissioned to run the sports information programs. We would write match previews, summaries and reviews, interview athletes after events, and generally provide the media with information they required. As part of the program, we worked with young Qatari men and women who had ambitions of later working in sports media and administration, a mentoring role I loved.

At the time, other than taxis, there was no public transport in Doha, and many of the main roads were still being built, fanning out around the main stadiums and venues that were being used for the Games. Sports were generally run from about midafternoon into the late evening, meaning my mornings were generally free. One morning, I had already walked several kilometres along the Corniche, mesmerised by the white sandy bottom so clear through the clean turquoise sea, when I noticed a small island not far offshore where multiple fishing boats appeared to be ferrying people back and forth. I found out it was known as Palm Island, a place mostly frequented by the locals looking for a cool escape from the city bustle and relentless daytime heat.

The Eye of the Dragonfly

There were deckchairs nestled amongst the palm trees, a small ice-cream shop that also served coffee, a change room, and water games and small pools for children. It was a small oasis that had been turned into a day resort, with barely a soul to disturb the peace. Well, do you think I waited for an invitation? This was heaven for me.

Each morning of the West Asian Games, I'd get up early, before any of my colleagues. I'd stand on the side of the road, and sooner or later, an air-conditioned car, ute or four-wheel drive would pull over and ask if I needed a lift somewhere. No matter where the car was headed, they would first drop me at the Corniche. This was my daily dose of Qatari friendship and hospitality. I'd pay a fishing boat a small fee to take me to the Palm Island jetty and arrange for them to pick me up in a few hours' time. I swam with the fish in the clearest water imaginable; I read on the beach as the wind gently rustled through the palms; I relaxed, sometimes dozed; then I swam some more and was totally refreshed and invigorated before heading to work. Again, I'd stand on the side of the road, waiting for a car to stop and offer to take me to whichever venue I was working at that day.

This was the Qatar I had first known. There were only a few office buildings between the famous marketplace Souq Waqif and the CBD; the Sheraton hotel was visible at the far point of the Corniche, with lots of sand and palm trees in between. Nobody would believe what it would become in less than 20 years' time, when it finally stood ready to host the largest single-sport event on the planet. Sadly, by the time of the 2022 FIFA World Cup, Palm Island had been stripped of its greenery. It served as a sandy platform for a large sculpture of the Qatar 2022 World Cup logo – a figure of eight, representing the eight World Cup venues, in the style of the infinite loop, symbolising eternal connectivity. No matter where you stood on the Corniche arc, it was visible.

From the start of our conversation, Sheikh Mohammed said that I could ask any question I wanted, and he would answer it. We were free to film the entire briefing. He had a model of the venues Qatar planned to build; he spoke of developing open-air stadiums with air conditioning to combat the desert heat; he answered questions about sustainability and white elephants; true to his word, he answered everything.

The model venues were futuristic. The bid was bold. Actually, it was better than bold, it was incredible. Nobody had previously heard of open-roof air-conditioned stadiums. As soon as we'd finished the interview, on the way back to edit the story, I rang my husband. Stan was always overseas somewhere – I think at the time he was in Pakistan. I told him that of all the major-event bids I'd ever seen, Qatar's for the FIFA Men's World Cup was by far the most amazing. 'Even if it delivers half of what it promises,' I told him, 'no other bid will be able to beat it.'

So in 2010, when FIFA President Sepp Blatter read out, 'The winner is . . . Qatar,' I was not surprised. I smiled for Sheikh Mohammed, who at age 22 had delivered his small but influential country one of the biggest shows on earth. But most others in the media were not smiling. They had not seen the brief; they had not been to Qatar. They were stunned. The only possible reason they won must have been bribery. Then the tsunami of criticism began, focusing heavily on workers' rights.

—

Workers' conditions in the Middle East were horrendous. Cheap labour, particularly in construction, was flown in from Bangladesh, Pakistan and Nepal, where wages were low, unemployment was high and there was little opportunity for construction workers to break the cycle of poverty. In Pakistan and Nepal today, the average yearly salary for a construction worker is about $4,500. In Bangladesh, construction workers might make $3,500 a year. Men from these countries took their chances and lined up for jobs in places like Qatar and the UAE, where they could earn about five times more, enabling them to save for a family home and hopefully send their children to school. The catch was, unlike in our society, workers' rights were virtually non-existent under what was the *kafala* system, a form of slave labour.

Workers were housed too many to a room, sharing bathrooms and cooking facilities that were often nothing more than a portable gas burner on the balcony of their tin living quarters. They worked six days a week, including during Ramadan, when eating or drinking during daylight hours is forbidden, despite the high temperatures. Workers were often indebted to agents in the countries they came from, locking them into fees that would take years to pay off. Once the workers were in Qatar, employers (including companies from the UK and Australia) confiscated their passports, only handing them back if bosses approved holidays, which they were under no obligation to do. Once the World Cup was awarded to Qatar, it did not take long for the spotlight to turn to the appalling conditions these workers lived in.

While the *kafala* system still exists in most Arab Gulf nations, it was dismantled in Qatar in the lead-up to the World Cup. A full-time office of the International Labour Organization was established there, leading to further changes, including the introduction of a labour court to rule on workers' grievances. Early changes began in 2013 with the development of the Workers' Charter and the Workers' Welfare Standard. Prior to this time, workers had not been able to leave their jobs if they had grievances. In the labour court, more than 384,000 applications to change jobs were approved. There is still much work to do to make sure the system functions as it should, but Qatar remains the only Gulf nation to have dismantled the *kafala* system.

Barely any media covered the significant and substantial changes that took place inside Qatar in the years leading up to the World Cup.

Much of the negative media coverage, to my eyes, was hypocritical, even racist. A lot of it seemed to question how such a small – read 'irrelevant' – place could host one of the greatest shows on earth unless bribery and corruption were involved. Interestingly, I did not recall seeing any of the journalists who wrote such pieces at the sheikh's on-the-record briefing session ahead of the vote.

Corruption and bribery headlines persisted. Then, a whole new round of controversy was kickstarted in 2014 after the FIFA-commissioned 'Garcia Report' was finalised. FIFA decided it would publish only a 42-page summary, rather than the entire 434-page report 'for legal reasons'. The American attorney who did the investigation, Michael Garcia, then criticised the FIFA summary for containing 'numerous materially incomplete and erroneous representations of the facts'.

FIFA was accused of whitewashing the investigation and faced unrelenting criticism. It was pressured into publishing the report in full when a German news agency said it had been handed a copy and threatened to publish it themselves.

I doubt many people read the full report. There were allegations of bribery made against every single bidding nation except Belgium and the Netherlands. Australia had its own chapter in the report, complete with dates, times, emails and meetings where a discussion took place about a pearl necklace bought as a gift for the wife of a visiting dignitary, Jack Warner. The former vice-president of FIFA and minister of national security in Trinidad and Tobago, Warner resigned from football's governing body in disgrace and was later banned for life from having any football-related role. The US justice department accused him of decades of corruption.

It wasn't just a pearl necklace the Warners appeared to have pocketed from Australia's bid. The Australian government contributed $45 million to the bid: almost half a million was promised to Jack Warner to upgrade a sports facility in his country. The money was transferred to an account controlled by Warner, the upgrade never happened, and an integrity investigation in his country later claimed Warner 'misappropriated' the funds. It appears Mr Warner was quite adept at attracting 'investment' money from any country involved in football.

What emerged from the 'Garcia Report' was that it was FIFA officials and associates who were corrupting the system, as opposed to the bidding nations themselves. The bids were predominantly following the rules – bad rules, which ended up being tightened after significant changes at FIFA headquarters. The US Department of Justice ended up charging more than 50 FIFA officials, associates and corporate defendants from close to two dozen countries. More than US$200 million was recovered and paid back to FIFA and its continental associations. Ironically, it was FIFA itself that was the victim in the whole sorry affair, as office bearers and associates had devised schemes to skim millions of dollars off the top of numerous deals.

Most people have never heard of the principle of 'autonomy of sport'. It refers to sport determining its own rules of engagement, free from government interference. What it generally means is that oversight from external parties is not encouraged or appreciated. Pretty audacious, isn't it? When a government is deemed to have interfered in the way a sport is run, it can suspend that nation from participating in their tournaments. Periodically, a scandal of such significance will arise that it leads to the tightening of the autonomous rules of sport, such as rules around gift giving.

For generations of sports officials, sport itself is the gift that just keeps giving.

—

The 2022 FIFA Men's World Cup was phenomenal, and for the entire month, Qatar was buzzing. The world's greatest player, Lionel Messi, captained his nation to a sensational victory over the defending champions, France. The Socceroos had their best-ever performance, going down to the eventual champions, Argentina, in the round of 16. Coach Graham Arnold, a former Socceroo – and the first Socceroo I ever interviewed, back in 1989 – was voted the coach of the tournament.

While I was waiting to do a cross one night during the tournament, a large Englishman – probably around 6'5", or close to

The Eye of the Dragonfly

2 metres, tall – with a shaved head, thick chains around his neck, and calves covered in tattoos walked up to me.

'I hope your tellin'em wot it's reeeelly like here,' he said. I wasn't sure whether he meant that positively or negatively. Having been threatened by English thugs at a World Cup previously, I was cautious in my reply.

'What do you think it's really like?'

'F***in' awesome!' He was too funny. He told me how he had been a football thug in a previous life (I might have even encountered him in France in 1998!) and spent some time in prison before 'growing up'. At first, he hadn't planned to travel to Qatar, he said, because he'd heard so much negativity in the media. Then he decided 'to check it out for me-self'. He was glad he did. Three games in a day, barely any queues as the entry and exits flowed so well, free metro rides between venues, and not a fight to be found! It was the first-ever FIFA Men's World Cup where no British person was arrested. Perhaps the alcohol ban had a positive outcome.

I described it at the time as the first non-white FIFA World Cup, since so many of the usual football fans stayed away while fans from the Middle East and North Africa streamed in daily. Saudis, Moroccans, Tunisians and more filled the souq each evening with their drums and songs, giving tourists from elsewhere incredible sights and sounds to be uploaded to their social media sites. One night while doing a live cross, some Qataris swapped my microphone for a sword so I could join in with their spontaneous traditional celebration. I accepted as graciously as I could before handing back the sword and claiming back the implement I felt much more comfortable with, my mic.

My mic and my iPhone were my constant companions in Qatar, recording the event as I watched it unfold. I knew I was speaking to people other media did not. I knew my coverage was at odds with most of the Western press. But I was glad I told the stories of those who were there, through their own eyes and in their words. People still stop me in the streets back home wanting to thank me for sharing stories they did not see or hear anywhere else.

One of the interviews I did was with a shop owner in the souq. His little store had the most incredible array of sporting antiques, including Olympic torches and old World Cup programs from eras past. Saban told me football came to Qatar in the 1940s, when the foreign oil companies, such as Shell, came to the area searching for the liquid gold the region has become famous for. He played in the national team himself in the 1970s and proudly summed up what it meant to host the biggest tournament of the biggest sport in the world as visitors from everywhere poured in:

'Now I can call Doha, Qatar, the smallest biggest city in the world.'

Matildas Mania
Australia and New Zealand 2023

> Data from Gemba, collected after the Women's World Cup, found the Matildas are now the most marketable national sports team in Australia – significantly more well liked and well known than the Australian men's cricket team and the rugby union team, the Wallabies.
> – *The Australian Financial Review Magazine*, February 2024

When it comes to the 2023 FIFA Women's World Cup, I am still trying to get my head around what it was about the tournament, and what it is about the Matildas, that galvanised the nation in such a remarkable way. Was it a post-COVID coming together? Was it the emotion of the world game that brings people together like no other sport? Was it so many Australians coming out to support teams from their country of heritage? Was it the authenticity of the Matildas players and their coach?

Was it that we felt like we knew this team as people, not just players? Was it partly media-driven hype?

I have an answer for the last question only. Most of the mainstream media was late to the story. After they saw the impact the World Cup was having around the country, they rushed to jump on the bandwagon. Media outlets and journalists who had largely ignored women's football beforehand rang the overworked media staff at Football Australia (FA) demanding access to Matildas players, with the implied threat that their coverage could make or break the team and the event.

Too many times I have heard people in the media say how the interest and impact caught them by surprise. Well, if they knew what they were talking about, it shouldn't have.

—

Australia and New Zealand were awarded hosting rights for the Women's World Cup by FIFA in October 2020. Who could forget the images of the Matildas players, including long-time goalkeeper Lydia Williams, sitting with officials from Football Australia, on chairs evenly spaced as COVID protocol required at the time, waiting for FIFA president Gianni Infantino to make the announcement? I've always felt a twinge of sorrow for the co-hosts, New Zealand, who never got to hear their name read out; the minute Infantino said, 'Australia and –' it was mayhem. COVID protocols were quickly forgotten as those in the room leapt in the air, bouncing up and down, arm in arm.

The Matildas would go straight from the COVID-delayed Tokyo Olympic Games in early 2021 into preparations for a home

World Cup. No doubt, for many of the players, it could end up being the pinnacle of their careers.

This moment hadn't come out of nowhere. The Matildas had been competing at World Cups since 1995 – although with barely any media coverage, few knew. Women's football had hit new heights throughout the 2000s, about 100 years after they first started playing matches publicly. At a celebration at the Sydney Football Stadium marking 100 days until the start of the World Cup, hundreds of fans came out to mark the occasion. The Matildas Active Support group were playing their drums and chanting, while politicians and administrators were on hand to make their speeches. As I stood behind my camera operator watching it all unfold, and thinking about whom I would interview, I noticed the absence of any former Matildas – except for Sarah Walsh, Matilda number 125, who was there in an official capacity as Football Australia's head of the women's game.

As it happened, the next day I had a call scheduled with Matilda number 170, Michelle Heyman, whom I hoped I could convince to join the ABC team for our upcoming coverage. (I couldn't, as it turned out, because just about every media organisation was offering more money than the ABC.) I asked why she wasn't at the 100-day celebration. 'I didn't know about it,' she said.

I rang Renaye Iserief, Matilda number 26, who was the recognised spokesperson for the Matildas Alumni, the group that represents past Matildas, many of whom had played in previous World Cups. She told me the same thing. 'We didn't know anything about it till we saw it on the news.' I confirmed the same story with several others.

I wrote an article for the ABC News website describing how many of the alumni felt left out of their own story. They had not even been offered tickets to matches, let alone been involved in promotional events the way England's Lionesses had been. All were thrilled for the current players and proud to have played a role in the sport's development, but as one put it, 'I suppose it's about a level of respect that we think we've earned, but maybe they don't think we deserve. Or they do, but they don't know how to do it.'

Many other mainstream media news outlets picked up the story, and Football Australia apologised, saying that they had always had plans to involve the alumni but dropped the ball while focusing on other priorities. It was an oversight they quickly fixed. The alumni were included in ticket allocations for group games and were made very much a part of the World Cup journey. It was fabulous to frequently bump into groups of them making their way into various matches. Matilda number 11, Leigh Wardell, has told me they rarely think of themselves as individuals but always as part of a bigger group that includes all those who supported them on their journey – the coaches, the parents and family members, and the various administrators who really pushed for their recognition.

'Individually we are all just blips trying to push the cause,' Leigh said. 'Together, we are a whole lot of little blips that then formed a critical mass. And that was happening here, in America, in Europe, everywhere. Some people thought this success and profile just happened. It didn't, it's taken a fair while.

'We could all see what we wanted to be, and we went about achieving that. If you can use your imagination, you won't be limited, you can achieve anything.'

—

The Eye of the Dragonfly

While I stood at venues around Australia waiting to do live crosses to the ABC, an astounding number of people came up to chat to me – every single one of them so happy, so energised. The last time the feeling on the streets was as palpable was during the Sydney 2000 Olympic Games, but that was just one city. Kids were excited to be wearing kit emblazoned with the names of their favourite players; parents were just as thrilled to be part of what seemed like a national celebration. Mainly, I was blown away by the number of diehard soccer blokes who made a point of telling me how impressed they were with the standard of the women's game. Many said they now preferred watching women's football over men's.

Matildas merchandise now outsells Socceroos merchandise two to one. In the first quarter of 2024, Matildas sales surpassed the total for the entire previous year. It's not just young girls driving consumption. This shift has happened because alongside the young girls there are young boys, sisters, brothers, mothers, fathers, football fans of every type, as well as people who previously would not have described themselves as sports lovers, walking around with the name and number of their favourite Matilda emblazoned across their back.

The games sold out and were watched by the biggest television audiences in the history of Australian TV. Usually, that level of support would signify the home team was winning. The Matildas did not win – they were beaten in the semifinals – but the outflowing of love and support for the team outshone that for many of our championship winning teams, such as netball's Diamonds, basketball's Opals, the men's and women's cricket teams, the Hockeyroos, rugby union's Wallabies, and others. Why?

In her book *The Matilda Effect*, Fiona Crawford explains that the term in her title was not coined with the football team in mind. Science historian Dr Margaret W Rossiter used the term to describe the historical exclusion of women from science. She was referring to an American writer and activist named Matilda Joslyn Gage, who was denied a place in medical school in New York in the mid-1800s, not because she wasn't smart enough but because she was a woman. There have long been women doing science, but the academies just didn't admit them. And believe it or not, women have been playing football in Australia and other parts of the world since the 1800s. But the sport's world governing body, FIFA, refused to hold a women's World Cup until 1991, 61 years after the first FIFA Men's World Cup.

An unofficial Women's World Cup, called a world championship, was held in Mexico in 1971. The final between Denmark and the host nation was played in front of more than 112,000 people at Mexico City's Azteca Stadium. Denmark beat Mexico 3–0 and were offered a reception at Copenhagen City Hall when they flew home, but the Danish Football Union refused to recognise the 'unofficial' result.

Australia's current women's football team, coincidentally sharing a name with Ms Gage, is the result of many Matildas who came before – the women who struggled to be taken seriously, to make ends meet, to have access to training and playing facilities, and to be recognised as equals to their male counterparts, the Socceroos.

One of football's strengths is the power of its player association. Globally, FIFPRO is a union representing 65,000 professional players, both men and women. Australia's domestic player union is Professional Footballers Australia (PFA). As a member of its inaugural advisory board in 2000, I was lucky enough to see up close how some of Australian sport's most dedicated, driven and well-intentioned people operate. Player associations are unlike governing bodies. Player associations have the welfare of their members as a driving motivator. Governing bodies tend to have their balance sheets as the number one consideration, reflected in the growth they chase. Player associations believe in growing the game too, but with their members as partners, not merely components in the machine of sport. Any time there is a crisis in sport, player unions are most often my first port of call for interviews.

With the support of the PFA, in 2015 the Matildas became the first Australian national sports team to go on strike. On the eve of a couple of friendly matches against the reigning World Cup champions, the USA, the players refused to go into camp because their contracts had expired and the sport's governing body – which was known at the time as Football Federation Australia (FFA) – had dragged the chain on renegotiating a new collective-bargaining agreement.

The imbalance between what the FFA demanded of players and the support it was prepared to give had been starkly demonstrated earlier that year. In preparation for Canada's FIFA Women's World Cup, players had been required to attend a six-month full-time training program. Some had to quit their jobs. Others were fired. The maximum annual salary the FFA paid female players at the time was $21,000. Some Matildas, heading off to represent the nation, prepared while on unemployment benefits.

(To prepare for the Sydney Olympics, the Matildas raised money by posing for a nude calendar. It didn't make them rich, but it certainly raised their profile. People who are too young to remember those Games are often surprised when they hear this story, but it wasn't unusual for the time. During the late '70s and into the '80s, Matildas players held their own raffles to raise money to travel overseas, as did many sports teams. There are players who tell of being handed tracksuits at the airport and asked to sew their own Australia patches onto them before they boarded the plane. And in many male-centric workplaces, calendars of naked women were commonly seen hanging in public view.)

The 2015 strike paid dividends. Two months later, a new collective-bargaining agreement was signed with a substantial increase in pay and a commitment from the FFA to provide better working conditions and a greater investment in the women's game. It was the start of increasing recognition for the Matildas. The next agreement, signed in 2019, guaranteed the Matildas the same business-class air travel as the men, and an equal split of all commercial revenues between the Socceroos and the Matildas. It was a smart move for the men to agree to the revenue split: with the continued growth and increasing success of the Matildas on a world stage, and if FIFA follows through on its promise for equal prize money at the next World Cup, it's expected the Matildas will earn more than the Socceroos.

—

The Matildas' mantra is 'Never say die.' It's perfect for them because, frankly speaking, they don't have time to stop, let alone die.

The Eye of the Dragonfly

Immediately after the 2023 World Cup finished, Matildas who played for overseas teams flew back to their European or North American bases, and got straight into training and competing for their clubs. Australian-based players returned to their A-league clubs to prepare for another domestic season. But there were constant windows in which they had to regather, having to play in qualification matches for the upcoming Paris 2024 Olympic Games. There were matches against Iran, the Philippines and Chinese Taipei in the space of a week in late October. Then back to their clubs.

Across four days in December, they played a home-and-away series with Canada. Then back to their clubs. In another four-day window in February, they took on Uzbekistan, home and away, before returning once more to their clubs.

Here's how that looks in kilometres travelled. Many of the players flew 5,470 kilometres from London to Dubai to join the pre-match training camp. They flew from the desert heat of Dubai to the snow of Tashkent, Uzbekistan, on the day of their match, a further 2,198 kilometres. After playing for 90 minutes, they showered at the ground, went straight to the airport, and flew back to Dubai, another 2,198 kilometres and another significant shift in temperature. They almost immediately boarded a plane to Melbourne for the return leg of the Olympic qualifier, another 11,658 kilometres. They played their 90-minute game, and within 48 hours were back on a plane to London to return to club duty, another 17,128 kilometres. In ten days, they flew 38,652 kilometres.

It didn't end there. They reassembled in San Antonio, Texas, in April 2024 for a match against Mexico; then, in the last week of May and the first week of June, they played China in Adelaide in order to remain 'match fit' ahead of July's Olympic Games.

And we wonder why there is burnout, and why there are mental health challenges and a disproportionate number of ACL injuries requiring surgery? We get to see the glamorous side of being a member of the Matildas. Rarely do we see its underbelly.

Olympic Moments

All people must be allowed in, without debate.
— Baron Pierre de Coubertin, founder of the
International Olympic Committee, 1894

Providing a window onto the soul of the world, that's how I see my job when I have a front-row seat to some of the most powerful moments in Olympic history. A journalist is not there to merely report the result; they are there to provide the detail and complexity of a moment in time, the brushstrokes a photo or image on a television cannot capture in its flattened two-dimensional form. A journalist needs to decipher the look of concentration on an athlete's face before the race begins, when a lifetime's effort to excel is distilled into one moment; to understand the depth of the celebration or despair once the race is over; and to know what impact this will have, psychologically or spiritually, in the athlete's home nation.

Athletes together on the starting line are alone with their thoughts. Different cultures, languages, political and religious beliefs mean nothing now; they equally feel the weight of expectation bearing down. Who will best control the adrenaline, simultaneously harnessing their pumping heart while quietening the voices in their mind that oscillate between hope and fear? The countdown begins. 'On your marks' – the sprinters crouch on their blocks. 'Get set' – their back legs straighten. The packed stadium is hushed. *Bang.* In the time it takes to count to ten, it's over; years of training, disappointment, injury, recovery, improvement, mental anguish and psychological preparation are done. The winner's elation is reflected in the cries from the crowd; the runner-up smiles, holding back the despair, knowing he will never get the chance to relive those ten seconds again. The last-place finisher has the national flag around his shoulders already; nobody expected him to get this far, but he believed in himself as those around him doubted, and now he has done his nation proud.

On the surface, these are humanity's most stunning physical achievements, yet they also have meaning buried deep inside the psyche and the soul. These moments, these athletes, hold a power even they do not often comprehend – the power to impact those around them. Witnesses to these moments leave inspired, with awe, with empathy, with a new level of understanding of what it takes to seek perfection. This is sport's version of Michelangelo's Adam reaching to touch the hand of God.

A handful of the most memorable moments I have witnessed (and they fluctuate from day to day), from one of the most privileged seats at the Games, would inevitably include:

- All of Usain Bolt's gold-medal victories for Jamaica on the track in Beijing 2008, London 2012 and Rio 2016, representing the sheer dominance of one man, from one small island, against the might of the world.
- Michael Phelps's 23 gold-medal victories for Team USA in Athens, Beijing, London and Rio. He was a swimmer for whom the water seemed to part, a man who overcame the monotony and the pain of training to emerge more motivated and inspired than the many who challenged him.
- Cathy Freeman lighting the cauldron at the Sydney 2000 Olympics, then stunning a packed crowd days later as she ran like the wind to win the gruelling 400 metres, a victory that said to Australia and the world, 'I am Indigenous, and I am free.'
- Watching Afghanistan's female runner Kimia Yousefi run a national record in the 100 metres at Tokyo 2020 after carrying her national flag into the opening ceremony knowing that the Taliban was advancing on the capital, Kabul, and that by the time the Games were over, her life would be in danger if she returned.
- Witnessing the elation of Australian men's basketball co-captain Patty Mills at winning a bronze medal ('rose gold', he called it) at the Tokyo 2020 Games after failing so many times before.
- Watching the tears of co-captain of the Kookaburras hockey team, Aran Zalewski, who had to put into words what it felt like to lose at Tokyo 2020 to Belgium, an opponent so evenly matched with Australia that the two could not be separated even after extra time. For those who have one hand on gold,

settling for silver is a punishment beyond words, especially when it is decided by a made-for-television event, a penalty shootout.
- In contrast, how different it was to watch the joy that filled an empty Japan National Stadium when two high jumpers, whose performance could not be separated after two-and-a-half hours, asked if they could share a gold medal. When the official said yes, Italy's Gianmarco Tamberi and Qatar's Mutaz Essa Barshim created their own shared history.
- Hearing the gasp of surprise at the opening ceremony in Atlanta 1996 when the final torch bearer and cauldron lighter was revealed: out of the darkness, a spotlight bore down to show 'the greatest' of them all, Mohammed Ali.

But all of those moments are the tip of the iceberg. It's the iceberg I seek to understand.

Nothing beats it. The more the world fractures, the more important the Olympic Games becomes. There are more than 200 countries on the planet and only two places where they agree to meet regularly: the United Nations and the Olympic Games.

Part Four
Developing Stories

The Games of a New Era
Paris 2024: Part One

Without hesitation, I can say that of the 14 Olympic Games I've covered, Paris was the best. It was not because of Australia's record medal tally, nor because it was without fault or drama. It was because one of the most important cities in the world showed that a single-minded belief and a determination to merge tradition with innovation could succeed, despite years-long media criticism predicting failure.

This is the challenge all host cities face. Once Los Angeles 2028 is done, the world media's attention will turn to Brisbane 2032. Is the Queensland capital ready for the intense scrutiny it will come under? Then again, will the media's opinion even matter so much in the future?

The media is confronting its own challenges. Mainstream media is in a state of flux, trapped in a bubble it finds hard to escape from as today's 20-somethings – the future generations of civic, corporate and government leaders – turn in ever greater numbers to YouTube, Instagram, X and other platforms for their news and information.

The former president of the International Olympic Committee (IOC), Thomas Bach, said in one of his final speeches before stepping down in 2025 that the Olympic movement must 'change, or be changed'. He recognised his own limits of influence and impact by announcing he would not seek a mandate to run for another term, instead suggesting the time is right for the injection of someone – and something – new as the Olympics forges its course for the future. It was his way of endorsing former swimmer Kirsty Coventry – Zimbabwe's most successful Olympian with two gold medals, four silver and one bronze – to succeed him as president at the IOC vote in March 2025.

When Coventry announced her candidacy after the Paris Olympics, she was the only female and only candidate from Africa alongside six men – two from Asia and four from Europe. Coventry's successful campaign to win the IOC vote was the perfect exclamation mark to Bach's presidency, during which he made a commitment to correcting gender inequality.

Another significant shift Bach recognised was in the way the Games are now consumed by audiences. A focus only on traditional media broadcasts, supported by mainstream news publications, is a thing of the past. The media is not exempt from the general public's loss of trust in institutions. Consumers seek voices they believe to be authentic, free of the shackles of media narratives and agendas. One perfect example is Snoop Dogg.

The American rapper earned around US$500,000 a day to turn up at the Games, and turn up he did. He was everywhere – at the swimming, the athletics track, the skateboarding, the equestrian events. Everywhere he went, he was a crowd favourite; and everywhere he went, he brought new fans with him.

'The Snoop Dogg Olympic partnership offers valuable lessons in authenticity, adaptability, and the power of choosing your personality wisely,' wrote Brand Rebellion's Bryden Campbell. 'As brands look to engage diverse and evolving audiences, they would do well to take a page from the Olympic playbook of this truly wacky – yet highly effective – collaboration.'

According to the IOC's marketing report, on their social media platforms during the Games, there were more than 16 billion engagements (a measurement of users who don't simply view a post and scroll but take the time to interact), and they gained 32 million new followers. The Olympic app became the number-one sports app in more than 70 territories, including key markets such as France, the USA and Italy. The IOC had succeeded in leaping into the world of new media.

Including all social media handles, Paris 2024 tallied 412 billion engagements from 270 million posts, representing a 290 percent increase compared to Tokyo 2020.

Paris significantly altered the shape of the Olympics in numerous other ways as well, starting with the opening ceremony. It did away with the predictability of a stadium-based opening and took the ceremony to a completely different stage by floating it down the river Seine, showcasing along the way the many landmarks the city boasts. It was a bold, creative, controversial and eclectic event. Like Parisians themselves, it was unafraid to confront history, modernity and difference; all were welcome at the table – black, white, and even blue.

Ninety-five percent of the Paris 2024 sports venues were already in existence, meaning money wasn't spent on new, unnecessary facilities. Paris organisers worked at providing numerous opportunities for spectators to watch Olympic events for free, on the streets and along the river, in the urban park precinct. This way, they capitalised on the nation's vast experience of hosting other events – such as the Tour de France – where sport is taken to the people, rather than demanding the people travel to the sport. And of course, there was the introduction of the new sport, the street's sport: breaking.

Olympic innovation is not easy. The challenges for the Paris organisers were immense. Security was always going to be complex and costly in a city not immune to terrorism and the sometimes violent escalation of political protests. But the Games, despite all the apprehension, ran much more smoothly than many had predicted.

There were costs to the economy because of the commercial and public transport shutdown of certain areas along the opening ceremony route. Roads, buildings, bridges, shops and all vantage points had to undergo security sweeps in the days leading up to the event, to guarantee the safety of the athletes and officials taking part.

Originally the plan was to provide seating for 600,000 spectators. That was reduced to 300,000 because of security concerns. There was a very visible 24/7 security presence at train stations, on the streets and, of course, at every sporting venue. According to reports, each day of the Games there were about 30,000 law-enforcement officers (and an extra 15,000 during the opening ceremony), 15,000 military troops and 22,000 private security staff on duty.

Each of the national Olympic committees with larger teams, including the USA and Australia, also has its own security detail, who works closely with local security experts during the planning and delivery phase of each Olympic Games. Since the 2001 terrorist attack on the Twin Towers in New York, security has become the single biggest cost for Olympic organisers. Team USA is particularly security conscious. In Paris, attached to the almost 600-strong American team were 70 agents from the US State Department's Diplomatic Security Service. That's more than one agent for every ten athletes.

Getting security right is not just a matter of public safety, it is also a case of making locals and visitors believe they are safe without the blanket of security being so obvious that it becomes intimidating. Despite teams of military personnel armed with automatic weapons cruising down suburban streets on regular patrols, and boarding the metro on particularly busy routes, they managed to blend into the surroundings and into the crowds, who felt comfortable going about their business.

London 2012 was the first Olympics where I saw this in action. At the last minute, when the security provider, G4S, admitted it did not have the required personnel to guarantee the safety of venues and public streets as they had been contracted to do, the army was brought in as a matter of urgency. The troops, who controlled all security access and checkpoints, were incredibly friendly and polite, despite being dressed in uniform and some of them armed. Olympic organisers often talk about the smiling, friendly volunteers at the Games making the experience so enjoyable for spectators, but in London it was the military that stood out.

As a member of the working media, I can go in and out of security checkpoints up to ten times a day. The process can be tedious and frustrating, especially in the humidity and heat, usually after having walked substantial distances from public transport stops to access points and, in the case of freelancers or camera operators, with heavy backpacks and numerous bags of equipment. To be greeted with a friendly smile and casual conversation can make all the difference.

Culture also plays a part. The smiling security forces in London were hardly going to be replicated at Russia's Winter Olympics in Sochi in 2014. They were more in line with the security operations in China, which has hosted all three editions of the games – the Beijing 2008 Summer Olympics, the Nanjing 2014 Summer Youth Olympics and the Beijing 2022 Winter Olympics. I was lucky enough to work at all of them. Over that decade and a half, China went from nervously inviting the world inside the country for the first time with its spectacular summer games in the nation's capital, to confidently expressing in Nanjing that it deserved to be on a world stage without having to copy or 'become' the West. By the time of the Winter Games in 2022, hosted during COVID, it had shifted again, to an attitude of 'Our country, our way – you're welcome if you follow our rules.'

On the eve of the 2008 Olympics, the International Olympic Committee's press commission, headed up by Australia's then senior IOC member Kevan Gosper and the head of press operations, Anthony Edgar, worked overtime to guarantee that Chinese officials would allow press freedoms for the tens of thousands of visiting media who would cover the games. At one point, it looked like all the hard work they had done was about to be undone by nervous Chinese officials, but at the last minute, with a lot of backchannel negotiations – including Kevan Gosper threatening to resign from the IOC if the president did not stand firm in demanding press freedoms from their Chinese hosts – the deal survived.

While freedom of the press was a delicate issue, there was praise in certain sections of the media for the 'ease' of Beijing's security. They planned it so well that they made it unnecessary for the accredited media to have to venture outside to do their jobs. From inside the secure perimeter of the media village, the media would board buses that would deliver them directly inside the security bubble of the main press centre, and from there to the secure zone of any sports venue. Reporters loved it because there was no need to go in and out of security checkpoints, unless you specifically wanted to leave the secure perimeter. It was also a clever ploy.

The downside for the media was that many didn't leave the secure perimeter at all to experience the real Beijing, crossing paths with locals and life in the *hutong*s and streets of China's large capital – exactly the type of interaction Chinese officials were nervous of. It helped ease the concerns of the Public Security Bureau, who never before had to watch over so many inquisitive foreigners all at once.

When the Nanjing Summer Youth Olympic Games rolled around six years later, China's confidence on the world stage had grown, and it was boasting about its might. Each day, before entering the media work area inside a cluster of venues, every accredited person had to walk past a massive black tank parked in front of the security entrance. Armed military personnel guarded the tank. They never spoke, never so much as made eye contact. The message was clear: 'Don't mess with us.' If you strayed too far from the village or venues, you couldn't help but feel there were uniformed eyes watching how far you went and making sure you came back. For those who had not experienced it before, it felt threatening.

In 2022, with the world still at various stages of dealing with the COVID pandemic, many of those who had been accredited to cover the Winter Olympic Games decided to stay at home, predicting that the strict COVID protocols – including daily swabs to test for the virus and the wearing of masks at all times, inside and outside – would be too much to bear. The media contingent was smaller than at most other Games.

Despite the many restrictions, it was obvious there had been a real shift in the mindset of the local officials. Police were friendly and spoke languages other than Mandarin. Security staff were approachable and helpful. The medical staff conducting daily COVID tests in the lobby of every apartment block in the media village and hotels were friendly, engaging and interested in the experiences their visitors were having. It felt as though China no longer sought the approval of the West; it was now confident in its place as a global superpower and didn't feel the need to overly flex its muscles in public. It didn't require the armoured tank used to welcome visitors to the Nanjing Summer Youth Games.

Whether it is in Nanjing, Beijing, London or Paris, the two-week Olympic sporting festival is like a time capsule, offering insights into the state of the world. Paris 2024 marked 130 years since the first Olympic Congress, held at the Sorbonne University, in Paris, where the foundations of the IOC were first laid out. Paris is one of only two cities to have hosted a Summer Olympic Games three times, in 1900, 1924 and 2024. The other city is London, which held it in 1908, 1948 and 2012. When Los Angeles hosts the Games in 2028, it will also be celebrating a third Olympics, following editions in 1932 and 1984.

Paris 2024 was a momentary burst of blue skies and sunshine in what had become a fraught world full of outrage. Israel continued the annihilation of Gaza, almost a year after the shocking Hamas terrorist attacks in which 1,200 people were killed and hundreds more kidnapped. The war in Ukraine was in its third year. Russia's invasion began just four days after the Beijing 2022 Winter Olympics came to a close. In the USA, there was an assassination attempt made on former President Donald Trump as he campaigned to become president again. New Cold War tensions between the USA and China were playing out through a sports doping scandal: the World Anti-Doping Agency had been accused of helping to cover up positive tests of 23 Chinese swimmers, even though WADA, World Aquatics and an independent review all came to the same conclusion that there was no evidence to disprove it was anything but a mass contamination event.

Afghanistan fielded a team in line with the IOC's gender-equal guidelines: it included three men and three women, although none of the women actually lived in Afghanistan. Since all 17 million women and girls in the country are banned by the Taliban from playing sport, Afghan women were selected from other countries. In a sad irony, the IOC Refugee Olympic Team had almost as many Afghans as the national team.

There were also geopolitical overtones when two women boxers were first wrongly accused of being transgender, then became the topic of daily news headlines in a debate over intersex athletes and whether they should be allowed to compete in the women's category of sport. The next chapter looks into the boxing saga in more detail, but in essence the situation was fallout from the bitter conflict between the IOC and the International Boxing Association (IBA), the only international sports federation to ever be expelled from the IOC. The Russian-run IBA was originally suspended because of governance and corruption concerns but with no progress the Olympic body took the decision to kick the IBA out and run the boxing tournament in Paris itself.

Try as it might to remain 'politically neutral', as the Olympic charter requires, the Olympics has and always will be used as a platform for current issues and challenges (also the subject of a subsequent chapter). Olympic athletes today are free to raise issues they feel strongly about, so long as they don't do it on the field of play or on the medal dais.

Refugee athlete Manizha Talash found out in Paris what happens when you test that rule. While competing in women's breaking, she unveiled a blue cape with the words 'Free Afghan Women' painted in block letters, in recognition of all the women in Afghanistan who were essentially living lives as prisoners in their own homes. Talash was immediately disqualified, but her message went around the world. The same would not have happened if she wore the cape outside the competition stage.

One of the biggest challenges for the Olympic movement in remaining politically neutral is defining what is political and what is not. At the Beijing 2022 Winter Olympic Games, Ukrainian athlete Vladyslav Heraskevych completed his skeleton run and unveiled a hand-painted sign in the colours of the Ukrainian flag with the words 'No War in Ukraine'. The IOC excused him, did not disqualify him, and suggested the world could all understand a 'call for peace'.

When Manizha Talash was disqualified, I asked the IOC why two athletes who were both supporting humanitarian causes – not political causes – were treated differently. As it turns out, the International DanceSport Federation – who administered the new sport of breaking – were so eager to be good Olympic citizens, they acted to immediately disqualify Talash without seeking the advice of the IOC.

When I posted on X asking why Vladyslav and Manizha were treated differently, one of the first to engage was Vladyslav Heraskevych himself, writing: 'Do not try to find consistency in the action of the IOC. There is simply no consistency. A brave and important act of an athlete and a caring person.'

It is a particular type of person who is courageous enough to stand against the establishment and the system to highlight an injustice, despite a consequence of enormous personal cost. In 1968 two high profile American sprinters, Tommie Smith and John Carlos, had to leave the Olympic village and struggled to find employment after they raised black-gloved fists during the medal ceremony highlighting the civil rights struggle in their country at the time. Many years later their image remains as one of the most famous in Olympic history. On the dais with them that day was Australian Peter Norman, who won silver behind Smith and ahead of Carlos. In support of their protest, he joined them in wearing an 'Olympic Project for Human

Rights' pin. Norman was never selected for another Australian team. I wonder whether the images of Vladyslav Heraskevych and Manizha Talash will carry the same weight in decades to come or whether they will fade into a mosaic of other protests in an era when everyone's outrage diminishes the impact of those that really matter.

At the Paris 2024 closing press conference, IOC President Thomas Bach described the Games as those 'of a new era'. They were, he said, 'more sustainable, more urban, younger, more inclusive, the first Olympic games with full gender parity'.

The IOC Refugee Olympic Team, another legacy of Bach's presidency, won its first medal on behalf of the 120 million displaced people in the world that they were representing: boxer Cindy Ngamba, born in Cameroon and living in London, won a bronze medal in the women's 75-kilogram category.

Boxing was also the sport that gave the 2024 Olympics its greatest drama. The world split in a fierce media-driven, social-media-amplified story characterised by disinformation, misinformation and propaganda, which emanated from the new Cold War geopolitical battle between Russia and the West. It's a story of such intrigue that it deserves its own chapter.

Boxing
Paris 2024: Part Two

On the eve of the Paris Olympics, stories were leaked revealing female boxers Imane Khelif, from Algeria, and Lin Yu-Ting, from Taiwan, had been banned from competing by the International Boxing Association (IBA) for allegedly failing undisclosed tests in 2023. The implication was that these were gender tests. Although the IBA would not confirm the nature of the tests, they said that the public could 'read between the lines', leading to the assumption the competitors were transgender.

The IOC was adamant that both Khelif and Lin were born women, were declared female at birth, and travel on passports identifying them as female. Legally, and socially, both are women and have always lived their lives as women.

An area of biology that is little understood by either the general public or most sports administrators is the difference between transgender and what is known as DSD – differences of sex development. They are not the same. Transgender refers to being born one gender and either self-identifying or medically transitioning to the other. To be overly simplistic, DSD refers to babies who are born with genitalia that looks like one gender, while their internal organs can exhibit a range of differences which can put them more in line with the opposite gender. The condition is often not discovered until puberty, if at all, or until they become elite athletes and others start questioning their physical attributes.

Debate had been raging for years over whether a particular category of DSD athletes should be allowed to compete in women's events or whether they should be banned. It is this debate that Khelif and Lin found themselves in during the Paris Games. Following the Games, Khelif lodged a cyberbullying lawsuit in France, naming author JK Rowling and owner of X Elon Musk in a social media harassment claim for the weeks of sustained abuse she received.

Each day of the Olympics, and for months after, there were headlines, broadcasts and editorials highlighting the Olympic boxing saga. Even Donald Trump, campaigning for the US presidency, had opinions on women's boxing. Knowing the facts seemed irrelevant in the media storm; bigoted opinions were fine.

To give you some insight into how the media machine works and how it is often manipulated by outside forces, I want to tell you an intriguing backstory to the boxing in Paris.

The IBA is run by Russian businessman Umar Kremlev, who has ties to Russia's President Vladimir Putin. It is the only international sports federation to ever be expelled from the IOC. Initially, it was suspended because of governance and corruption concerns. When the IBA failed to address those issues, the Olympic body took the decision to kick the IBA out and run the boxing tournament in

The Eye of the Dragonfly

Paris itself. When the IBA leaked the previously undisclosed information about its ban on Khelif and Lin, without providing any documented evidence, it knew this would create a drama for the IOC on the eve of the Games. Both athletes were well known on the boxing circuit, having competed at numerous events, including Tokyo 2020, where neither of them won a medal.

In Paris, Khelif won her first bout when her Italian opponent, policewoman Angela Carini, threw in the white towel after only 46 seconds. Through tears, outside the ring, Carini told journalists that she'd never been hit so hard. Later, two puzzling lines of reporting emerged. The first was that Carini had been offered US$50,000 by the IBA, and her coach was to be given a handsome cash payment as well. The second, even stranger, report was that in preparation for the Olympics, Khelif had trained in Italy with its national team – presumably including Carini. Twenty-four hours after her teary, painful withdrawal, Carini offered an apology to Khelif, saying she was just angry because her Olympic dream had ended so quickly.

The IBA held a press conference outside the Olympic Games to fan the flames of their already headline grabbing story about banning the two boxers whose gender was being questioned, while inside the Games, the IOC was working just as hard to defend their decision to include the Algerian and Taiwanese athletes. The IOC said IBA officials had no credibility and that the IBA minutes from the World Championships in 2023 appeared to back up the IOC's claims that a unilateral decision was taken to ban Khelif and Lin without any process in place. A social media frenzy continued to raise questions over 'men competing in a women's event'.

Another piece of the puzzle fell into place when Russia raised the topic at – of all places – a United Nations Security Council meeting in Geneva. The forum was discussing the expansion of the rights of women in peacekeeping forces around the world, an issue that has been debated for at least 30 years. Russia's deputy ambassador to the UN, Dmitry Polyanskiy, accused the West of 'monopolising the Olympic movement' and pursing 'an LGBT agenda', which was 'damaging women's rights and dignity'.

'At the Olympic Games in Paris, female boxers are being publicly subjected to violence on the part of athletes who have previously failed hormonal tests done by the International Boxing Federation and according to the Federation, and according to common sense, [these athletes] are men,' Polyanskiy told the members of the Security Council.

'This is absolutely repellent . . . from all angles. It shows what damage to women's rights and dignity is done by the LGBT agenda the West so regrettably imposes on the rest of the world.

'We think it is that in many traditional societies the impact on women, wives and mothers on political and social processes is done through ways hewn over centuries and can in fact be even much more effective than those done within the frame of liberal ideas.'

Algeria's deputy permanent representative at the UN, Toufik Koudri, rejected the remarks.

'I apologise for taking the floor a second time,' the Algerian said. 'However, my delegation did not wish for politics and sport to be conflated and mixed, especially in the context of the current Olympic Games.

The Eye of the Dragonfly

'We have listened to an implicit reference, but it was a very clear reference to an Algerian female athlete. I would like to stress the following: the courageous boxer, Miss Imane Khelif, was born a female, she has lived through her childhood and upbringing and adult years as a woman.

'She practised sports as a fully-fledged woman. There isn't a shred of doubt on that matter, except for those who have a vague political agenda . . . I would like to refer everyone here to the Olympic Committee itself that has clearly and beyond any doubt entered a testimony that would silence all those who would question our proud, courageous female athlete who is the granddaughter of the free women of Algeria.'

For anybody who had any doubts, what this exchange in a UN Security Council meeting showed was how strategic and politically motivated the Olympic boxing saga was, reaching into the highest echelons of international diplomacy. In a place supposedly dedicated to maintaining global peace or finding solutions to issues that threaten it, debating a boxer's gender at the Paris Olympics should have been completely out of place. That it wasn't tells you two things: sport and politics are so closely intertwined they are impossible to separate, and major events such as the Olympics become the rope in an international tug of war between different cultures and ideologies battling for supremacy. Sadly, the welfare of the individuals at the heart of the matter is rarely considered.

There are still those who say sport doesn't matter. This shows why it does. As society wrestles with identity and who gets to define it, there is no bigger stage than the one sport provides. In ancient times, the arena was the Colosseum; today it is whichever city happens to be hosting the Olympics.

Identity politics has become a flashpoint around the world. Science once told us that every human was either XX and female, or XY and male. Now we know there are people born who scientists describe as XX males, and others who are XY females. There is a continuum between the XX and XY extremes, with several categories in between.

On a day-to-day basis, as we play footy or cricket, or go running down at the local park, most of us are not equipped to understand the complexity of today's science, nor is sport equipped to navigate the spaces in between definitive male and female categories. I looked out at a room of sports bosses recently at a conference where I was hosting a series of panel discussions about the most pressing issues facing the industry. I'll be frank, the room lacked inspiration and energy. Sports administrators are trying to stay afloat in oceans they have not swum in before – washed this way and that, faced with a thousand demands and too few answers, leaving them wiped out and lifeless, unable to deal with complexities like these.

Who'd want to run a sport in today's environment packed full of seemingly impossible challenges and dilemmas? Get it wrong and the outrage brigade will shout you down or succeed in having you cancelled. It's not just complex questions of gender taking up the time of those who run sport: there is global warming melting winter sports locations and making summer sports impossible to play. Then there's doping. While a gallant attempt has been made to eradicate drug cheats, tests have become so sensitive they are picking up minute traces of banned substances that can be found in food and drink, leaving athletes with no way of being able to prove their innocence. Adding to the complexity is the announcement of the 2026 Enhanced Games, backed by billionaire investors in the biotech industry, where athletes will be able to take performance enhancing substances banned in Olympic sports in pursuit of world records and hitherto impossible human feats. There is also the gambling industry, with its fingers reaching into every aspect of sport with little regard to the equally invasive impact on families and societies.

In 2032, Australia will host its third Olympic Games, in Brisbane. Between now and then there will be several election cycles, offering up governments with different approaches and priorities. People are right to ask about the need for new sporting facilities at a time when many are suffering horribly from high cost-of-living expenses and a lack of affordable housing. At a more basic level, there are boxers, both at home and abroad, wondering if their sport will even make it to the start line in 2032 given the dramas it faced in 2024.

Imane Khelif continues to train, adamant she will defend her gold medal at the LA 2028 Olympics, despite President Trump continuing to falsely describe her as transgender. He signed an executive order in February 2025 banning transgender women and girls from competing in female sport.

When I chatted to Imane in Doha, where she was training during April 2025, she told me how her outlook has changed, believing her world was one thing prior to Paris and something very different afterwards.

'My perspective changed significantly after the Olympics because of everything that happened during Paris. I hope we are careful about what we do in the future . . . the world has changed a lot. And it will continue to change.'

Khelif's ambition was thwarted further when in March 2025 the new governing body for Olympic-style boxing, World Boxing, announced it would introduce gender testing. In its announcement it named only one athlete, later issuing an apology to the Algerian federation for naming its gold medal champion, Khelif.

There has never been a time when the Olympics has not faced challenges, its demise is often predicted but, till now, it has survived world wars, pandemics, terrorist attacks, fascism, and culture wars.

Sport, a Cold War Propaganda Weapon

For nearly 50 years, the Cold War raged between the USA and Russia, each trying to fortify its own dominance in what was an ideological and political struggle between democracy and communism. It reached its zenith at the time of the Moscow 1980 and LA 1984 Olympic Games, with both hit by multi-nation boycotts. Many thought the Olympic Games were finished.

With the Olympics now thriving once more, a new Cold War is being fought – this time between the USA and China, with Russia playing a bit part from the sidelines. Again, sport is being used as a weapon of propaganda, nowhere more so than in the pursuit of clean sport.

Anti-doping is a multimillion-dollar industry in the global battle against performance-enhancing drugs in sport. Overseen by the World Anti-Doping Agency, it involves a multi-pronged strategy of in-competition and out-of-competition testing, intelligence gathering and investigations, scientific research, and educational programs for athletes and others involved in the sports industry. (It also involves a lot of acronyms, as we will see.)

WADA was established in 1999 as an independent agency funded equally by the IOC and governments. A network of national anti-doping organisations (NADOs) ensure sports are following the WADA rules. In Australia, the organisation is Sport Integrity Australia (SIA). NADOs work with accredited laboratories in various countries to conduct the testing of samples, and increasingly partner with policing units globally to tackle crime gangs involved in the illicit drug trade and illegal gambling. Also growing in importance is the International Testing Agency (ITA), contracted by a host of sports to conduct the testing of athletes at numerous competitions. Once an athlete is notified of an anti-doping rule violation, they will usually front a domestic sports tribunal, with the potential for the case to progress to the international Court of Arbitration for Sport (CAS).

From top to bottom, it is a complex system to navigate and an expensive system for athletes who get caught up in it.

Leading up to the Paris 2024 Olympic and Paralympic Games, German broadcaster ARD and well-known anti-doping investigative journalist Hajo Seppelt revealed 23 Chinese swimmers had failed anti-doping tests at a national swim meet held *before* the Tokyo Games in 2021. Despite testing positive, they were not sanctioned, and some of the same swimmers competed in Tokyo and won medals. Some of them were subsequently selected for China's Olympic team for Paris. *New York Times* journalists Michael Schmidt and Tariq Panja had also been investigating the story and released their findings at the same time as the German broadcaster. The media alleged there had been a cover-up after

Chinese authorities cleared the swimmers, ruling they had been contaminated by food in the hotel where they were staying and that WADA had chosen not to intervene.

China has struggled to free itself from reputational damage sustained in the 1990s when numerous high-profile swimmers and middle-distance runners were found to have doped. Like Russia, China has an enormous sports system funded by the state, meaning the state is always blamed. In high-profile doping cases in the West, the athletes are held solely responsible, even when they are part of a doping program like the one run by a pro cycling team sponsored by the US Postal Service during the 1990s. The head of the US Anti-Doping Agency (USADA), Travis Tygart, called it 'the most sophisticated, professionalised and successful doping program the sport has ever seen'. The team's star rider, American Lance Armstrong, had all seven of his Tour de France titles stripped and was banned from cycling for life after Tygart spent years gathering the necessary evidence.

There have been plenty of other doping cases in the West. Canadian sprinter Ben Johnson was stripped of gold for testing positive at the Seoul 1988 Olympics. American track star Marion Jones was sentenced to six months in prison for perjury and had her five Olympic medals, including three golds from Sydney 2000, stripped following revelations she was a client of the Bay Area Laboratory Co-Operative, which had been supplying performance-enhancing drugs to numerous high-profile athletes.

There is no way back for any athlete who has been labelled a drug cheat, no matter which country they are from. Even after serving their suspensions, if they return to sport they are often shunned by others. Any subsequently good performance is viewed with suspicion. The stigma exists even when, on rare occasions, athletes are later declared to have no fault or negligence, meaning their urine or blood test might have returned a false positive, or one of only a few other explanations accepted by the anti-doping authorities.

What differs, though, is that the collateral damage varies depending on which side of the Cold War you are on. If you're from a Western nation, you're a rogue cheat and all your compatriots remain innocent. If you are from China or Russia, you are deemed to be from a rogue nation, and it is suspected every other athlete from your country is also a cheat.

These narratives are repeated over and over. They lead to suspicion of the other country and a loss of trust in the strict anti-doping system in which athletes are always considered guilty unless they can prove their innocence.

In the case of the 23 Chinese swimmers, competitors from Australia, the USA and Team GB voiced their displeasure over the lack of action against those who'd tested positive, suggesting they should have been named publicly and suspended. There were other competitors from the same nations who were more pragmatic, not as willing to denigrate the entire Chinese swim team despite the media persisting in asking them the same questions almost daily.

WADA held two lengthy media briefings to answer all questions put to them. WADA also invited media to attend an online briefing session for any interested stakeholders as they released full details of the case involving the 23 Chinese swimmers. I was on both briefings; I can't say how many outspoken athletes tuned in, but from their ill-informed commentary, I presume not many did.

The Eye of the Dragonfly

According to WADA, the China Anti-Doping Agency (CHINADA) had followed all the rules after they received erratic results for minuscule amounts of the banned substance TMZ, which is a heart drug, found in the swimmers' samples. The nature of the positive tests, and the tiny amounts of TMZ they picked up, were not consistent with either systemic doping or microdosing, where athletes take tiny amounts of a banned substance hoping to evade detection.

WADA asked for the entire CHINADA case file to be handed over to be investigated thoroughly. WADA reviews between 2,000 and 3,000 cases a year, and it can appeal decisions (such as it did with Essendon Football Club). One of the most high-profile appeals WADA has ever been involved with was the one against Chinese swimmer Sun Yang. He had been issued with a warning for refusing to allow his urine sample to be taken by testers after he questioned anomalies in their accreditation. Given that he had failed a doping test years earlier, WADA appealed the warning to the Court of Arbitration for Sport (CAS). After an 11-hour hearing in front of three arbitrators, none of whom spoke Mandarin, WADA succeeded in having Sun banned for eight years, effectively ending his swimming career.

But in the case of the 23 Chinese swimmers, they found no reason to appeal. WADA sought the opinion of external forensic toxicologists, and the latest research from the company that manufactures TMZ, legal experts and others. All of them concluded that CHINADA's finding of contamination was not only plausible, but there was no concrete evidence to challenge the finding.

While the case was playing out in the media, one of those most vocal in calling WADA's decision into question was USADA's

Travis Tygart, the anti-doping chief in the USA who succeeded in going after cyclist Lance Armstrong all those years ago. It was later revealed that it was Tygart who had contacted WADA with allegations against the Chinese swimmers just ahead of the story being released by the *New York Times* and ARD. WADA asked Tygart to supply any evidence he might have. They say none was provided.

Publicly, Tygart accused WADA of giving China 'special treatment' and being in need of 'significant reform'. The USA has used the case as a reason to withhold its annual fee to WADA (over US$3 million), putting a dent in the global anti-doping watchdog's balance sheet.

An independent review of WADA's handling of the case, commissioned by the organisation, disagreed. It found that WADA had shown no favouritism to the Chinese swimmers, that there was no evidence of interference from outside organisations (such as CHINADA), and that WADA's review of the case before determining not to appeal was detailed and covered all the relevant issues. Finally, the decision not to appeal CHINADA's determination that the positive tests were the result of contamination, likely from meals eaten in the hotel where the swimmers were staying, was deemed reasonable. The review did suggest, however, that WADA should review and codify its internal review system for a more efficient treatment of future investigations.

The new Cold War environment under the second presidency of Donald Trump may have real implications for the world's two biggest sporting events, both being hosted in the USA in the next few years: the FIFA Men's World Cup in 2026 and the LA Olympic and Paralympic Games in 2028. While the politics play out in cases like this, my thoughts always remain with the athletes who are used as pawns. Twenty-three swimmers in China have been named and shamed, and they will carry the slur of being 'dopers' without being found guilty of such a sporting crime. On the other side, athletes from Western nations are frequently encouraged by others to pour scorn on their rivals and organisations such as WADA, often without being aware of all the facts.

Captaincy, a Bad Night Out, and the Emperor's New Clothes
Sam Kerr

An hour before kick-off in Australia's first match as host of the 2023 FIFA Women's World Cup, news broke that the much-loved captain, Sam Kerr, would miss the game with a previously undisclosed calf injury.

When I think back now to all the camera cutaways of Kerr sitting on the bench during the match, I ask myself what was running through her mind, given the secret she was harbouring that had far greater consequences than a mere calf injury.

The national coach, Tony Gustavsson, looked pale at the post-match press conference. Despite the Matildas winning 1–0, he was peppered with questions about the secrecy around Kerr's injury. Was it so the fans still turned up – a money decision? How bad was the injury? How long would she be out? What chance would Australia have to finally win a World Cup without Kerr playing? These questions, so newsworthy at the time, would appear insignificant five months later when it became public that she'd been charged with a criminal offence.

In early 2023, just months before the World Cup and the Matildas' biggest opportunity for silverware success, Kerr had been involved in a drunken, abusive, violent incident in a London cab and with a police constable. She had spent a night in a cell, originally charged with criminal damage to the taxi, before she sobered up and agreed to pay repair costs. A second charge of racially aggravated harassment of the policeman was still to come.

Presumably with the advice of those closest to her – bad advice, in my opinion – Kerr decided against telling those who pay her national captain's salary about the incident even though she was at the heart of a nationwide marketing and publicity campaign ahead of the biggest women's sports event in history.

I cannot imagine what the weight of such an enormous pressure would feel like. Then again, maybe Sam didn't feel any pressure at all. It was another night out, got out of hand, but so what? And what business is it of anyone's anyway, least of all a bunch of suits sitting in head office somewhere, whom she'd much rather never have to speak to?

Kerr has a testy relationship with the media and is perceived to have an 'if I have to' attitude to Football Australia. She bristles if a press conference takes her in a direction she doesn't want to go. If media analysis of the team's performance is not complimentary, it seems to sit inside her turning acidic.

Kerr was named captain of the national team ahead of the 2019 FIFA Women's World Cup in France. The Matildas had been under pressure but came back to beat heavyweights Brazil 3–2. In a post-match interview, she said, 'You know there was a lot of critics talking about us, but we're back, so suck on that one.'

Quick as a flash, the crew at retro clothing brand Futbol Cult printed up T-shirts showing a figure resembling Kerr kicking a ball and the words 'Go suck on that one.' I joined thousands of others who bought one. Why? I like her spunk. I like it that she is not afraid of anybody, will give as good as she gets – and then some – and will stand up for her crew. But witty banter and jovial one-upmanship can easily turn that great Aussie barometer, the pub test: instead of seeing humour, people start to see an attitude problem.

Four years after her captaincy debut, with a home World Cup to play, Kerr was now a multimillion-dollar player. She was a star striker for Chelsea in the UK's Women's Super League, had a million-dollar contract with Nike, had been named by ESPN as Australia's most influential sports star (male or female), while others ranked her the most influential athlete in women's sport. A Nike executive said she was that marketable because she was so humble. Humility is not a word I would choose to describe Sam. Her quietness in a room of people she neither knows nor trusts is more a sign of the guarded lion, sizing up her environment before having to pounce.

As the World Cup began a month-long celebration in Australia, Football Australia had been counting the money pouring through the gates. Kerr was very much at the centre of the marketing strategy. The highest-selling piece of merchandise for Football Australia was the Kerr jersey emblazoned with her number 20, more popular than those of the male players in the Socceroos team. In some ways, though, the extra demands put on Kerr's shoulders might have fuelled a deep resentment burning inside her. She was a star footballer who just wanted to play, not have to deal with all the extracurricular activities demanded of her.

The construction of the Matildas story reached almost mythical proportions in 2023, given they had not ever come close to winning a World Cup or an Olympic gold medal. They were riding the crest of a wave of national support. It all could have splintered into a thousand pieces if headlines emerged during the World Cup connecting captain Kerr with a drunken vomit in a taxi, an argument over the fare, a smashed window, and the less-than-humble video of her calling a cop 'fucking stupid and white', flashing her bank balance and declaring, 'I'm not paying for fucking some fucking dodgy cunt's window' and that she would, 'get the fucking Chelsea lawyers on to this'. When it emerged, video of the exchange went viral, circling the globe faster than an Elon Musk satellite.

The first the public (and the media) knew of it was early in the afternoon of 4 March 2024, London time, when a journalist from the UK's *Daily Mail* happened to be sitting in courtroom number 5 at the Kingston-upon-Thames Crown Court in South West London, waiting to see if any interesting cases were being heard that could make for a good story. Boy, did he find one.

One name was read out by the clerk of the court and suddenly the reporter was wide awake. 'Samantha Kerr, you are charged on this indictment with racially aggravated intentional harassment, alarm or distress.'

The public's surprise was only surpassed by the surprise of officials at Football Australia. It was early the next morning, Australian time, when the news filtered through. Still celebrating in the afterglow of the World Cup, Football Australia CEO James Johnson and Matildas coach Tony Gustavsson were scheduled to announce a two-match series against China to be played in Adelaide and Sydney in the lead-up to the Paris 2024 Olympic Games. The Kerr headlines completely overshadowed the announcement. Both Johnson and Gustavsson admitted the first they knew of the Kerr arrest was when they saw the news at the same time as everybody else. The media, cynical after the secrecy around Kerr's World Cup injury, weren't sure the football officials were telling the truth. Whispers started spilling out from HQ making it clear they were blindsided by the news along with everyone else. The relationship between head office and Kerr was barely functional: FA didn't know Kerr was injured ahead of the World Cup, let alone that she'd been charged with a criminal offence. What else didn't they know? Who was running this operation? The tail, it seemed, was wagging the dog all over the place.

Publicly, FA were supporting Kerr, but privately, they were fuming. They wanted answers to some questions of their own but would be kept waiting for more than 48 hours for the chance to talk to the player. Interaction between Kerr and FA was clearly on her terms, not theirs.

Kerr's personal management team would argue she was not a playing member of the Matildas at the time the news broke, so she owed them nothing. She was also recovering from knee surgery, which was preventing her playing for her club in England. However, in today's sport, the promotional aspect of captaincy doesn't work that way: whether she was playing or not, Kerr was always referred to as the captain of the Matildas, and brand building for prestige and commercial return never stops, for either the player or Football Australia. Despite her injury, Kerr was expected to play a similar role at the Paris Olympics to the one she performed during the early stages of the FIFA 2023 Women's World Cup: a leadership role from the bench. Having her in the team was good for the group, it was said, whether she was playing or not.

Football Australia held an emergency board meeting to address two separate issues. They had to confront the very real situation that an Olympic Games campaign might be derailed by Kerr's unresolved legal case and, secondly, decide whether Kerr's captaincy should be stripped.

Football Australia had been in a similar situation before. Only months out from the 2019 FIFA Women's World Cup in France, the Matildas' head coach, Alen Stajcic, was terminated, with a payout in lieu of notice, on the back of two damning reports examining the culture of the team. Football Australia admitted Stajcic was not in breach of his contract, nor had behaved inappropriately, but decided to act on a 'culturally unsustainable environment' by cutting ties with him. With his departure, Sam Kerr was promoted to Matildas captain. Nobody has ever explained what the toxic culture was, who was orchestrating it or, more important, whether it continued. But by sacking the coach, the Matildas had their scapegoat; it was time to move on.

The Matildas finished their France 2019 campaign in the round of 16, falling short of their own expectations. Two years later, under new coach Tony Gustavsson, the Matildas were on the rise again. In the Tokyo Olympic Games held in 2021, the team made the semifinals, hoping for a spot in the gold-medal game, but went down to Sweden 1–0. They missed out on the bronze medal also, losing to the USA 4–3. Still, it was the first time any Australian team, men's or women's, had made the final four at the Olympic Games.

Despite a massive push from FA, which saw improvements in the team's performance against higher-ranking nations and an added layer of depth to the playing ranks, the Matildas repeated their fourth-place finish at the 2023 FIFA World Cup, defeated by Sweden 2–0 in the third-place playoff. It was the first time an Australian team (male or female) had reached the semifinals of the World Cup, but it was clearly upsetting for a team and coaching staff who knew they were capable of more. The focus immediately switched to the Paris Olympic campaign less than a year away, with the hope that the Matildas might finally return home with a medal. The campaign was an abysmal failure. For the first time since Sydney 2000, the Matildas failed to progress beyond the group stage, with losses to the USA and Germany, and a single win over Zambia.

The coach, Tony Gustavsson, (unsurprisingly) carried the can and reportedly left the team camp before the players had their bags packed. Sam Kerr's absence from the pitch was used as a reason for the team performing so badly. An article in the *Australian* newspaper cited unnamed sources in describing the Matildas' camp as a 'shit show' and their performance 'a mess' and 'disorganised', all laying blame at the feet of Gustavsson, despite him coaching them to their best-ever performances at the previous Olympics and the home World Cup. Explaining the relative success of finishing fourth at the World Cup only a year earlier, it was said Kerr 'was there on the bench giving guidance when there was none coming from elsewhere'. Anyone with eyes could see that wasn't true. I'm sure Alen Stajcic was watching on with interest as Gustavsson paid the price again without any indication of an internal review to see if the toxic culture evident in 2019 might still have been impacting the squad in 2024.

There were other stories, too, that have gone unreported. When Tony Gustavsson took on the role of Matildas head coach, off the back of two World Cup victories as assistant coach of the US women's national team, he sought guarantees from Football Australia that he would have their complete support in running the program he thought would deliver medals and titles. They agreed. It didn't take long, though, before that commitment was tested – some insiders say as early as Gustavsson's first camp in charge. A core group of the players didn't like some of the conditions he laid out for maximum rest and recovery to support his demanding (but not unreasonable) program, which was designed to extract the best from each of them. Despite Gustavsson being a collaborative leader who encouraged player input, he also had a set of values he was unwilling to compromise. He found out early that if there was an arm wrestle between what he wanted and what some of the players wanted, head office would appease the players.

There is a pattern I have seen repeated several times with the Matildas. Despite having enormous talent, they promise much, fall short and then criticise the coach, who is inevitably replaced. Kerr continues to be highlighted as the team's superstar, at the expense of others, placing unfair pressure on her shoulders and banking on her continued success for the cash registers to keep pinging. The continued failure of the team to reach its potential must be examined more broadly than simply blaming the coach. Despite having some of the best players in the world today – extending far beyond Kerr – almost a year after the Paris collapse, and with less than a year to prepare for a home AFC Women's Asian Cup in 2026, the Matildas remained without a full-time coach. Had word spread that coaching the Matildas – a team with so much promise – was a job some of the best coaches were steering clear of?

In early 2025, a seven-day criminal trial in London's Kingston-upon-Thames Crown Court finished with the jury's unanimous decision that Kerr was not guilty of racially aggravated harassment. Her star lawyer, Grace Forbes, had successfully argued that Kerr and her partner, Kristie Mewis, had feared for their lives before smashing their way out of a taxi that had delivered them to Twickenham police station. The two women said they believed they were being taken hostage. There is plenty written elsewhere about the merits of the case – whether it should have gone to court at all, and whether Kerr, who identifies as a lesbian and a white-Anglo-Indian, was in a subordinate power play against a white police constable in a force that had been found by an independent review in 2023 to be 'institutionally racist, misogynistic and homophobic'.

Questions have also been asked about whether Sam Kerr's power and privilege as one of the most recognised footballers on the planet were superior to those of a lowly paid police constable, no matter what his colour. Her behaviour in the police station – abusing a cop, flashing a bank balance, threatening the police with the might of the Chelsea lawyers – did not resemble that of someone afraid for her life, but of someone who knew she had access to all the money and legal power she needed.

Court case aside, my interest was in how Football Australia dealt with the matter and what the Kerr case teaches us about sport, leadership and the rise of women. There is one aspect about which I can hypothesise with the highest degree of certainty: a captain of the Socceroos, the men's or women's national cricket team, or the Olympic team would have been immediately stood down from their role. Innocence of the criminal charge is one thing, reputation as a national sporting captain displaying such behaviour is another. A frequent complaint about sport is that all sorts of public behaviour is excused if the player is seen as crucial to a team's success. While such leniency does exist, it rarely extends to national captains.

As women athletes call for equal recognition and equal pay, they must expect equal scrutiny will come. What was revealed in this incident was that neither Football Australia, nor few in the media, were prepared to treat it in the same way they might treat a similar scenario had it involved an Australian men's captain.

It is widely accepted that a criminal charge would most likely trigger a 'no-fault stand down' clause in a player's contract, which commonly requires a player to step down or aside while a serious incident plays out. Notwithstanding that under the law everybody is innocent until proven guilty, in elite sport bad headlines are bad for business. It's part of the commercial model every athlete should understand.

There are those who lament that Australian sportsmen and sportswomen should be held in such high regard. Yet, travel the world and you'll find out that what most people in most places know about Australia is the success of our sporting teams and athletes. Overwhelmingly, Australia's reputation on a global stage is built around sport. Sport is not just about what happens on the field, it is about the doors it opens off the field, the relationships forged from cultural to commercial and political realms, extending all the way through to issues of national security. The Australian government's 2025 release of 'Australia's Sports Diplomacy Strategy 2032+' spells out the growing importance sport can play in international affairs and relationship building, even more so in times of global uncertainty. In the big scheme of things, the results of a match or a game may be trivial, but sport itself is no trivial matter. Captains of our national sports teams do and must shoulder a heavier burden than their teammates, because they have a responsibility in platforming our national reputation.

All of that said, I am mostly reluctant to use the term *role model* to describe a person who plays sport well. The term carries a weighty burden for many people who just play sport because they are good at it and, if they are lucky, can make a living from it. Making athletes role models is an easy excuse for the rest of us to absolve ourselves of our responsibilities as mates, parents, teachers, coaches, or community leaders and instead lay these responsibilities at the feet of those who, by virtue of having a global profile, are somehow expected to teach our kids what it means to be the best humans possible.

However, to be a captain does take something special. Leadership means accepting a higher responsibility and ability to hold yourself as an example to others. I have never understood why Kerr did not have a press conference the day after her police station incident, explaining the situation honestly: that she'd had too much to drink after scoring a hattrick for Chelsea, was involved in a mishap and misunderstanding in a taxi ride on the way home, had behaved in a way that embarrassed her, and apologised to those she'd abused, and then explained that she'd paid for the damages to the cab and that she'd learnt from her experience.

A good adviser would have convinced Kerr that it was the right thing to do. It is unlikely the incident would have progressed any further, and the most natural reaction from most would have been one of understanding and forgiveness. Instead, when a national poll was taken after the story became known, it showed that 60 percent of the previously adoring public believed Kerr should not captain again.

Economies of (Male) Scale

Measuring the success of a sport is not an exact science. As far as 'biggest' sports or 'most successful' sports go, they can be measured by the number of registered players or the size of the broadcast audience, rights fees or revenue. It is like the never-ending stream of sports statistics: you can dress them up any way you like, to support whichever argument you might be trying to prove.

People are always surprised by which sports are the biggest in terms of registered participation rates. Almost everyone thinks it's football (as in soccer). But dwarfing every other sport is volleyball. It's by far the most popular, with almost 1 billion registered players worldwide, more than double the sport sitting in second spot, basketball (450 million). Then comes table tennis (300 million), while football is in fourth spot (265 million). The only other sport with more than 200 million registered players is badminton (220 million).

When it comes to ranking sport according to how many people are watching, you get a very different top five. Football is the juggernaut. Four billion people watched the FIFA Men's World Cup 2022 in Qatar, and almost 2 billion tuned in for the FIFA Women's World Cup co-hosted by Australia and New Zealand in 2023. Cricket sits in second place with 2.5 billion global viewers; field hockey has 2 billion, and tennis 1 billion. Audiences start to fall away after that: volleyball has 900 million viewers around the world, table tennis 875 million, and basketball 825 million.

But if revenue is the marker you choose, you get a different list again, with American leagues filling the top three positions. NFL (American football) has an annual income of US$19.2 billion, MLB (Major League Baseball) US$11.6 billion, and the NBA (National Basketball Association) US$10.6 billion. Sitting in fourth spot is football's EPL (English Premier League) with an annual income of US$7.6 billion, then it's back to North America to round out the top five, with the NHL (National Hockey League) generating annual income of US$6.4 billion. However, while America is a field of dreams for men's sports, representing 61% of the globe's major league revenues, the sun shines elsewhere for women.

The most lucrative cricket competition in the world is the men's Indian Premier League (IPL), which began in 2008. Television rights for the 2023–2027 period sold for US$6.2 billion – meaning, on average, that each match was worth US$15.1 million. The competition is held over two months each year, with the lowest-paid players earning around US$24,000 and the highest-contracted cricketers more than US$3 million for their eight weeks of work.

It took 15 years for a women's equivalent in India, the Women's Premier League (WPL), to be introduced. While it still has a lot of ground to make up, its initial five-year broadcast deal was worth US$128 million. The highest-paid player, for what amounted to a three-week tournament, was Indian opening batter Smriti Mandhana, who was signed for US$400,000. Australia's Ashleigh Gardner was signed for US$377,000. It was cricket that provided Australia with its biggest crowd for a women's sporting contest: the 2020 final of the Women's T20 World Cup at the MCG was attended by 86,174 people.

In England's professional women's football league, the Women's Super League (WSL), North London club Arsenal conducted a record-smashing spree during the 2023–2024 season. I was lucky enough to be at the match between Arsenal and Chelsea in early December, when a record crowd of 59,042 cheered on a home victory. Matildas players Steph Catley (the Matildas' captain during Sam Kerr's injury absence) and Caitlin Foord played for Arsenal at the time, while Kerr played for Chelsea. Weeks later, Arsenal fans did it again, with 60,160 turning up for the match against Manchester United. The club's average attendance for the season was greater than half of the men's teams in the EPL.

It's men's sport, though, that continues to bring in the lion's share of the money. The tradition of networks outbidding each other for broadcast rights for men's games is a bubble that has never burst. In recent years, it's been inflated further as companies such as Netflix, Amazon and YouTube have got in on the act. Once all the accounting was done for the 2024 Olympic year, the combined total of global sports rights would surpass

US$62.61 billion. According to the 2024 'SportBusiness Global Media Report', just over 34 percent of that would come from football (soccer) rights. Just as football is the most valuable sport, the most valuable market is the USA, contributing just under 50 percent of the entire sports rights total.

The president of football's world governing body, FIFA, warned broadcasters ahead of the 2023 Women's World Cup that if they weren't serious about the rights offers they made, he would choose to not sell them at all, starving the markets of access to some of the biggest women's teams in the world. Gianni Infantino said FIFA knew how big audience numbers were, with FIFA's own research suggesting the audience for women's football in some markets was almost 80 percent of that for men's football. So why, he wanted to know, was there such a vast discrepancy in broadcast dollars offered by networks for the men's game compared to the women's game?

'Often public broadcasters in big countries offer us one hundred million US dollars or more to broadcast the Men's World Cup; they offer us one million or less to broadcast the women's World Cup,' Mr Infantino told delegates at a FIFA Congress in early 2023. He was goading the broadcasters to step up, as FIFA itself had done with prize money.

In 2015, prize money at the Women's World Cup was US$15 million, but by 2023 it had grown to US$150 million. If parity is to be reached at the next World Cup tournaments in 2026 and 2027, as the FIFA president predicts, women's prize money will be in excess of US$400 million.

It appears the men who still run most media outfits are reluctant to gamble on bidding for the rights to women's sport, which relies on sourcing around 55 percent of its revenue from commercial sponsorships. Deloitte predicts revenue generated by global women's sport is on target to crack the US$1 billion mark for the first time, with the most popular individual teams worth as much as US$100 million each. The single-biggest men's team franchise is the Dallas Cowboys, worth a whopping US$9 billion. FIFA claims the 2023 Women's World Cup was the first to break even, generating revenue of US$570 million.

Football (soccer) hasn't always dominated the women's sporting ranks, though. For many years, netball enjoyed top spot as the sport of choice for girls and women in Australia. It stood out in an almost deserted television landscape for women's sport. Even so, a 2016 television broadcast deal with the Nine Network saw no money flow from the broadcaster to the sport's governing body. Instead, Nine covered production costs (a much scaled-back version of men's sports production, with limited cameras and staff), and the network agreed to share advertising revenue with Netball Australia. Unlike football and cricket, netball did not have a big brother with a large bank account to help catapult the women's league. Netball, like the Commonwealth Games, is struggling in a now crowded marketplace where their product has been left in the wake of others.

Sport has always been played by women, but the idea that it could be as skilful, entertaining and commercially viable as men's professional sport has taken a while to sink in. Over the decades, it has been predominantly men who have run sport and the media. There is still a long way to go, but the curve has hit the inflection point where gains in sports played by women are becoming steeper, more quickly.

The Eye of the Dragonfly

Two of the most recent professional leagues launched for women in Australia are the NRLW (rugby league) and AFLW (Aussie Rules football). Despite there being a men's rugby league competition since 1907, the women's equivalent wasn't created until 2018, 111 years later. The AFL took even longer, introducing the AFLW competition in 2017, 120 years after the men's competition began.

Women's competitions have always struggled with head office wasting time debating the 'chicken or egg' theory – what comes first, growing interest leading to greater investment, or greater investment to grow interest? I'm a fan of the Nike sportswear motto 'Just do it.'

Early in my time at the ABC, I came to know two hugely influential women in Australian sport, who helped carve a path for the many others who have followed in the decades since: Ann Mitchell, president of the Australian Women's Cricket Council, and Heather Reid, executive director of the Australian Women's Soccer Association. It does not surprise me that cricket and football have surpassed all other women's sports in Australia in terms of professionalism, given the groundwork these two women did before the associations they led were united with the men's national governing bodies for their respective sports, creating a single body enabling further growth.

In 2015, as the juggernaut of the Women's Big Bash League (WBBL) took off, putting women cricketers into the lounge rooms of Australians everywhere, the Australian Cricketers' Association did an interview with Ann Mitchell in which they asked her about the future of the game. Remember, she had been around in the days when women played by funding themselves and without any media attention at all.

'I was surprised by the success of the WBBL . . . but it just shows the power of free-to-air commercial TV and the interest of the Australian public in exciting sport,' she said. 'I have always maintained that the game for women simply needed exposure to the general public; the success of the WBBL last season is evidence of that. The T20 concept has taken off and seems to be what suits this generation, so administrators will have to use this form of the game to keep cricket at the forefront.'

Mitchell was right. Exposure, engagement and free-to air-television – as well as India's potential to deliver a billion fans – has seen cricket make its way into the LA Olympic Games in 2028.

Heather Reid is a women's football visionary. Alongside other like-minded women, she lobbied for a women's World Cup, which happened in 1991, and the inclusion of football in the Olympics, which happened in Atlanta 1996. Having become the first CEO of a state football federation, in the ACT in 2004, Reid knew a thing or two about being the only woman in the room. Australia did not qualify for the first FIFA Women's World Cup in China in 1991, but Heather Reid was there. She still has the notebook where she recorded the appointments during the tournament to phone in for her regular interviews with me on *ABC Grandstand*.

While much has changed, with women and girls now able to play any sport of their choosing, she speaks of challenges women still face in reaching the top of sports administration and media.

'Cronyism, nepotism, mismanagement, incompetence, lack of mutual trust and power struggles. Why would anybody want to get involved with that?' Reid told me. Correct. Power does funny things to people, and there is still a massive power imbalance in sport when it comes to those who govern it and those who report on it. A big part of the problem is that many of those seeking 'the top job', whether in media or at sports governing bodies, are not reminded often enough of why they are there. Hung on the wall of every office should be this message:

> You are here for a short time.
> In the future you will be forgotten.
> Use your time wisely.
> Serve the people for their benefit and the benefit of sport.
> Do not serve yourself for the benefit of personal power
> and ambition.

—

After the FIFA Women's World Cup in 2023, the Paris 2024 Olympic Games celebrated equal numbers of female and male athletes competing for the first time in the 128-year history of the Olympics. How disappointing, though, that there was a lack of gender equality in the media reporting on the Games.

People are often surprised that there can be up to twice the number of media personnel accredited for the Olympic Games than there are athletes. In Paris 2024 there were just over 24,000 media representatives, 5,733 of those were press, 18,434 were rights-holding broadcasters and Olympic Broadcasting Services (OBS) staff. OBS is a subsidiary of the IOC responsible for producing television, radio, and digital coverage of the Games which is distributed to broadcasters around the world. Ahead of Paris, OBS introduced several programs designed to boost the number of women employed in the industry. As a result, for the first time, broadcast accreditations surpassed press accreditations in terms of female representation, but a significant gap remains. Women accounted for 26.42 percent of broadcast accreditations, and 23 percent of press accreditations. Without the OBS staff, the broadcast teams from television networks attending the Games would be skewed even more heavily towards men. The category with the lowest representation remains photography with women accounting for only 15 percent. There was one standout media organisation: Reuters. The international news agency's team at the Games was 57 percent female overall, and an impressive 49 percent of photographers.

American broadcaster NBC always has the biggest media contingent at an Olympic Games, with more than 400 personnel. They are also the rights holder that pays the most to the IOC for the privilege. Its last rights deal was signed in 2021, for exclusive rights in the American market to cover the Winter Olympics of Beijing 2022, Milano-Cortina 2026 and the French Alps 2030, as well as the Summer Olympics of Paris 2024, Los Angeles 2028 and Brisbane 2032. It came with a price tag of more than US$7.75 billion.

NBC first began covering the Olympics at Tokyo 1964 but are yet to have a female prime-time host. This is despite NBC's executive producer and president of Olympics production being a woman, Molly Solomon, who is respected across the industry. In 2023, the *Journal of Sports Media* looked at a 25-year period of NBC coverage and found that 80 percent of their non-athlete presenters, reporters, commentators and analysts were male.

Ahead of the Paris Games, OBS published its report, 'Framing the Future', detailing its commitment to shifting what has been stubbornly slow progress in opening up Olympic opportunities for women:

> The broadcast industry, as a whole, has long struggled with gender diversity, but when it comes to sports broadcasting, the gender gap becomes even more pronounced. Historically, televised sports have predominantly focused on male athletes, and the teams working behind the scenes have often been dominated by men as well . . . There remains a glaring underrepresentation of women in technical positions, particularly as camera operators. It's a challenge that Olympic Broadcasting Services has recognised and is determined to address.

There's some irony in the fact that the media, so good at calling out inequality in sport, doesn't even pass its own litmus test.

The 'Conversation of Sport: Representation of Women in Sports News Coverage' report, published in 2024 with support from Victoria's Office for Women in Sport and Recreation, found only 15 percent of sports news coverage in that state was focused on women's sport. Women journalists had only 27 percent of by-lines but were 62 percent more likely than their male colleagues to report on women's sport.

The USA and Britain are similar markets, with similar statistics to ours. There have been significant rises in viewing audiences and interest in women's sport there, but the amount of airtime women's sport gets hovers around 15 percent of the total. Australia set television ratings records at the 2023 FIFA

Women's World Cup, with the nation's most-loved team, the Matildas, showing how much interest there is despite such limited supply.

—

Deloitte's prediction that revenue from elite women's sport would reach US$2.35 billion in 2025 remains on target. That's a 240 percent rise from revenue in 2021. There are now portfolios valued at more than US$150 million investing specifically in women's sport. The list of sponsors aligning with women's sport is also growing. Attendance figures keep setting new benchmarks, meaning match-day revenue and merchandise sales are also shooting up. The biggest winners are football and basketball, with tennis and golf next. The biggest markets – the USA, Europe and the UK – are all witnessing exponential growth. Sport is ranked by the Global Sports Insights report as the ninth-largest industry in the world in 2025. Sports participation, sports products and fan engagement combined generate more than US$2 trillion a year. By the time Brisbane hosts the Olympic Games in 2032, the market value of the sports industry will have grown further, with women's sport expected to carve out a much larger slice than it currently enjoys.

Despite all the positives, not one woman, even in a FIFA Women's World Cup year, has made it into sport's top 100 earners list. In 2024, footballer Cristiano Ronaldo was the world's highest-paid athlete, with earnings of US$260 million. The 100th ranked athlete was the NFL's Minnesota Vikings quarterback, Daniel Jones, with US$37.5 million. Well outside the list, American tennis player Coco Gauff was the top-placed woman, earning

US$34.4 million. And we haven't even started applying the blow torch to the ranked earnings of coaches, managers and officials. Most sports-governing-body heavyweights still do not look like the communities they serve.

Deloitte warns women's sport must carve its own path – not simply replicate men's sport, which has worrying challenges such as drug, alcohol and gambling abuse, as well as concussion and debilitating injuries. But there's a much bigger, more fundamental question that needs to be asked about the future of sport generally. How relevant is it – locally and globally – to the future?

Should we maintain the pyramid model that emerged out of Europe? Elite-level sports at the top of the pyramid are fed by pathways that draw talent from children playing at the community level. Sports are governed by international federations whose members are national federations, dropping down to state-based federations who oversee community sport. Or, as many sports are doing, do we chase the for-profit entertainment model so prominent in the USA and increasingly evident in European leagues such as the EPL? Professional teams are franchises that are bought and sold. Through their player associations, the athletes are more like partners – or investors – in their own game, and matches are spectacles. At the other end of the scale is school and college sport.

There is a third model too. Increasingly, people are going back to basics. Meeting up with friends for a swim at the local pool, joining groups for non-competitive park runs or simply walking solo – a rediscovered delight during the COVID lockdowns. As people adjusted to working from home, they found other, simpler activities that kept them fit and gave them more spending money for other interests. Some have decided they are happier with their new habits and are not returning to the way things were pre-COVID. This is a trend that must concern sport. Highly organised, heavily scheduled contests are either becoming too expensive for parents to afford for their kids, or they are impractical to fit into modern living. The lack of flexibility is detrimental to shifting attitudes and lifestyles. The traditional European model of sport favoured in Australia will feel the brunt of this shift. It is the constant pursuit of relevance in an ever-changing world that occupies much discussion inside IOC and international sports offices.

In the same way some nations have come and gone through a century in which the Olympic Games has survived, it would seem inevitable that some sports will shrink into oblivion, as new pursuits capture the imagination. Football and athletics are the two exceptions. All over the world, from the poorest favelas in Brazil, to the mountains of Kenya, to refugee camps around the world, and to the ritziest streets in New York, Paris and Beijing, every child runs and every child kicks a ball. This will never change. What has changed is that women are no longer viewed as imposters in this previously heavily male-skewed world of sport.

Wrestling with Power

Power has always fascinated me.

As I see it, there are usually two different kinds of power at play: one of politicians and high-ranking officials (including sports officials); the other is in the hands of the people. It is the interplay between both types of power that I find intriguing.

Sport has never been far from the most dramatic events in our history. Sport is the partner that promises peace, joy, and celebration, an escape from the trials of our daily lives, which can range from the mundane to war-torn oblivion and genocide.

Power has become a dirty word – and yet, still, most people seek it. It is not power itself that is negative, but the way many of those who have it choose to use it.

During the Cold War, the Olympic movement became hostage to the geopolitical standoff between the USA and the USSR. After Russia's invasion of Afghanistan in 1979, the United States lobbied other nations to join it in a boycott of the Moscow

1980 Games. The Australian prime minister, Malcolm Fraser, agreed with the request from US president Jimmy Carter – but in a split decision, the Australian Olympic Committee voted not to support the boycott.

As a result, at the opening ceremony in Moscow, the Australian team marched under the Olympic flag, not the Australian flag. In her excellent book *Boycott*, Lisa Forrest documents the enormous pressure athletes were put under. Some resisted, choosing not to give in to politics. Others were promised money if they elected to stay home. Many of those who decided to compete were labelled traitors, received death threats and faced constant harassment.

Sport is used for political power, economic power, social power, diplomatic power and, of course, the pursuit of personal power. It is evident from the bottom to the top – from those who volunteer in grassroots and community sport, through to the world's most influential presidents at international sports organisations such as FIFA and the IOC – that sport carries sway.

In the pursuit of power, sport is a malleable tool, because we all so easily fall under its spell. As well as being used by nations, governing bodies and sponsors, it has memorably been used by individuals to stand up against power, often with dire consequences.

Muhammad Ali was one of the most recognised people on the planet when, after being conscripted for the Vietnam War in 1967, he refused to fight because of his religious beliefs. He also had social and political motivations, which he captured this way: 'Man, I ain't got no quarrel with them Viet Cong. No Viet Cong ever called me nigger.' He was stripped of his title, banned from boxing, given a hefty fine and sentenced to five years in prison.

'Some people thought I was a hero,' he later reflected. 'Some people said that what I did was wrong. But everything I did was according to my conscience. I wasn't trying to be a leader. I just wanted to be free. And I made a stand all people, not just Black people, should have thought about making, because it wasn't just Black people being drafted. The government had a system where the rich man's son went to college, and the poor man's son went to war.'

Ali's jail sentence was overturned on appeal. Over many years, his place in American history was reshaped from hero to villain to hero again as the rear-vision mirror has allowed us to view the events of time more objectively.

Ali's bravery is rare, although the 1960s produced quite a few others who were equally motivated. It was a time when the children and grandchildren of those who fought in World War II were becoming leaders of their era. The stories of their elders created a generation of ambassadors for peace. Mexico City 1968 will forever be remembered as the Games with the Black Power salute of the 200-metre gold and bronze medallists, Tommie Smith and John Carlos of the USA, as they each raised a black-gloved fist during the medal ceremony to highlight the civil rights struggle in their country. They were supported on the dais by the Australian silver medallist, Peter Norman. When Carlos discovered that he had forgotten to pack his gloves into his backpack on the way to the track, the Australian runner had suggested Smith and Carlos wear one glove each. Norman borrowed an Olympic Project for Human Rights pin from American rower Paul Hoffman to wear during the medal ceremony.

Like Ali, the 200-metre medallists were scorned by Olympic officials. Norman, who had also been a critic of the White Australia policy, was never picked to represent Australia again. The IOC described the black-gloved fists in the air as 'a deliberate and violent breach of the fundamental principles of the Olympic spirit' and demanded Smith and Carlos be expelled from the village and suspended from the US team. When the US officials initially refused, the IOC threatened to expel the entire US team. Smith and Carlos were sent home, were subjected to death threats and would struggle to find work. *Time* magazine's reporting of the story started: '"Faster, higher, stronger" is the motto of the Olympic Games. "Angrier, nastier, uglier" better describes the scene in Mexico City last week.' It went on to describe the protest as 'petulant'.

Rule 50.2 of the Olympic Charter states, 'No kind of demonstration or political, religious or racial propaganda is permitted in any Olympic sites, venues or other areas'. After canvassing the thoughts of thousands of Olympians, the IOC said most were in favour of keeping the Olympic arena free from politics and demonstration as a mark of respect for athletes from everywhere. And yet, for the brave, there is no place like the Olympic games to platform a message.

Protests at the two most recent Olympic games could not have been handled more differently. After finishing his run at the Beijing 2022 Winter Olympics, Ukrainian skeleton racer Vladyslav Heraskevych held up a piece of paper hand painted in the colours of the Ukrainian flag, with the words, 'No war in Ukraine', and despite the image going viral, the IOC decided Heraskevych was not in breach of Rule 50.2, deeming his hand-painted sign a 'general call for peace'. When Manizha Talash unveiled her cape painted with 'Free Afghan Women' during her breaking performance at the Paris 2024 Summer Olympics she was immediately disqualified. What has happened to fifty percent of the population in Afghanistan has been labelled gender apartheid. South Africa was banned from the Olympics for almost 30 years because of its apartheid regime separating people based on skin colour. It is a shame gender apartheid in Afghanistan was not viewed by officials the same way in 2024, even while celebrating Paris as the first ever gender-equal games.

Strangely, even while funding a handful of athletes from Afghanistan as members of the Olympic Refugee Team, the IOC also did all it could to support a team marching under the Afghanistan flag at the Paris games. Female athletes living in exile were given permission to compete for their home nation, the IOC arguing it sent a strong message of support to the young women back home. Others, like Afganistan's first female Olympian, Friba Rezayee who competed in judo in Athens 2004, disagree. She says the IOC was allowing women who live in exile to compete for a country where women are essentially banned from public life, are persecuted – or worse – for practicing sport, and where sports stadiums today 'are better known for public executions than athletic competition'.

It is not as though there was no precedent. When the Taliban previously ruled Afghanistan in the 1990s the country was banned by the IOC from competing at the Sydney 2000 Olympic games because of its hardline stance against women. Two steps forward one step back is a common pattern when it comes to gender equality. Real power lies in leadership. It doesn't take a genius to figure out that it is the small acts of defiance in the face of adversity that live on beyond tyrannical oppression. The Mohammad Alis, the Tommie Smiths, John Carloses, the Vladyslav Heraskevyches and Manizha Talashes are the people I look to for the stances they take – despite the lifelong consequences they bear for their powerful acts of leadership placing the greater good above themselves. For continuing to speak out against the Taliban from her home in Canada, Friba Rezayee, has been targeted and threatened by religious extremists who believe in the strictest form of Sharia law, essentially preventing women from playing any active role in society.

Those who are younger than me may need to head to the record books (or my earlier chapter on South Africa) to know who JJ Fouché and Idi Amin are. Those who are older will know I am referring to two men – one white and one Black – who presided over South Africa and Uganda, two nations where the abuse of power had horrific repercussions.

Through their brutality, these men and their governments taught me that all people can be discriminated against, regardless of colour. As a kid, I was too young to decipher the complexity of such behaviour; my simplistic understanding was that if all people can be discriminated against – somewhere – then all people really are equal. Of course, I now understand the deeper issues at play but hold on to the value that all people should be treated equally.

Today, I still wrestle with this: why do people of all colours and nationalities turn on those who are different? Why are there some Palestinians who can't see that the Hamas attacks in Israel on 7 October 2023 were abhorrent and should be widely condemned? Why do some Jews not see that Israel's Netanyahu-led obliteration of Palestinian men, women, children, hospitals, schools and lands was excessively disproportionate and will lead to another generation of anger, mistrust and violence?

Growing up, I remember playing with Black children and being aware of the deference their parents gave to mine – their humility, because a white child was playing with their child. Equally, I was aware that there were Black people, so angry at how they were treated in their own country by people who looked like me, that they would never let their children play with me.

I have seen these forms of discrimination both as a child and as a parent, witnessing the experiences of our own children both in Australia and overseas.

We are all subconsciously trained to recognise the traits of the bad guy; they are framed by the politicians and the media environments we grow up in. For those of us who have been lucky enough, by a pure accident of birth, to be born into a liberal democracy, it does not mean we are immune from this conditioning. We need to watch and listen critically to both sides of politics, to all our media, to understand the impact of the words being used and the manipulation being exercised. Likewise, we cannot judge an entire population on the behaviour of its religious or political leaders.

Those who use power to turn an entire population against another, or even sections of a domestic population against others, are committing manipulative abuse, plain and simple. Turning Han Chinese against Tibetans or Uyghurs, fanning Islamophobia or antisemitism, denying the history of Australia's First Nations people – these are just a few examples of many that are currently playing out in our world. But entire populations are not criminals, cheats and despots because of their religion, nationality or skin colour. Violent rogues, would-be dictators and law-breakers exist everywhere. Yet I guarantee when we walk down the street today, you and I will both make a series of judgements about the people we walk past, based on what – experience? What we've been told good or bad looks like? How we've been conditioned to accept some and not others? Because of the colour of their hair or how many piercings they have on their face? Or the colour of their skin and what they are wearing?

We exercise our own power every day by the decisions we take and choices we make, each one carrying its own consequence. Would Muhammed Ali make the same decisions today as he did in 1967 in refusing to fight for his country in a war on a foreign land? Would Tommie Smith and John Carlos raise their black-gloved fists if they stood on the Olympic medal dais again? Would Australian prime minister Malcolm Fraser decide our athletes should boycott the Moscow 1980 Olympics if he was asked to do so again? Without a doubt, I believe the athletes would stand by the convictions they displayed decades ago, while the Australian prime minister said in later years that his decision to ask athletes to boycott the games was a mistake and he would not do so again. Political decisions without a moral foundation do not age well.

Many people view sport as a quick fix: a momentary high for the masses, a seat at the top table for those in suits, a marketing jackpot for the balance sheet, or a three-minute wrap at the end of a nightly news bulletin, providing little more than a score. Sport means so much more than that. The power sport can provide is seductive but can also be harmful or dangerous if exercised without quality leadership. It's one of the greatest challenges sports officials face, and an area where few excel.

The Olympics in a Fractured, Political World

As the world prepared for the Paris 2024 Olympic Games, the Geneva Academy of International Humanitarian Law and Human Rights was monitoring more than 110 armed conflicts spread throughout the world. Western media rarely reported on any of them, the two exceptions being Russia's war with Ukraine, and Israel's war in Gaza.

As sovereign states picked their sides and agitators agitated, the IOC came under pressure to ban athletes from the nations recognised as the aggressors in those two wars. Which nation you identified as the aggressor depended largely on your passport, your country's allegiances, your personal politics and how far back your historical rear-view mirror could focus. In previous wars (Vietnam, Afghanistan, Iraq for example), when the USA was the aggressor, supported by allies such as the UK and Australia, there were never serious calls for athletes from those nations to be banned from competing at the Olympics. One thing

30 years of covering sport has taught me is how hypocritical the West can be.

The IOC's reluctance to ban athletes based on the actions of their national governments is often reported as a weakness. The IOC, a self-declared apolitical organisation, is often accused by the media of playing politics. It is a simplistic view on the part of the media, and a half-truth from the IOC. Of course politics impacts the Olympic movement: how could the Olympics be immune when politics is everywhere? How could it be immune when athletes come from nations immersed in their own political struggles and battles? Try as it might, the Olympic bubble is not a bubble at all – but the Olympics do try to create a politically free moment in time amidst turmoil, when athletes from everywhere can gather together. Those who want the Olympic movement to judge the athletes according to their nations' politics ignore the very foundations of the movement itself.

The IOC banned the Russian flag, national anthem and government officials from the Paris Games because of its 2021 invasion of Ukraine. It also suspended the Russian Olympic Committee because it had taken control of sports organisations in seized Ukrainian territory. However, the IOC allowed a small number of Russian athletes to compete as 'neutrals' if they could prove they did not support the war in Ukraine and were not part of the Russian military. The same applied to athletes from Belarus because of their country's support of Russia's invasion of Ukraine. But still, that wasn't enough for many in the Western media.

Israel's war in Gaza was viewed differently. Given Israel's position that the months-long war was a matter of self-defence, the IOC did not consider it in the same light as Russia's war on

Ukraine. A handful of legislators in France's parliament did, as did the Palestinian Football Association and a group of others who started a petition demanding the IOC suspend Israel as a nation, while allowing its athletes to compete, as neutrals, like the Russians. The IOC said the Olympic Committee of Israel had not seized control of sports bodies in occupied land as the Russians had done in Ukraine, so the same penalty would not be applied. Critics of the IOC's position argued that although Palestinian sports bodies or teams had not been seized, Israel has for years included in its national competitions sporting teams it created on illegally occupied Palestinian land. As the number of Palestinian athletes killed by the war continued to mount, so did the anger inside Palestinian territories. Gaza became barely recognisable, certainly much of it uninhabitable. How can the children who survived US bombs launched by Israel not carry lifelong scars, physical and mental? How will they think of Israel in the future? Are they likely to be peace advocates extending a friendly hand to resolve a generations-long dispute with deep roots in religious, political and ideological differences?

What of Jewish children? For them, the stories of Auschwitz will never be forgotten. The Hamas terrorist attacks on 7 October 2023, with its resulting carnage and kidnapping of 250 people, was a piercing reminder that they are still the target of a particular type of ideological hatred. Will today's children of Israel become tomorrow's wary adults, believing they will always be walking targets?

We had come to know the Rabbi who serves the Jewish population in China because he lived across the street from us in Beijing. His kids would play street soccer with our boys and the

German kids who lived next door. One of Jesse's best friends at school was a Jewish boy whose mother became one of my friends. We are all still in touch today. I remember her telling me how they felt, that wherever they went in the world they had a target on their back.

During one of Stan's stints in Israel for CNN, he asked me to fly over to spend some time with him as he was feeling a little low; apparently he had his own target on his back. Each time he walked from home to the CNN bureau he would be stopped by police and questioned. He did not look Jewish, they presumed he was Palestinian. They often didn't believe his Australian passport was real. He didn't look like what they imagined Australians looked like.

The first coffee shop I visited had security at the front door. They inspected my handbag and after a quick rummage through the guard looked at me and asked where my gun was. I laughed. She didn't. 'What's funny?' she asked. 'I don't carry a gun,' I said. 'Everyone in Israel carries a gun,' she said. It was a good lesson to learn on day one.

CNN's bureau is in Jerusalem. We've all heard of Jerusalem, it's a holy city for Judaism, Christianity, and Islam. On the day I had planned to visit Bethlehem, the Israelis had closed the gate, or checkpoint, in the wall they've built separating Israelis and Palestinians, meaning people like me, without an Israeli approved pass, could not enter. Stan had been filming in Bethlehem and explained that there was another way in.

I had to get a taxi to an area where a section of the wall had almost disappeared behind a rather large, hilly sand dune. If I climbed this dune, from the top I would see a rubbish tip on the other side. If I ran through this rubbish tip to the bottom of the hill, a car would be waiting there for me.

I was now on the other side of the wall. Bethlehem was quiet. When the checkpoints are shut randomly, Palestinian businesses are left with no tourists to sell to. A university educated travel guide was pleased I had turned up. As he took me through the narrow alleyways, to show me the manger where it is believed Jesus was born, he told me he could speak seven languages.

'I can speak to anybody in the world,' he said, 'and yet, more and more I have nobody to speak to.'

I will never forget that man. I do not know if he is still alive. I will never forget the Rabbi in Beijing, or Jesse's friend, who was doing his compulsory service in the Israeli army in the war following the October 7 Hamas attacks. All of them good people and yet they are all implicated when we judge entire populations by the worst amongst them.

When the IOC is confronted with such complex situations, I often imagine myself in the shoes of all parties and wonder what I would do. Firstly, I'd like to ban all national flags from the opening ceremony at the Olympic Games, so the parade of nations isn't a parade of politics. Imagine if every team of athletes – still holding up a sign with the name of their country – marched into the arena carrying the Olympic flag. Wouldn't that make a powerful statement about keeping politics out of the Olympic Games as much as possible? Of course, this will never become a reality because governments of every nation have too much invested in sport and the Olympics. The politics are too entwined.

People have forgotten that Australia once marched under the Olympic flag instead of the Australian flag, at the Moscow

Games in 1980. The president of the IOC during the Paris 2024 Olympics, Germany's Thomas Bach, wasn't as fortunate when he was an athlete back in 1980. At the Montreal 1976 Games, Bach was part of the West German team that won a fencing gold medal but was prevented from defending it four years later in Moscow when his country opted to join the US boycott. He, more than most, understands the cost of political interference in sport. Germany's own past carries a particular complication when it comes to the Olympics and Israel.

The Berlin 1936 Olympics remain a stain on the history of the Games, used as a propaganda exercise for the Nazis, who would plunge the globe into World War II and exterminate more than 6 million Jews. The next time Germany held the Olympics, in Munich 1972, a militant group known as Black September, which was an affiliate of the Palestine Liberation Organisation, snuck into the Olympic village and took hostage 11 Israeli athletes and coaches. Black September demanded the release of more than 200 Palestinians being held in Israeli custody, in return for the release of the Israeli Olympic team members. A failed rescue mission mounted by the West German authorities resulted in all the Israeli hostages being killed, along with a West German police officer and five of the eight Black September commandos.

To this day, there are calls for the IOC to do more in recognising the Munich massacre. At a ceremony to mark the 50th anniversary of the tragedy, which was held in Munich 2022 and organised by the German government, the IOC president, Thomas Bach, said: 'September 5, 1972, was the darkest day in Olympic history. What began so peacefully and joyfully ended in inconceivable suffering. We share the pain of the relatives of the eleven Israeli victims and the German policeman. To this day, the barbaric attack fills us with horror, shame and disgust. This attack was also an attack on the Olympic Games and the Olympic values.'

It is clear Thomas Bach's experience as an Olympic gold medallist – the first to lead the IOC – played a significant role in shaping his views and the decisions he took in his 12-year leadership of the organisation. During his presidency, he added the Latin word *Communiter* to the long-established Olympic motto, so it now reads: '*Citius, Altius, Fortius – Communiter*', meaning 'Faster, Higher, Stronger – Together'. When 205 national teams paraded along the river Seine to mark the opening of the Paris 2024 Olympic Games, around half the nations represented were involved in armed conflict. Yet there they were, together, with one exception: the independent athletes from Russia, who were not invited to be part of the parade.

Given the nature of sport, essentially a contest between two sides agreeing to play by the same rules, there is an underlying attitude that external events that impact sport should be adjudicated the same way: by applying the same blunt rules in every situation. When wars and other significant challenges are instead judged on their individual circumstances, it opens the door for critics to suggest that politics are at play; often they are, but we should not underestimate the attempts that are made to neutralise the politics so that the world can come together, and hopefully return home with a refreshed understanding of their place in a complex world.

Whether it is war, human rights violations, corruption scandals, doping or issues regarding gender and safe sport, the

Olympics provides the world's biggest stage on which political actors of all shapes and sizes are keen to parade their particular causes, meaning the Olympics can never truly be free of politics.

Navigating politics with a long view is even more difficult. It is tempting to believe that the political divides we see today have always been there. Take, for instance, the constant reporting of impending war with China, stirred up by Western media, quoting almost daily the hawkish think tanks doing the work of American politics. The relationship between China and the West wasn't always thus. China was supposed to make its long-awaited return to the Olympics at Moscow 1980 after an absence of almost three decades. But it agreed to join the US boycott of the Moscow Games and delayed its return for another four years, making its grand entrance at the opening of Los Angeles 1984. It was also the first time in the history of the Olympics that China and Taiwan both took part – a major diplomatic feat that took many years and ultimately the diplomatic prowess of then IOC president Juan Antonio Samaranch to achieve. Now here's a story . . .

China competed in the Olympic Games as far back as Los Angeles 1932. In 1949, Mao Zedong took over after a long and bitter civil war, declaring the creation of the People's Republic of China (PRC). Officials from the previous government, the Republic of China (ROC), including sports authorities recognised by the IOC, fled to Taiwan. The IOC continued to recognise the same officials as the legitimate representatives of greater China. That shifted when Chairman Mao's government established relations with the IOC, claiming it should have legitimacy as the true representatives of China. Toing and froing continued into the 1970s, with Taiwan unwilling to give up its position, and both Taiwan and China refusing to compete if the other was recognised by the IOC. The Olympic body's preferred outcome was that the two would accept each other's legitimacy.

Now for a condensed 100-year history in a couple of paragraphs.

What may surprise many is that in 1973, the Japanese Olympic Committee wrote to the IOC in support of China's recognition and to advocate for the expulsion of Taiwan. Why? Politics. In the 1890s, Japan had colonised Taiwan and integrated it into the Japanese economy. In the 1930s, Japan invaded China, with troops including Taiwanese who had been recruited and later conscripted. Nearing the end of World War II, with Japan's surrender imminent, the US and British governments agreed the territory of Taiwan belonged to China and helped facilitate its return to Chinese rule. Four years later, in 1949, the defeated leader in China's civil war, Chiang Kai-shek, fled to Taiwan with more than a million supporters. With the support of the United States, which was increasingly concerned about the Korean War, new political battle lines were drawn. Communist nations Russia and China sided with each other against the capitalist democracies of the West, which supported Taiwan. Fast forward 20 years or so, and the sport of table tennis – or ping-pong as it was known – played a major role in one of sport diplomacy's greatest breakthroughs.

Japan hosted the 1971 table tennis world championships, in which a team from China competed. A chance meeting with the American and Australian teams opened the door for separate visits to the mainland by US President Richard Nixon and Australia's opposition leader, Gough Whitlam. Months after Mr Whitlam's visit to China, he won the federal election and became prime minister. Three weeks after taking office, he delivered on a pre-election promise to establish diplomatic relations with China. The USA took a little longer, with its relationship normalised in 1979. Ping-pong diplomacy delivered.

Politically, most of the world recognises the PRC's One China policy, while the Olympic Games continues to host separate teams from China, Taiwan and Hong Kong.

This is just one example of the increasingly fraught and complex geopolitical landscape the IOC operates within, as competing interests pressure the Olympics to bend to whichever political campaign is being fought at the time, all the while endeavouring to remain true to an idealistic mandate of inclusion for all. It is an impossible ideal, meaning it is impossible to satisfy all the people all the time.

And yet the Olympic movement has survived plenty of challenges, all well documented: bribery, corruption, the Cold War and the boycott era, a reluctance to shift away from amateurism as the rest of sport professionalised, state-sanctioned doping in East Germany and Russia, the Nazi Olympics in Berlin in 1936, and the Israeli hostage crisis in Munich 1972.

The Olympic movement has not had an easy road to navigate since it grew out of Europe's fledgling peace movement in the late 1800s. Whenever another crisis hits the Olympics, I wonder to myself whether the world would be better off without it. The answer is always no. Unlike the UN, the Olympic Games is an arena of possibility, where hope lives, where each athlete strives to be better tomorrow than they were today.

The IOC recognises 206 member nations, while the United Nations recognises only 193 member states. The thirteen additional territories, which compete under their own flags and anthems, are Hong Kong, Taiwan, Palestine, Kosovo, Cook Islands, American Samoa, Guam, Puerto Rico, US Virgin Islands, British Virgin Islands, Bermuda, Cayman Islands and Aruba.

The UN replaced the League of Nations after World War II with the aim of maintaining international peace and security. It represents the best in us but sadly cannot stop the worst in us. In the moments of greatest turmoil, the UN is rendered a toothless tiger as sovereign states choose self-interest in voting against resolutions designed for the greater good. Intriguingly, the most successful UN treaty in terms of the number of signatories and the speed with which it was ratified was the UNESCO International Treaty Against Doping in Sport. It was adopted in 2005 and came into force in 2007. Less than 20 years later, there remain only seven nations that have not signed: Lebanon, Afghanistan, South Sudan, Niue, Guinea-Bissau, Mauritania, and São Tomé and Principe.

The IOC has observer status at the UN. Ahead of each Olympic Games, the UN reiterates its traditional call for an Olympic Truce, asking warring nations to put down their weapons, even if only for the two weeks of the Games, so they can be celebrated in peace. It's a tradition echoing the ancient Greek Olympics, during which all wars ceased. Today it is a symbolic gesture only, one that attracts media criticism each year it is pronounced – but is it not better to have aspirational symbols than to have no aspirations at all?

At its most simplistic, the Olympic Games is a bunch of grown people running, jumping, kicking balls and throwing sticks around. Other than proving who can run fastest, jump highest and throw farthest, it is pretty meaningless. And yet, in a much fuller context, it represents so much else.

Our athletes symbolise who we are. Participating on a world stage is important. Winning is remarkable. We watch humans, like us, who have overcome enormous odds to get there. The Refugee Olympic Team reminds us that not all have the same opportunities and shows us how the human spirit can soar despite life dealing a dud hand. The Games provide an opportunity for world leaders to meet, not in battle, debate, or anger, but in a spirit of mutual celebration.

The Olympic Games will always have its challenges. Politics will always try to tear it apart, to remake it in its own selfish image. Resisting those challenges is a battle all leaders of the Olympic movement – and sport generally – must face. How those challenges are navigated reveals much, not just about the calibre of those in charge but about who we are and what we believe collectively. The Olympic Games is the world's barometer.

Part Five

Future Stories

Brisbane 2032

At the closing ceremony of the Sydney Olympics in 2000, celebrated rock band Midnight Oil performed one of their protest songs, 'Beds Are Burning':

> The time has come to say fair's fair
> To pay the rent, to pay our share
> The time has come, a fact's a fact
> It belongs to them, let's give it back.

What the band didn't tell Olympic officials ahead of time was that they'd be wearing outfits emblazoned with the word 'sorry', the most politicised word in Australia at the time. In big white block letters on their black pants and shirts, front and back, no matter which way Peter Garrett staccatoed across the stage and his band of merry men turned for the cameras, you saw the apology.

Prime Minister John Howard, who could not bring himself to utter the word to Australia's Indigenous population for deep historical wrongs, was sitting in the royal seats along with the IOC president, Juan Antonio Samaranch, and other dignitaries. The volume of the roar from the pulsating crowd and the reaction of the athletes to Midnight Oil's apology sent a deafening message to the PM on that October night. As if that wasn't enough, immediately following Midnight Oil, around 200 young Indigenous dancers made their way to the stage to form a guard of honour for Yothu Yindi, who performed their anthem 'Treaty'.

Now that Brisbane will get to host the Olympics in 2032, it's time to ask: how have the messages of 'unity, forgiveness and resilience' referred to on the IOC's website played out in the quarter-century since Sydney's cauldron was extinguished? The answer is badly, although you'll never hear that from the politically neutral IOC.

Indigenous people are still the most impoverished in the country, still the most incarcerated people on the planet. Queensland, the state hosting the XXXV Olympiad, suspended its human rights act in 2023 so it could continue to detain children as young as ten in adult facilities. Indigenous people make up 4.6 percent of the Queensland population, but Indigenous children account for 63 percent of those in detention and 84 percent of those placed into solitary confinement over a 12 month period in 2022. In 2023, every state and territory in Australia except the ACT overwhelmingly voted 'no' in a referendum asking all Australians to recognise Indigenous people in the Australian constitution.

Queensland's human rights legislation was shelved without sufficient warning or debate, described as a 'dog act' by Greens MP Michael Berkman. A year later, in November 2024, a newly elected Liberal state government repealed the inclusion of its

Path to Treaty Act contained within the *Brisbane 2032 Olympic and Paralympic Games Act*. Much has been made of the Olympic organising committee's commitment to Aboriginal and Torres Strait Islander involvement and legacy, yet with the stroke of a pen, one of the most important pieces of legislation supporting that commitment was deleted.

When asked to respond to the news, an IOC spokesperson said they 'weren't involved'. An Australian Olympic heavyweight said he didn't recall a treaty ever being a part of Brisbane's Olympics candidature. That's funny. Memories can play tricks, can't they?

If you take a look at the IOC's Future Host Commission report into Brisbane's candidature, presented to the IOC's executive board before they voted to award the games to Brisbane, it says: 'The intention is to build on the progress made during the Commonwealth Games, and in alignment with the AOC's First Nations Reconciliation Action Plan and the Queensland Government's Path to Treaty.'

Brisbane's Olympic website states: 'We recognise it is our collective efforts and responsibility as individuals, communities and governments to ensure equality, recognition and advancement of Aboriginal and Torres Strait Islander Peoples across all aspects of society and everyday life, including sport. We are committed to building a deeper connection with First Nations Peoples through meaningful listening and authentic engagement. We celebrate and honour all Aboriginal and Torres Strait Islander Olympians and Paralympians past and present and we are committed to honouring their unique cultural and spiritual relationships to the land, waters and seas and the rich contribution they have made and continue to make to society and sport.'

What does all that really mean? It sounds like blah, blah, blah . . . connection, blah . . . meaningful listening, blah . . . honouring their unique cultural and spiritual relationships, blah blah.

Brisbane's Games are still years away, but I reckon it's a pretty safe bet that what the glossy-brochure spiel means is that Indigenous people will be asked to dress up in traditional costume, make everyone feel welcome, and then disappear to the wings to let the important people take over for the real business of the Games.

Words are easy, action is not. Some years ago, when embarking on what has become a long-since stalled PhD at the University of Technology Sydney, I met Professor Stewart Clegg, a world expert on the theory of power. He introduced me to the work of Professor Nils Brunsson, an institutional theorist from Sweden, who wrote *The Organization of Hypocrisy: Talk, Decisions, and Actions in Organizations*. The entire book could have been written about sport. I'll describe it crudely and cynically this way: a bloated and dispensable layer of middle management listens to stakeholder concerns, passes them on to senior management and the board, who will do what they were always going to do (make decisions that will make money, generally), then someone in middle management is made a scapegoat, and the loop begins again.

The Australian government initiated its Closing the Gap framework in 2008, targeting seven areas where the disparity between Indigenous Australians and other Australians could be closed. In over a decade, results had been achieved in only two areas: early childhood and high school education. Ten more standards were introduced by the government in 2022, with only four on track to be met by 2031, with another four going backwards:

The Eye of the Dragonfly

Indigenous suicide, incarceration rates, children in state care, and the percentage of children developmentally ready for year 1.

As 2024 came to a close, Queensland's neighbour the Northern Territory was trying to overturn a landmark court ruling requiring the government to provide safe drinking water to remote Indigenous communities. It's to be expected that news like that barely makes the headlines in Australia despite our reputation for 'brave athletes' who call out human rights abuses in other countries. Also in 2024, in its first week of parliamentary sittings, the newly elected Northern Territory government lowered the age of criminal responsibility from 12 to ten. There was silence from some of the most vocal advocates who work in the human rights space, constantly highlighting abuses in the Middle East or China. They continue to ignore what's happening in our own backyard. I don't know why, but it still astounds me. Whenever I raise it, I am accused by some of 'whataboutism'. They are absolutely right, what about what is happening right here in our place?

If Anglo-Saxon Australians made up less than 5 percent of the population but their children made up more than 60 percent of those being detained, the outcry would be deafening. If the government went to court to overturn legislation requiring it to provide safe drinking water for the rest of us, would there be outrage? Damn right there would be. So, what's the difference? There's only one thing that stands out as the obvious difference to me: colour.

We have a history in Australia of treating people differently according to their skin colour. Some might have forgotten one of the first pieces of legislation in this country's federal parliament in 1901 was the White Australia policy, limiting non-British migration. It wasn't dismantled until 1966, and only completely eradicated in 1970 with the passing of the *Racial Discrimination Act* in 1975. Ask many migrant Australians how they overcame discrimination, abuse and sometimes violence, and almost all of them will tell you it was by excelling at sport. Being a champion athlete in Australia is akin to winning the lottery. It is your 'get out of jail free' card.

Ought this hypocrisy – declarations of equality, actions of discrimination – impact Australia's right to host the Games? If human rights were a determining factor, which country would qualify to host the world's biggest sporting events? I cannot think of a single sovereign state that would make the cut. Nowhere and nobody is blameless.

So where does this leave us? Short of staging the Olympics on the lawn of the UN, should we scrap the thing altogether and wish everyone well?

Or persist, hoping that apart from the myth building there are genuine steps taken to encourage us all to understand the other a little more, while playing our individual part in leaving the world we all occupy in a better condition than how we found it?

The Future Is Abbie from *HER WAY*

When I first met Abbie, she was 12 years old. It was 2022 and she was already one year into publishing her startup monthly digital magazine called *HER WAY*, designed to fill a void she'd noticed in the market, for coverage of women's sport. Started during the COVID lockdown with help from Abbie's mum and dad, *HER WAY* soon grew into what is now a daily multimedia enterprise featuring interviews with players, reports from press conferences, and updates on everything that moves and shakes in women's sport, including regular exclusives.

At a media event marking a year out from the FIFA 2023 Women's World Cup, a throng had gathered in a small area called 'the mixed zone', a walkway where athletes and dignitaries file past the media, usually separated by a rope or some other barrier, for a string of short interviews. But the 'talent' doesn't have to stop for everybody and plenty of journalists have left mixed zones with nothing to show for their efforts. Experience counts and

I've refined my tactics over the years: I am used to arriving early and working out the best place to position myself to guarantee early eye contact with any guest entering the mixed zone, thereby maximising my chances of getting an interview.

On this day everybody was waiting for the FIFA Secretary General Fatma Samoura, the only woman to have ever held the position – she was also black, African, and a Muslim. (Talk about breaking several moulds all in one go.) I noticed Abbie swallowed up in the media throng behind me, shorter than the rest of us and without a hope of being seen by the secretary general, so I waved her through to come and stand in front of me. When Ms Samoura entered the zone, I got her attention first, asked a couple of questions and then pointed to Abbie who got the opportunity to ask the most powerful woman in the world of sport a question or two, despite being the youngest journalist there.

From the moment I met Abbie I could see she had what it takes to succeed in her chosen career. She is intelligent, hardworking, not daunted by being the only person at a press conference that looks like her, and – best of all – she loves what she does and grows closer to it every day. Still a teenager, Abbie is too young to get accreditation to cover the biggest events, but when the Brisbane 2032 Olympic and Paralympic games take place, she'll be 22, probably about to graduate with a university degree, and already a ten-year veteran of sports journalism and an accomplished digital creator. Abbie is exactly what the future looks like to me: not the depressing vision of diminishing opportunities in established media, but a future full of opportunities for those who are willing to back themselves and have a go.

Where does Abbie's drive come from?

'I think I've always been really passionate about equality,' Abbie tells me. 'I was like, I really want to see some changes, and I'm only eleven years old, but there are some other kids doing cool things out there, so why can't I do it in a totally different area?'

Abbie's father, Chris, gave her a magazine about the entertainment industry before she was in high school, thinking she might be interested in it. She was adamant: what she wanted was something about female athletes.

'If you can't find it, go and invent it for yourself, which is, you know, the best way,' she says.

Sports governing bodies such as the IOC, FIFA and World Athletics know that to reach the next generation and continue their market growth, they need to head where the eyeballs are and target digital content creators. Traditional media argue content creators are not journalists and should not be accredited alongside working media. New categories of accreditation are being offered instead, and no doubt, there will be a reduction in the number of traditional media accreditations as sports turn more towards influencers and content creators. This is a modern twist on an historical theme – we shifted from the printing press to the cinema, to television, and now from television to streaming on laptops and social media apps on mobile phones. Social media has had a profound effect on the societies we all live in but I don't believe the net result is negative. New mediums provide new opportunities for storytelling. Like all mediums, there will be a range of products created – from fake news, to clickbait, to documentary, to fantasy – in exactly the same way newspapers, cinema and television have served up stories to their audiences in the past. If it is quality journalism you seek, you will find it on whatever new platform takes your fancy.

Abbie describes herself as a journalist in a traditional sense, but one who utilises modern media for her storytelling.

'The definition of sports journalism is kind of evolving ... Before, I would just write articles, but now I'm posting 30-second clips on TikTok, and that's also a form of sports journalism. I think it's really evolved.'

So, too, have government responses to social media. Abbie's arrival onto the sports media landscape has coincided with political debates about restricting younger users. If government legislation makes it impossible for her to continue using various platforms, as an early-career professional, she would suddenly be prevented from following the people she writes and talks about, and it would be a whole lot harder to access athletes to line up interviews, let alone distribute her content.

As the debate swirled in Australia and traditional media bought into the government's agenda (driven by self-interest, in my opinion, to try to prevent their declining audiences), I couldn't help but think back to my own childhood in South Africa, where politicians banned television because they thought the population would be negatively impacted if exposed to this mass communication tool that opened up the world.

Social media has redistributed power to athletes, too, who can build their own profiles now without relying on traditional media coverage. Some athletes who have built their brands on social media are also creating their own production companies, inverting the whole traditional media model and changing the way the stories of sport are told, and even changing the way sport is contested.

The Eye of the Dragonfly

Tennis player Naomi Osaka struggled with the day in, day out relentless pursuit of titles on the tennis tour. Her love of the game gave way to a never-ending loop of flying in, competing, media commitments, flying out, repeat. Her mental health suffered. Ahead of the French Open in 2021, she told officials she would not be attending the mandatory daily press conferences; they responded by saying she would be fined US$20,000 for each one she missed. Rather than capitulating, she withdrew from the competition altogether, placing her wellbeing first. It was an inspirational lead others followed – US gymnastics champion Simone Biles pulled out of a potential gold-medal performance at the Tokyo 2020 Olympics.

'Athletes' journeys will always ebb and flow, and the expectation of us all is sometimes crushing,' Osaka told me for a feature in *Harper's Bazaar*.

'Being on top of your game in both mind and body is challenging, and I am so glad to be a part of the important conversation trying to change that for future athletes. Athletes have more of a voice than ever before. How one uses that voice can vary dramatically. I respect athletes that speak out and disrupt the status quo. I suppose I have done that over the years,' she said.

Osaka launched a production company for creative storytelling, which produces a podcast hosted by Australian tennis player Nick Kyrgios, who has fought his own battles with the media. These athletes bring a raw honesty and authenticity to their storytelling that traditional media cannot replicate.

One of the greatest footballers of all time, Cristiano Ronaldo, has more social media followers than any person on the planet, a combined total of more than 2 billion. In 2025, he partnered with a friend to create a production company focused on action films. Basketball legend LeBron James has been involved in media production since 2007, with his latest venture focused on 'creating stories of the future'.

None of this means that journalism is becoming extinct. It means journalism is changing, and journalists must continue to adapt to the ever-shifting environment. Abbie is perfecting her skills of the profession at an exciting time. Interestingly, even though her career started three decades after mine she has noticed the profession remains heavily male dominated.

'We definitely need more women and girls in this industry, because it's very male dominated at the moment. It would be good to see that in the future. It would be really cool,' she says.

It still amazes me that female trailblazers in the media are not only *not* celebrated, they also remain relatively unknown compared to many of the men whom they worked alongside. So let me give these three Australian pioneers a shout-out:

- Judith Joy Davies, an Olympic bronze medal swimmer from the London 1948 Olympics who went on to become Australia's first female sportswriter in the 1950s.
- Marg Ralston, appointed the first female sports editor of a major metropolitan newspaper in the late 1970s, *The News*, in Adelaide.
- Debbie Spillane, who started with the ABC in the 1980s calling cricket, rugby league and many other major sports.

By the time I started as a broadcast trainee with the ABC in 1989, there was a small group of other female journalists working in sport. Names such as Margie McDonald, Amanda Lulham, Jacquelin Magnay, Louise Evans, Nicole Jeffrey and Karen Tighe, spring to mind, since we were often all at the same events or press conferences. While the number of women in sports media has grown, sport remains the only media category in Australia that is heavily dominated by men. I hope that when Abbie reaches the same stage of her career that I am at in my own, the gender ledger may look a little more balanced.

One of the reasons for my optimism is that I've always tried to keep one eye on the future. Since 2010, I have gone to each edition of the Youth Olympic Games, both summer and winter, to mentor the IOC Young Reporters. A group of around 30 international students nearing the end of their university studies or journalists early in their career is selected for the Summer Youth Olympic Games, evenly split male and female. After the Games, the best of the best are selected to attend the next Winter Youth Olympic Games where the program becomes a little more intense as the young reporters build on their skills.

Nothing gives me more satisfaction than to see where the hundreds of young reporters I've helped mentor throughout my career end up in their own careers.

Everywhere I've worked, I have always taken an interest in the younger media professionals coming through, offering them any advice they ask for and providing feedback which they don't otherwise always receive.

For many years, I've also taught or lectured at various universities and colleges – including the University of Canberra, University of Technology Sydney, the Australian Film Television and Radio School, and Macleay College. I've always said that I learn as much from my students as (I hope) they learn from me.

In the spirit of which: what does Abbie see in the future?

'I think social media is going to be dominating it all. At the moment, nightly news and morning shows promote sports, but they're not really promoting the sports. They're just showing the scores from two sports, mostly men's NRL and AFL from the night before.

'If there's a really cool story from the Olympics or the Paralympics, then maybe they'll chuck that in too, but that's only for a couple of weeks every four years. So, I think if we actually want to see coverage of a large variety of sports, which is what I want to see . . . we'll come up with ways, hopefully, to do that.

'On a similar note, a lot of the female athletes that receive a lot of attention now, they're not getting that [attention] because they were shown on TV or because their results were shown on these shows – it's because they built a platform for themselves.

'Ilona Maher is a great example. She's a Rugby Sevens Olympic bronze medallist for the USA, which is a tiny sport over there, but she's given it a huge platform because she's created her own social media. I think she gained over 2 million followers after the Olympics, which is crazy, because she already had, like, a million before.'

'I think it's going to be interesting to see how much impact AI has, because I've seen it generate some really, really creepy images, like, realistic images of people. It's kind of crazy how fast it's evolving, but we'll see if that steals anyone's jobs in the future. But I hope it doesn't steal mine.'

I'm with you on that one, Abbie.

The Future is Technology

There is power in sound. Racist booing inside Australia's sporting crucible, the MCG, carried an ugly energy as it made its way to the ears of the man it was aimed at: Adam Goodes.

It's an experience inflicted upon him at many football grounds around the country during the final two years of his AFL career. There was the uplifting sound also, when his supporters stood and cheered for him as one, like a modern-day King Canute ordering the tide not to rise.

Imagine the heartbeat. Pounding faster, harder. Imagine the rise in temperature. Imagine the oxygen flowing through his veins. Imagine his thoughts and the physical responses they generated.

Through each of those experiences, the AFL was collecting Goodes's biometric data, and that of every other player.

The AFL was capturing performance statistics ten times a second via a small device on his back connected to a global network of satellites. But surveillance of Indigenous people carries extra meaning in Australia. It has a dark past.

The words above are the start of a story I wrote for the ABC in 2022 after interviewing AFL Brownlow medallist and 2014 Australian of the Year Adam Goodes. Those familiar with the Goodes story will know about his rise to the top of his game, only to suffer two years of booing at every ground he went to after he called out racism from a spectator at a game in Melbourne. Unwilling to endure it anymore, he walked away from the game he loved and has never looked back.

Goodes, together with Professor Angie Abdilla (a technologist from the University of New South Wales and founder of Old Ways, New) and contemporary artist Dr Baden Pailthorpe reclaimed the data that had been collected and stored by the AFL measuring his heart rate, bodily rhythms, brain patterns and all associated reactions during every moment of every game. In an exhibition commissioned by MOD (the Museum of Discovery) in Adelaide, visitors could sit and absorb an algorithm's blending of Goodes's game-day data, his voice speaking in the language of his Adnyamathanha people, and the wind blowing through the leaves of a sacred 500-year-old Wirra (river red gum) still standing in his ancestral homeland.

It is extraordinary what technology can already do.

And we're on the cusp of a technology revolution.

The IOC is exploring the possibility of using AI to identify talented athletes in remote areas of the world who would otherwise never come into contact with talent scouts. Artificial intelligence may also provide opportunities for athletes from remote areas, such as Indigenous communities, or countries in Oceania without access to an institute of sport, to stay at home and train. Using computer-generated training programs, these athletes could monitor themselves and send biometric feedback to coaches thousands of miles away.

Earlier in the book, I recalled my interview with Algeria's Olympic gold-medal boxer Imane Khelif. During our conversation, she spoke to me mostly in Arabic because she felt more comfortable using her own language. When I edited her interview for *The Sports Ambassador* podcast, I ran it through an AI program that copied her voice and translated it into English. You could not tell the two voices apart. That's incredible.

I shared an Uber to the airport with another podcaster after the 2025 SportNXT conference in Melbourne, where the latest developments across the entire sports industry were examined. He was telling me how he writes a script then runs it through an AI tool that has his voice stored in its memory. He instructs it to convert his text into a podcast, inserting music where appropriate. The entire podcast is AI generated using his own voice. The negative side to that, of course, is that anyone's voice that is easily accessible from the internet can be loaded into AI and be made to say anything.

This is now: imagine the future. Where there are positives, there will also be negatives.

Viewing the future through a negative lens means journalists would all fear the loss of our jobs. Viewing it through a positive lens, we should be excited about learning new ways of storytelling, enabling us to do journalism better, to reach wider audiences, to engage more thoroughly. How do we measure the positives and the negatives? How do we find the balance? Is there a balance?

Professor Toby Walsh is a world-leading researcher on AI at the computer science and engineering department at the University of New South Wales and author of the book *2062: The World That AI Made*. Writing in 2018 he said that 2062 would be the inflection point at which computers will at least equal human intelligence, if not having already surpassed it.

There are some people you are lucky to meet in life because they have the ability to challenge, enthuse and inspire you. For me, Professor Walsh is one of those people. He always leaves me feeling more energised because of his extraordinary knowledge and his ability to make it relevant. Toby believes AI will have a major impact on three distinct areas of sport: the athlete, the fan and sports governance.

The year Toby's book discusses is the year sandwiched between two Summer Olympic Games, in 2060 and 2064. It will be the year of a Winter Olympics to be staged at a place yet to be determined, quite possibly a city of the future, like NEOM, currently under construction in Saudi Arabia, described as a city with 'nature first principles' to protect and regenerate an eco-friendly environment ranging from ski slopes to coral reefs.

Athletes will continue to push the limits of human performance, but how far is it possible to go? Toby's view is that as sport becomes more data-driven, athlete training will continue to improve.

'Sport is becoming much more data driven, and so they're [the athletes] going to be able to work out how to get that last epsilon out of their performance, and that might mean things like swimmers swimming less.'

That's just the beginning of the story, though. The greater impact on human performance will be AI's ability to accelerate the refinement of scientific techniques that can change the human form, like gene editing. In the same way animals and crops have been genetically modified, it is possible to do the same with humans.

Chinese geneticist He Jiankui was responsible for gene-edited babies named Lulu and Nana, who were allegedly created to be resistant to HIV. He was sentenced in Beijing to three years in prison for 'illegal medical practices'. Where technology is concerned, the pace of legislation keeping up with the pace of possibility has always been a problem. Then of course, there is the constant ethical question: just because we can, should we?

Australian businessman Aron D'Souza ruffled feathers in the strict-liability, anti-doping sports world when he announced he was creating the Enhanced Games. His vision is a global sporting contest where athletes can dope, under medical supervision, to test the limits of the human body. To entice athletes to join his alternative games, he promised that any world-record performance would earn the athlete US$1 million.

D'Souza's games would give the trillion-dollar wellness and anti-aging biotech industry a high-profile platform for spruiking the benefits of their wares. The public's insatiable appetite for artificial supplements that will make us look better, perform better and live longer is a danger zone for athletes, who are bound by the World Anti-Doping Code. While many supplements may not be performance enhancing on their own, plenty of athletes have found themselves facing serious bans because products they ingested were contaminated in the production process or failed to list all of the ingredients on the packaging.

Increasingly, the general public is heading down an anti-aging path with few restrictions, while athletes remain under tight regulation in order to protect what is termed by sporting officials as 'clean sport' and what is described (but not defined) as 'the spirit of sport'. What will happen if D'Souza's Enhanced Games challenge the accepted spirit of sport? What if the general public prefers to watch athletes who are pushing legal and ethical boundaries to run faster and jump higher?

In December 2024, the second conference on human enhancement held in Oxford addressed this specifically. Its 'Declaration of Human Enhancement' was ratified by experts in attendance, including the following:

> We declare that athletic excellence is the exemplar of the human spirit, and athletes have the innate right to elevate their physical and mental capacities. Excellence can not be confined by arbitrary boundaries, and true greatness flourishes in the freedom to explore, enhance, and evolve beyond what once was.

It's no surprise that those who govern world sport are not enamoured with the experimental nature of the sporting event proposed by D'Souza. The World Anti-Doping Agency labelled it a 'dangerous and irresponsible concept', while the IOC said the idea of the Enhanced Games 'does not merit any comment'. Olympic officials believe the concept of 'fair play' would be destroyed by such an event, which without 'accepted rules or values . . . is completely at odds with the idea and values of the Olympic Games'.

Sport is all about pushing boundaries, but from within acceptable limits. Defining those limits has changed over time: women were originally prevented from competing at the Olympic Games, and for almost a hundred years, Olympians had to be amateur, unable to earn an income from sport. The limits of sport are being challenged again, and they will continue to be so, according to Toby Walsh.

'Sport is the genetic lottery that you just happen to be born with. But if we can have a say over that genetic lottery, perhaps it's not as fair, not as even a playing field as it was. In some sense, we do try and design sport to give the underdog a bit of a chance. I mean, otherwise, what's the point if it's only the survival the fittest?'

—

When sport professionalised and migrated towards the entertainment industry, harvesting vast sums of money through television rights, sponsorship and gambling, the importance of fans grew significantly. As social media and streaming services also bought into sport, athletes found they could create their own lucrative fan bases by speaking directly to their supporters. Athletes can now be compensated independently from their sports.

YouTube pays its content creators between US$1,200 and US$6,000 per million views. Advertising on a YouTube channel will net creators a further US$18 per thousand views. When Cristiano Ronaldo started a YouTube channel in August 2024, he had 22 million subscribers on the first day. One month later, he had 63.5 million subscribers and 517 million views. Do the maths.

When it comes to fan engagement, Toby says AI is a game changer.

'Ronaldo has got a billion social media followers, but you will now have Ronaldo talking to you personally about your own football team. The fan experience is going to become that much more intimate, that much more immersive, that much more interesting – but also that much more invasive into the lives of the sportspeople themselves.'

In the future, the line between what is real and what is virtual will be further blurred. In generations to come, virtual might be the only reality – if avatars will suffice, who will need human athletes at all? Superstars of the past could be brought back to virtual life to compete against one another in a virtual Olympics, staged in any city of your choosing. The line between 'real' sport and Esports could be erased.

The collection of athlete data, is another area that enhances the fan experience but is challenging ethical and legal limits. What's being done with the data? What about breaches? What about data theft? Where does the privacy of an athlete start and stop? It's a conversation most professional player associations have started having with sports governing bodies.

And Toby Walsh identifies another sector hungry for athlete data: gambling.

The global sports betting and gambling market, according to Statista, was worth more than US$340 billion in 2022. Given that gambling is illegal in many parts of the world, the size of black-market sports gambling is also huge, and it comes with associated concerns about match fixing and corruption. According to the World Lottery Association, illegal sports betting is worth between $500 billion and $2.45 trillion, a figure calculated using an AI app developed by the lottery company Singapore Pools.

Many professional sports have thrown their future in with gambling companies, ensuring a percentage of every dollar gambled on their sport comes back to the sport itself. Ironically, as the social cost of problem gambling rises – a massive concern inside professional football and cricket codes – the sports are spending more money on safeguarding, wellbeing and education programs for their athletes who are at risk of becoming addicted. And sadly, once their athletes have retired, many sports deem them no longer to be the governing body's responsibility.

Still, the cost of those programs, does not come close to the amount of revenue the sports are earning from their gambling deals. And, as Toby Walsh points out,

> [T]he data that's going to come, and the opportunities that's going to bring, is going to change what people can gamble on and how they can gamble. We've always observed players on the field and while training, but now they're being monitored around the clock, when they're at home and even sleeping. People will want this data to get the edge on the betting market. It's also going to introduce more ways for people to cheat. We'll have to worry about that as well.

Traditional media houses are not happy to have to share a stage with social media voices they cannot control. They are going to be even less impressed when they are told they will not get the number of accreditations they are used to for sport's biggest events – whether it's the Olympics or the FIFA World Cup or the Cricket World Cup or the NBA playoffs – because they'll be wrestling for access to the athletes with influencers, content creators and YouTubers, many of whom have much bigger audiences.

Walsh is surely right to point out that more independent content creators lowers the barrier to entry and therefore allows new voices – younger voices, coloured voices, people who had perhaps not been represented before – to be heard. AI also allows more sports to be covered, as large sets of raw information can be distilled into palatable commentary. Esports and even fantasy leagues lend themselves to this sort of coverage. But he also worries that AI will undermine fragile rights income streams for smaller sports, and concentrate resources around the big brands.

'So if you're Formula 1 and you've got a Netflix special around you, then there's plentiful money in your coffers. But I do worry that some of the other sports get less time and attention, perhaps because they're less of a television spectacle.'

What would Toby identify as the green flags and red flags when it comes to AI and the governance of sport?

Officiating is clearly one area – AI can clearly replace a lot of referees in deciding whether the ball was over the line or not. But Toby doesn't see the eradication of the human official: 'Actually, I think we're going to have just as many judges, because rules need to be interpreted. In every sport, it always comes down to issues around sportsmanship – or sportspersonship,' he says. 'The rules can't always anticipate the strange circumstances that are going to happen in a competitive situation.'

Zooming further out, the IOC is also working on how to use AI to find talented athletes who would otherwise never be discovered by the system as it exists now, either due to their remoteness or lack of financial resources to join elite sports programmes. AI will enable sports to scout far afield to get the most talented people, and would-be elite athletes to input their data to say, look, I'm here, I'm ready, willing and able if you can help me.

'I've got this amazing thing, a Fitbit, that monitors every run I've ever done, and [the runs] of millions of other people around the world,' says Toby.

'They haven't capitalised on it yet, but they're sitting on a goldmine of information about performance: how performance changes with age, potentially whose performance is increasing significantly, who needs to perhaps have a scout check them out?

'Of course, it's also incredibly invasive. I don't own my heartbeat. Fitbit owns my heartbeat. If, for example, Fitbit noticed that there's some sort of fibrillation on my heartbeat and that I should actually go and see a specialist immediately, they're not obliged to tell me that. Indeed, they could charge me any amount of money to tell me that wonderfully important piece of information that I need to go and see a specialist ASAP because there's something troubling happening with my ECG.'

The strict anti-doping code that all Olympic sports have signed on to means that every athlete's very personal medical information is known and stored. Athletes have what is known as a biological passport, allowing drug testers to compare certain markers in urine and blood tests against the athlete's baseline to see if there's been any unusual deviation, which could imply doping.

Anybody familiar with the name Caster Semenya, a world and Olympic champion 800-metre runner from South Africa, would also be familiar with the term DSD. A small percentage of people in every country are born with DSDs – differences in sex development, sometimes referred to as intersex. When they are babies, their external genitalia may be ambiguous, and doctors decide whether the baby is more likely a girl or a boy. Caster, is legally a woman because she was identified as female at birth, raised by her family and community as a girl and a woman, only to be told by sports officials that their testing revealed she was DSD. World Athletics officials changed the rules of the sport so she, and others like her, could not compete in their favoured events – unless they agreed to take testosterone blockers or have surgery – against the advice of the World Medical Association which believes naturally healthy human beings do not require medical intervention. They say it is unethical.

Toby acknowledges this is a deeply complex subject, but points to a fundamental contradiction: sport relies on individual differences (if we were all the same, every race would be a tie), 'but equally, we somehow try and square that circle by saying we want a level playing field and everyone's going to have an equal chance. Well, that's never really exactly true'. We already make some acknowledgement of fundamental differences (for example weight categories in boxing) to make things fair within a group when they wouldn't be fair without. Science may help us make other categories that help fairness.

This raises important questions for all of us. Should we always opt to know rather than not know, just because we can? Should

I go and get tested to see if I might be prone to getting Alzheimer's at a younger age than most people – do I need to know that? Will it impact on my positive outlook on life if it turns out I am?

Moreover, the sense that technological developments are without bias is itself questionable. In his book Toby mentions 'the sea of dudes' involved in researching AI – and I'd guess overwhelmingly white men, in the West at least. He sent me an AI-generated conversation between two people discussing a paper he had written – an accurate analysis, but with a female asking the questions and a man giving the answers. Did AI decide for itself that it was a woman who would mostly ask the questions in this made-up discussion with the man providing most of the answers? Or was it told to do it that way? Would it be perceived as not having the same level of authority if, for instance, it was two women discussing the paper, or the male asking the questions? These are genuine questions. Early in my career I was told women's voices don't have the same authority. It is a battle women still face when it comes to selecting journalists to cover the stories of most significance – whether it is war, politics or sport. This is confirmed by the number of male versus female accreditations sought by media companies to cover the Olympic Games.

'AI is a product of the training data it's given in many respects. Training data, by its very nature, is just historic and reflects the biases of the systems in which it was collected. And so we do have to be incredibly mindful that we don't continue to perpetuate and hold back the small wins that we've had in terms of giving recognition to female voices in sports, or giving recognition to Black voices, or giving recognition to other minorities that have not been properly represented in the past – and AI, If it's used unthinkingly, will only add to that.'

Here too Walsh is both optimist and pessimist. In the short term, he sees tech as a destabiliser – one of the numerous major issues the world faces, like climate and global insecurity. We might have 'a decade or two' in which this affects our quality of life.

'But in the long term, I'm optimistic that if we embrace these technologies and use them in careful ways, we can help it improve the quality of our lives.'

The Future Is Now

The path to the future is challenging. Just writing that excites me. While I don't fear the pace of change and where the world is heading, I also don't minimise the challenges we face.

Sadly, we live in an era in which the media is less and less objective, instead amplifying angst and fear – in my opinion out of all proportion – often because of its own biases. It's those biases I'm particularly passionate about challenging, and that eventually contributed to my resignation from the ABC.

The mainstream media is capable of remarkable acts of hypocrisy, especially while invoking the values of 'free speech'. Outlets that call on governments to mandate social media restrictions, often themselves rely on social media posts to fill half their nightly news bulletins. They ask for social media to be sanitised while filling their programs with negativity and fear, magnified by social media, which they then blame for societal breakdown.

Covering the Qatar 2022 FIFA Men's World Cup I saw a country undergoing significant social change, from what I witnessed working on one of their earliest international sporting events, the 2005 West Asian Games, including the significantly positive change in workers' rights. Unlike their neighbours (all of whom our governments and businesses trade with) Qatar had opened an office of the ILO (International Labour Organization), was rewriting legislation to include workers' rights, and had opened an employment disputes court. The changes were necessary given the appalling conditions foreign workers had previously suffered under. While some of these changes may have been planned, they were no doubt sped up given the sustained criticism from human rights groups and Western media after the country was named as host of the World Cup in 2010. For a time, the criticism was justified. Then it became relentless and myopic.

Yet, as I found out, every print article I filed for the ABC would be sent to one of the editorial bosses for an added layer of scrutiny above the standard procedure of the desk-subs and lawyers, if needed. Many of my firsthand observations were challenged and deleted back at the Ultimo bunker. One such observation was that for the first time this was a non-white World Cup. Many Western fans had succumbed to the opinions of their media and chose to boycott the event, meaning tickets were snapped up by those from the region – Saudi Arabia, UAE, and countries further afield such as Morocco, Algeria and Tunisia.

I was asked to 'define *white*'. I won't print what I wrote before deciding not to respond at all. They could spike the story for all I cared; I was too tired and had too much else to do to waste time worrying about it. More than a year after my husband

and I had resigned from the ABC, it released its long-awaited report that found systemic racism inside the organisation. Maybe now, that same editorial chief can answer his own question about defining *white*.

The obsessive nature of the one-eyed view of Qatar struck me as being hypocritical. This was proven in the following year, when barely a mention was made of Australia's own human rights issues in the lead-up to and during the FIFA 2023 Women's World Cup. It makes me question whether any of the media's concerns for workers' rights in Qatar were genuine, or whether they were simply used to enforce a stereotype. Since the final whistle blew on the 2022 Men's World Cup, there has barely been a mention of workers' rights in Qatar.

On many occasions, my husband and I stood up for good, talented young journalists at the ABC who feared standing up for themselves when they were subjected to racist behaviour or professionally demeaned in ways other (white) colleagues weren't. It is a shame that some of those same young men and women, who really should have been nurtured into the ABC's stars of tomorrow, also decided to leave the organisation, many of them with their dreams shattered.

—

Everybody, from journalists to university lecturers to the general public, is now operating in a system where you have to pick a side, because if you don't, you're seen as a supporter of the other side and then vilified as such. As a direct result of this polarisation, some commentators feel that we are already in the throes of another great war. There are more local wars and conflicts taking place around the planet than at any time in history. We are definitely in a new Cold War between the USA and China (with Russia an erratic third component), with perhaps only the complex links of global trade preventing it turning into a hot war.

This necessity to pick sides is one of the drivers leading people to tune out of mainstream (or legacy) media, returning to a more grass-roots approach that's freer of the vested interests of large organisations. It's no surprise that the least-mediated media channel – YouTube – is growing in popularity.

The bigger outlets – traditionally seen as the most reliable – have seen large numbers of redundancies, with a 9 percent reduction in the number of journalists in Australia in the decade between 2006 and 2016. The adoption of AI to replace humans in the production of stories continues to increase. The shift has seen advertisers turn away from the mainstream and head to where the audience is – mostly on YouTube and Facebook.

The Reuters Institute's *Digital News Report 2024* found that growth is focused on the platforms that are predominantly video-based networks. Almost a third of the people in the global sample from 47 markets across six continents use YouTube for news each week. Online platforms account for 72 percent of news video consumption, compared to just 22 percent for publisher websites.

When it comes to watching online news-related videos, YouTube has almost closed in on the outright dominance Facebook once had. The two platforms are the most dominant, although Instagram, TikTok and X are still growing.

Overall, according to the Reuters report, social-media video platforms are used by 86 percent of 18–24-year-olds, 81 percent of 25–34-year-olds, 76 percent of 35–44-year-olds, 69 percent of 45–54-year-olds and 60 percent of those aged over 55. The key reasons people gave for using social video content were:

1. Seeing is believing – 'You can trust it more.'
2. Convenience – 'It aligns with my interests.'
3. Diverse perspectives – 'Variety of opinions, not just mainstream media.'

However, close to four in ten people say they sometimes or often avoid the news, which should sound alarm bells for the way traditional media reports the most important stories of the day. The report stated:

> In exploring *user needs* around news, our data suggest that publishers may be focusing too much on updating people on top news stories and not spending enough time providing different perspectives on issues or reporting stories that can provide a basis for occasional optimism.

Legacy media's failure to adapt means the role of individual voices are gaining popularity, generally described as *content creators* and *influencers*. I don't like either term, because the reality is that good, strong voices in the media have always been content creators and influencers. What we are really seeing is not something new, just a modern adaptation in the delivery of it.

Meta, the parent company of Facebook and Instagram, decided in 2024 it would no longer follow the Australian government's 2021 News Media Bargaining Code, under which $200 million from Meta and Google has been distributed to mainstream news companies for the right to republish their stories online. Facebook and X have changed their algorithms so that links to news stories on other platforms, including mainstream media, are not promoted as they once were. Rather than losing eyeballs by users clicking through to another platform, these companies want you to stay on their site so their own data can be maximised for commercial value. Reuters says this has led to a sharp decline in traffic from social media, worsening the situation for mainstream media.

Is it a coincidence, then, that mainstream media began running what appeared to be a campaign against social media companies, criticising the spread of fake news, misinformation and disinformation? I saw numerous programs and articles on the subject, always pressuring the government to do something, and yet I cannot recall a single mainstream article that investigated its own failings in this area. One might point to the failed vote for the Indigenous Voice to Parliament as one example where mainstream media coverage played a major role in sowing seeds of doubt and fear built on misinformation. Misinformation is everywhere – not just on social media. It has always been thus.

The Australian government's move to restrict access to social media platforms for those under the age of 16, while popular with some parents and teachers, has significant negative consequences. Driving users underground, where there would be virtually no protections, is one concern cited by the eSafety Commissioner. Queensland University of Technology's director of digital media research, Daniel Angus, said the government's decision showed 'utter disregard for evidence-based policy'.

How much better would it be if instead of banning devices in schools and preventing teenagers access to some sites, they were taught how to recognise misinformation and disinformation, and how to develop resilience and strength? It is a frequent conversation I have with young reporters I mentor around the world.

What I've found, anecdotally, is that by shifting our mindset and reclaiming power over the (mostly anonymous, and therefore gutless) online abusers, the psychological impact of their abuse is drastically minimised. The psychological impact of social media is still contested, although most argue the technology companies themselves need to take more responsibility.

Those in charge of sport today are having to navigate, at a frightening pace, changes in technology and social media, plus shifts in culture, politics, economic wealth, climate change, personal priorities and the expectations of the next generation. I have been amazed by the IOC's awareness of these shifts, and their investment in researching ideas and future strategies. I was lucky enough to be invited on to a working group, as part of the IOC's press committee, investigating the very real changes in media consumption, the rise in social media, and the potential future role of influencers in the media mix. Simply, the athletes themselves are the best advertisements for sport. Look after the athletes and have them tell your story well, since they are the ones who'll be listened to. The media has some work to do to ensure their storytelling remains relevant to a rapidly changing market.

While sports governing bodies still receive the lion's share of their income from mainstream television broadcast deals, there are signs the market may cool with advertisers following the crowd to new platforms. If the rights-fee bubble bursts, where will sports turn? More and more they are turning to gambling revenue.

For now, the IOC has resisted the lure of gambling money, holding onto the values it was founded on – to build a better world through sport by encouraging friendship, togetherness and fair play – but the challenge will come should the economic realities outstrip the value of their values. And are all 'values' universal? I've discussed the big questions of Qatar, trans and boycotts, but here's a smaller-scale snapshot: in the Paris 2024 Olympic and Paralympic Games, competitors from outside nations competed in hijabs while no French athlete could be selected to represent the home nation if they wore one.

The issues sport has to confront have no easy answers. They are complex, fluid, dynamic and, above all, emotive. As people search for answers, they need leaders – in politics, business and sport – who are honest and unafraid of genuine debate, and who can listen before they talk, putting our multitude of similarities ahead of our differences. Likewise, our media needs to uphold those same values and skills, by asking questions of those with power to elicit answers that not only explain the current crises we are confronting but also lead to solutions for a positive future.

Circling Back: The Zakia Khudadadi Story

On the verge of collapse, in a putrid moat outside Kabul airport, Afghanistan's first female taekwondo Paralympian, Zakia Khudadadi, had barely enough mental or physical energy to make the single biggest decision in her life: give in to the Taliban or push on, somehow, hoping one of the last military planes out of her country would deliver her somewhere in time to get to Tokyo. Beyond that was completely unknown, but she could deal with that later.

She caught the plane. She made it to Tokyo.

Zakia is around my height, probably weighs half what I weigh, and is sharp as a tack and fit as hell. With a missing lower left arm, she competes in taekwondo's K44 category. In an interview from the Tokyo Paralympics, she told me she was proud to be at the Games but while her body was in Japan, her heart remained in Afghanistan, where her family was facing a tough time under Taliban rule.

Three years later, I caught up with Zakia at a coffee shop on the outskirts of Paris, where she now lives with 12 of her family members, all sponsored by her and attached to her refugee status. She had learned to speak French and English fluently and was in training as a member of the IPC (International Paralympic Committee) Refugee Team for the upcoming Paris Games.

'I did not have anything, just my passport with me,' she told me about her 2021 evacuation and arrival in Tokyo. 'The most difficult thing was that I was not able to speak about the situation. And I was going through a lot. It was obviously very emotional for me. Now I'm in Paris, and I want to make my dream come true to get a medal from the Games. I am very grateful France gave me these opportunities.'

Her dream did come true. Not only was Zakia the only woman on the eight-member IPC Refugee Team, she will be remembered for winning the team's first-ever medal – a bronze, which sits nicely alongside her gold medal from the European championships. Access to state-of-the-art training facilities and coaching in Paris meant that within six months, Zakia had won half a dozen medals from competitions across Europe.

Zakia's dream now is to go to a third Games in LA 2028, then potentially a fourth in Brisbane 2032 – but her end goal is to go back to Afghanistan to help others like her. She is driven by the vision that her experience will give hope to Afghan women amidst the misery they are living with.

'I want to show the power of me to every girl from the disabled community; I want to show that power to them, because this is very important. Back in Afghanistan, I did not have this opportunity or the facility to do so, but here in France, I have, and someday when Afghanistan is in a better situation, I hope to return and form an all-girls Paralympic team. I pray we will have peace in Afghanistan. I want these girls to not think about who they should marry. I want these girls to have hope and dreams for the future. I want other girls with a disability to have their own identity and to fight for their rights, to be able to walk outside without harassment or judgement but to walk comfortably with freedom. Please, don't ever forget Afghan women.'

After Paris, there was more to celebrate. Zakia was informed she had been offered a Global Talent Visa to live and train in Australia ahead of the LA 2028 Games. But her elation was short-lived. She could bring only her parents, none of the other close family members currently living in France because of her visa.

'It is possible that the conditions will be difficult for them because they came with my invitation. They have only temporary residence, and it is possible it will be cancelled after I leave as no-one will be responsible for them. I am the one responsible for them.

'I was hopeful but unfortunately the situation is very difficult for me.'

We all know what responsibility entails, but few of us will ever know or understand the level of responsibility that rests on Zakia's slim shoulders. I listened back to our Paris interview and was struck by her last words:

'Never give up.'

Whatever else happens in the future, I always see a role for sport in promoting peace over war, cultivating understanding over disagreement, and friendship over hostilities.

Sport is so much more than a game. It teaches children that winning and losing is part of the same journey; it is the pursuit of excellence; it is the striving for unobtainable perfection; it is the place where we learn about friendships and power dynamics. Sport is a microcosm of the larger world.

Can I imagine a world without sport? Yes, I can. But it is not a world I want to live in.

Acknowledgements

Ben Ball must be the most patient and thoughtful publisher any writer could hope for, finally succeeding in knocking my rambling stories into something that resembles a book. The entire team at Simon & Schuster have worked tirelessly on every aspect – from one cover to the other, and planning its launch around the country, going above and beyond to negotiate with one stubborn author. Vanessa Mickan managed to dot more 'i's and cross more 't's than are in the book, meaning her finely tuned editing skills are incredible. I am so grateful Simon & Schuster are my publishers, so to Michelle Swainson and all of her staff, thank you.

When publishers started calling me about writing a book, I was both flattered and lost. My husband's agent Tara Wynne, at Curtis Brown, came to the rescue and has been beside me on this journey ever since. I could not have done this without her. Tara, thank you.

While people I've worked with will recognise this trait, my husband and kids became familiar with it during my writing: they would talk to me but I wouldn't hear them, they could ask me questions but I wouldn't answer, they would say goodbye but I didn't even know they had gone until they returned. It is easy for me to bury my head into my work even if all hell is breaking loose around me. To Stan, Jesse, Millie and Dylan, thank you for letting me disappear into these words on occasion to surface later as though nothing had happened.

My journey through sport was only possible because of the doors to the world my parents first opened, influenced later by some incredible teachers who taught me to always be curious. A heartfelt thanks for teaching me the value of questions and the constant search for knowledge and new experiences.

To the many athletes, administrators, officials, academics, lawyers and rogues who throughout my career have helped me understand the issues more fully, to seek the answers more thoroughly, and to tell the stories more passionately, my story is nothing without you. A heartfelt thanks.

The few bosses I have had would probably all agree that I can be a challenge. Those of you who figured out how to give me the space I needed while putting in the guard rails required, you have helped me grow significantly. To the few who decided to take me on, with the hope of containing me, I am sorry. Actually, I'm not sorry.

I tried not to single any of my bosses out because it inevitably means leaving others out. Without diminishing the role all of them played, there are three people to whom I owe enormous gratitude because they have shaped me and my career in the most extraordinary ways: my first boss Kim McKay, my boss during two of my three stints at the ABC Peter Longman, and one of my closest friends whom I rely on every day for guidance even though he is no longer on earth – my boss at SBS Les Murray. It was not only the support they gave me but the examples they led by, exuding understanding, confidence, belief in values, and a love of the most important stories humanity reveals every day.

Finally, to my husband Stan with whom I have experienced so much: oh my God, Stan, how interesting is the world and how lucky are we to be in it? I am so glad I have got to share so many of the highs and lows with you. Thanks for putting up with my astral travelling and associated weirdness.

About the Author

Tracey Holmes is one of Australia's most recognised and rewarded journalists having spent almost four decades reporting on the world's biggest sports stories. Her work is focused on the intersection where sport meets politics, business, culture, and news. Her weekly podcast, *The Sports Ambassador*, explores in detail the stories behind the headlines. It can be found on Patreon, Spotify, YouTube and across most social media platforms. As Deputy Chair of the Oceania Australia Foundation, a Council Member of Indigenous Football Australia, a member of the IOC Press Committee, and a Mentor for the IOC Young Reporters program, Tracey is actively involved in promoting sport as a tool for social change and empowerment. Tracey has a Master's degree in Communications, is currently studying a Master's in Sports Diplomacy at the Hungary University of Sports Science, and (when time permits) will finish her Master's in Sports Law at Melbourne University.

www.ingramcontent.com/pod-product-compliance
Lightning Source LLC
Chambersburg PA
CBHW020517080526
44583CB00013B/626